PSI, What Is It?

By Louisa E. Rhine

HIDDEN CHANNELS OF THE MIND
ESP IN LIFE AND LAB
MIND OVER MATTER

PSI

What Is It ?

The Story of ESP and PK

LOUISA E. RHINE

Harper & Row, Publishers
New York, Evanston, San Francisco, London

To my grandson Ronnie, who at age 11 wished for a book about psi "without all those big words," and to all the other young and older people who feel a similar need.

To JBR for his part in and out of all of this.

PSI, WHAT IS IT? Copyright © 1975 by Louisa E. Rhine. All rights reserved. Printed in the United States of America. No part of this book may be used or reproduced in any manner whatsoever without written permission except in the case of brief quotations embodied in critical articles and reviews. For information address Harper & Row, Publishers, Inc., 10 East 53rd Street, New York, N.Y. 10022. Published simultaneously in Canada by Fitzhenry & Whiteside Limited, Toronto.

Library of Congress Cataloging in Publication Data

Rhine, Louisa E 1891–
 Psi, what is it?

 Includes bibliographical references and index.
 1. Extrasensory perception. 2. Psychical research.
I. Title.
BF1321.R555 1975   133.8   74-25697
ISBN 0-06-066826-1

75 76 77 78 79 10 9 8 7 6 5 4 3 2

Contents

SECTION ONE 1

Psi, a significant discovery. The new field of parapsychology: its objective. How to tell tested from untested claims.

1. The Need to Know about Psi 2
2. The Reason for Parapsychology 11
3. The Fringe 18

SECTION TWO 25

Discovering psi ability: clairvoyance, precognition, telepathy, psychokinesis. Who has it?

4. Starting on the Trail: Clairvoyance Suspected 26
5. Roadblock: Clairvoyance Discovered 32
6. Detour: Precognition 37
7. Telepathy at Last—Or Was It? 43
8. Moving Dice, Not Mountains: Psychokinesis, or PK 49
9. Are ESP and PK Relatives? 56
10. Who has Psi Ability? 61

SECTION THREE 71

Advances in psi research: in the schoolroom, in dreams, in various mental states. PK on static systems, on lower organisms, in the healing of disease, and ESP and PK in animals.

11. ESP in School 72
12. Experimental Dreams and ESP 84
13. Psi and Various Mental States 89
14. PK on Static Systems 101
15. The PK Effect on Lower Organisms 106

16 PK and the Healing of Disease   112
17 ESP and PK in Animals   119

SECTION FOUR   133

Psi in life situations. The forms it takes in consciousness, their psychological aspects.

18 The Forms of Psi Experience   134
19 Focus on Intuitive ESP Experiences   141
20 A Study of Hallucinatory ESP Experiences   146
21 Dream Copies   152
22 Dream Drama   157
23 Close-up on PK Experiences   162

SECTION FIVE   167

Life after death.

24 Psi Experiences involving the Dying and the Dead   168
25 Can the Dead Speak through Mediums?   174
26 Hauntings and Poltergeists.   181

SECTION SIX   189

The bearing of psi on the concept of man's nature.

27 The Meaning of Psi   190

SECTION SEVEN   197

Miscellaneous Topics. How to do it.

28 The Occult in School   198
29 How to Get into the Field of Parapsychology   210
30 How to Make a Successful Psi Test   216

APPENDIX   223

Methods and techniques of testing for psi, and tables for evaluating results.

ESP Tests   224
    Evaluating ESP Tests   230

PK Tests   232
    Evaluating PK Tests   234
Areas of Problems   235
References   237
Index   243

SECTION ONE

Psi, a significant discovery. The new field of parapsychology: its objective. How to tell tested from untested claims.

1. The Need to Know about Psi

One of the most significant advances of science is the discovery that psychic or psi ability is real. But the world has heard too little about it and of its meaning for humankind. Even today, decades after its reality was well established the majority of persons, if asked if they believe in psi, would answer No. Yet good evidence for it now exists. The question no longer should be, "Do you believe in psi?" but, "Do you know the evidence for it?"

The evidence, however, has not been widely enough or easily enough available to the general public to make widespread appreciation of its meaning possible, or to clarify its application to individuals who need to understand about it for personal reasons.

The personal reasons generally arise when an individual suspects that he has had a psychic experience. Even among those who would say that they do not believe in psi are many who would add, "But something happened once that makes me wonder. . . ." That something then turns out to be an instance when the person seemed to know about an event that happened at a different place or time which he could not have known by ordinary means. It was not within reach of his senses, even indirectly.

A college girl in Washington D.C. one morning slipped and fell down a short flight of marble stairs. She dislocated her coccyx, but though in pain she did not call her parents in New York City. No use worrying them she thought. She could manage by herself.

That evening she had a phone call from her mother. "What happened," her mother asked, "and how badly are you hurt?"

Playing dumb, the girl asked why the question.

"I had a dream last night. I saw you fall off a ladder and hurt your back."

Although the dream occurred before the fall, and though it involved a ladder instead of a flight of stairs, still the girl could not believe it was all just a coincidence. She wondered if her mother's dream could have somehow been connected with her fall. Could it have been a psychic experience?

A woman in Rochester one day had an experience for which she could not account. She was at home alone sitting in an easy chair reading when she heard a ticking like the ticking of a watch. She was not wearing a watch, and all the clocks were electric.

As she listened, absentmindedly she pushed her hand down under the cushion of the chair—and pulled out the watch her ten-year-old son had lost some weeks before.

The loss of the watch had been a minor family calamity. It was the second one the boy's father had given him, and the second one he had lost. The search for it had been long and thorough, but finally tearfully given up when it seemed certain that the watch was gone for good.

Half unbelievingly the woman shook the watch, but it must have run down weeks ago. It did not give even a solitary final tick. She wound it then and stuffed it back beneath the cushion where it had been. She listened, but could not hear it ticking.

No one took seriously her account of the ticking she had heard. Her husband just laughed and said she must have imagined it. She could not have heard a watch that was run down. But—she was not convinced. She *did* hear it. Could it have been a psychic experience?

A sixteen-year-old girl in Boston had a double date one night. Eventually the foursome went to the other girl's home some five miles from hers to listen to the late television show. It was midnight and the plot was just getting interesting, when suddenly she wanted to go home. In spite of remonstrances she prevailed upon her boy friend to take her home at once.

As they approached the house a doctor was entering it. He had been called because the girl's mother, who had not been sick before, had had a heart attack. She died a few hours later. That girl could not convince herself it was just a coincidence, as the rest all said. Was it perhaps a psychic experience?

Those few cases, chosen here mainly because they were fairly simple, could be multiplied many times. The main feature would be only that the person seemed to get information without using the senses. But in no case could anyone be sure whether anything but coincidence, imagination, or other such counter-explanation was involved. The person himself could feel that those explanations were not good enough, but his friends thought they were. So what?

However, puzzling experiences of this general kind have served a good purpose in the past. They suggested that experiments should be made to find out whether it was possible to get information without using the senses. By the 1930s this kind of experimenting developed into the field now known as parapsychology, a name selected to show that the field is both like and unlike that of psychology. The name was first used publicly in 1935 when a laboratory for the study of the psychic side of human life was established at Duke University in Durham, North Carolina.

As soon as people heard about this laboratory they began to write letters telling about experiences that puzzled them and that they thought might be psychic. Many of these persons expressed satisfaction in just knowing that serious research was being undertaken to discover the actual facts about psychic ability. They were ready and eager to contribute accounts of their own puzzling experiences in the hope of being helpful.

Over the years thousands of such letters have come to the Parapsychology Laboratory, formerly at Duke, now the Institute for Parapsychology under the Foundation for Research on the Nature of Man. Certainly it would not generally be supposed that so large a number of people, who of course are only a small percentage of all persons, should have personal reasons to be interested in psi research.

From practically all of these persons the same background question is implicit. Whether it is put into words or only implied when they report their own experience, they are asking, "What does this mean? How can it be explained?" They want reliable information to help them understand. They are not content to turn to dream books, horoscopes, and other remnants of the unscientific past. They want and deserve to know the results of parapsychological research.

Since the 1930s the results of this research have been reported regularly in scientific journals; and books have been written on the subject. But few of these are easily available—or understandable—to nonprofessionals. Besides, they are usually devoted to some special phase or problem of parapsychology, and are not intended to give a comprehensive, not to say, comprehensible, survey of the entire field. Such a survey is obviously needed, and especially now when research results permit new insights into the meaning of personal experiences.

Recently an additional need for more, and more readily accessible, information about psi has arisen. Until a few years ago all inquiries to the Parapsychology laboratory for information came from adults. But now, with items about parapsychology appearing in school leaflets and newsletters, an avalanche of inquiries come from schoolchildren too. Most of them are requests for information, which they find difficult to get elsewhere, for school assignments. Sometimes they want directions for experiments which they can carry out at home or in school, as in the following letter:

My name is Rosemary Able. I am thirteen and in the eighth grade. I am doing a science fair project because we have to. I have decided to do it on ESP. I have read six chapters of your book, *ESP in Life and Lab*. Before I started reading I didn't believe in ESP, but now I believe in it, and I think it's a very nice subject to read on.

In reading I was wondering if you might be able to send me some ESP cards so I can use them in finding out if intelligence affects how much ESP is in a person. And does age affect how much ESP comes out of the unconscious to the conscious?

If these questions make any sense to you, well if they do, could you send or write something having to do with them? If these questions are really bad, could you suggest some really good questions to find out? Could you suggest some tests to do for kids between the ages of 5 and 13 to find out if they have ESP that is very noticeable? Because a lot of kids at school don't believe in ESP, and I was wondering if there was a test to prove to them that they have ESP or show that some people have it.

I would like you to try to send me some information and those ESP cards and answer my questions before the end of January because my teacher will yell at me for not starting the project. I will pay for the postage. Please.

Requests from schoolchildren to the laboratory are handled by a secretary who routinely sends out such pamphlets and lists of books as can be recommended. Of course, many sensational "occult" books and articles are constantly being published, but the laboratory lists only items with a reliable research basis. Even so, these items were not written with a young student group in mind. And, at this younger level, sometimes more is needed than just pamphlets for school assignments. Questions of a more personal nature may arise, as this letter from Susie R. shows:

The reason I am writing is that I am not sure my experiences are psychic. I am fifteen years old, and ever since I can remember I have been an active dreamer, and on many occasions my dreams have come true.

The one that happened last week was the most disturbing. I dreamt something dreadful happened to my father. I could actually feel the tight sensation I get in my throat when I hold back the tears. When I went down to breakfast, my mother was crying because my father had had a slight heart attack. I didn't want to cry and make everyone worry too, and so I tried to hold back my tears. I had that same awful tight feeling in my throat.

Well, I don't know if my dreams are psychic or not. But I hope it's not that I'm crazy, as my mother says.

Or take this letter from Penny:

I am only thirteen. So maybe you wouldn't want to hear about my experiences with ESP.

One summer a couple of years ago I dreamed that my grandfather was dead. When I woke up my mother was leaning over me and told me that my grandfather died late that night. Then this winter before New Years, my grandmother died and I had dreamed it the night before.

Another time when I had an operation on my ear. While I was under the ether I dreamed about a road, a road I had never been on before. A couple of weeks later I went on that very road the same way I had dreamed.

Two years ago when I was in another school I dreamed I was going to dance in a school exhibit. So this February I danced in the same dance with no changes.

I was eating lunch and suddenly I thought of my little sister. I thought I heard her screaming. I did not think of her again until I finished lunch. Then I went over home. There she stood crying and holding her hand. I went over and it was cut almost in half. I went and got the doctor just in time. She could have died from loss of blood. I was all upset because I hadn't gone in search of her when I heard the scream. I couldn't really hear her scream because nobody else heard it and I can't hear very well. It has haunted me so.

My mother thinks I should not write about this because she thinks I am goofy anyway, throw it away if you want.

These girls are not alone, of course, in needing to know the answer to questions like theirs. Nor are their mothers alone in being unable to give better ones. Many young persons like Susie and Penny are ready to take seriously the possibility that an experience is psychic, but many an older person still will not even consider such a thought. This difference of viewpoint is not difficult to understand.

Most of the younger generation never knew much about alleged psychic phenomena. But they are quickly interested in experiments which they can try themselves, and which in any event concern unusual, even unsuspected, aspects of their own minds. They have few wrong attitudes to correct, and therefore they can be spontaneous and unprejudiced.

The older people, however—those who say, "No, I do not believe in psi"—long ago made up their minds about all the old debatable topics, from fortunetelling to haunted houses, from poltergeists to apparitions of the dead. They knew that tall tales about such things had been told from the dawn of time, that science had proved none of them, and that scholars in general did not believe they were real. It was easy to decide, therefore, that all of them were probably the result of ignorance, credulity, imagination, and mistakes of many kinds. It was only sensible to disbelieve them.

Now parapsychology comes along. Few members of the older generation have had the opportunity to learn that it is a research field and not just another superstition, or to realize that considerable truth has been found mixed in with those old superstitions. A new idea always has a difficult time securing its place when a wrong old one is there before it. The old one, in this instance, produced a strong bias against parapsychology in many of those of the older generation. In these situations, the younger ones *want* more information, and whether they are aware of it or not, the older ones *need* it. The pressure of the younger generation is strong. The older one slowly gives way before it. Eventually the effect here will probably lead many older persons to take a fresh look at an area they have been slow to take seriously.

In addition to these various kinds of needs to know, come troubled requests like these:

I have had some unusual and frightening experiences relating to the supernatural. Could you restore my peace of mind?

I have a unique problem that is causing me no end of trouble and embarrassment. I have got to find a way to put a stop to all this. Very simply, my mind is being read. It is not just a once-in-a-while happening, but on a 24-hour basis.

And on the younger level:

Lately I have discovered facts about ESP. I have really scared myself thinking about it. While writing this letter to you I had a feeling, should I write this letter, could it hurt me? Well, could it?

My grades in school are dropping. I really try not to think about ESP, but it is something I just cannot help. *Or* could I?

For such as these, the need to know and understand psi is urgent. With that understanding, in many instances at least, the unhealthy overtones would disappear.

A somewhat different need to know is represented by this letter from a young coach and recreation director:

I was reading a book called *Haunted Houses* to a young friend of mine. I enjoy reading about ghosts and monsters. I noticed that throughout the book Duke University was called upon to investigate reports of ghosts and poltergeists.

I was wondering if you could send me some results of tests and conclusions you have reached by your investigations. I would appreciate something rather simple to explain as I will be showing it to an eleven year old.

Explain to an eleven-year-old? Scientists write mainly for other scientists. It is the easiest and quickest way for them. But even so, the facts of parapsychology are relatively simple. There is no reason why they cannot be presented so that any intelligent person, even a smart eleven-year-old, could fairly well understand them.

The main difficulty with parapsychological research reports is that some of the ideas they present are radically different, even revolutionary. And so, to many people, they are not easy to believe. Validating them necessitates the use of statistical methods, and such methods are hard for nonstatisticians to follow. But the ideas without the statistics can be presented to laymen—with the statistical data reserved for professionals.

The statistics behind life insurance tables need not be mentioned when someone takes out a policy; and similarly, here too, they can now be taken for granted. The experts have found some of the answers and the rest of us can take their word for them, remembering only that when the experts say a result is statistically significant, it means that the odds are too great to be reasonably considered the result of chance.

Accordingly, this is an account of parapsychology today, written for inquiring minds of any age. In this book are outlined a sufficient number of the more significant aspects of the field to give a general concept of it. It should help those with personal problems better to understand them, and all the rest, better to appreciate their own inherent nature.

For simplicity and brevity, actual experimental data are omitted and only general suggestions and conclusions given. For those who wish to make a more detailed study and want to examine the data themselves, references are included, but limited as much as possible to general sources like a book or article in which a full list on the topic under consideration can be found. Figures in parentheses throughout the text refer to references at the back of the book, which are numbered by chapter.

2. The Reason for Parapsychology

The discovery that psychic ability is real is one of the most significant advances of science because it tells something very important about human nature. When parapsychological research began, the objective was to find out if any of the strange experiences people reported (like those described in Chapter 1) did mean what they seemed to mean, if the person actually did know about something without using his senses.

If the mind could get information about the objective world in this way it would call for a kind of mental ability that psychologists had not recognized. And it would fall in their field because it would be a mental phenomenon. Psychologists study such aspects of the mind as memory, learning, and the operation of the senses, motor skills, etc. All these generally obey the laws of time and space. But the psychic kind apparently do not. Instead, they seem to occur without regard to where or when the item "known" is located. On this account psychic phenomena were not included in the kinds studied in psychology.

However, the very reason for keeping psychic phenomena out of psychology made them seem especially interesting to a few individuals who came to call themselves parapsychologists. They undertook the basic research necessary to find out if psychic phenomena were real. If no trace of psychic ability could be found when proper controlled experiments were made, then it was time the world knew it and the old question settled finally in the negative. If, on the other hand, evidence of an extrasensory kind of knowing were obtained, it would mean that the deeper nature of man includes more than just the physical body. To find the answer to this question was the initial reason for undertaking research on the psychic side of human life.

The question whether the deeper nature of human beings includes more than just the physical body is not always stated so simply or in just these words. Yet nearly everyone in one way or another asks it when he wonders what life is all about and what the meaning of his existence in this world really is. The question, "What am I and why am I living?" is still being asked explicitly or implicitly by almost everyone. It may have been asked by the first cave man. Perhaps that was the sign that now he was a man.

The cave man did not write his thoughts in books. But everyone today knows that the question about man's deeper nature has not been finally (i.e., scientifically) answered even yet. Because of the bearing on this deeper question the results of parapsychological research need to be known and appreciated by the world in general. It is significant for this reason even more than for the answers it can give to those who need to understand their own personal experiences.

Even though the name "parapsychology" has been in use since 1935 and is becoming generally familiar, considerable confusion exists as to the topics it includes. Some ask about auras, UFOs, astrology, demonology, and other occult topics. None of these, however, is a proper parapsychological one. Then again, some think this field covers another set of beliefs in a class with religious cults or doctrines.

Instead, parapsychology is a scientific field, not a cult or "ism" of any kind. It is an attempt to find out the facts about a definite class of phenomena and to do so by carefully controlled experimentation just as the older sciences, like physics and chemistry, biology, and psychology, have established their respective domains.

The problems of parapsychology, however, are more difficult and complicated than those of psychology, because they have to do almost entirely with unconscious, rather than conscious, aspects of the mind, aspects so hidden that they have been almost completely overlooked by science in general. Yet they have now proved to be very real and to have effects that can be studied and measured.

For several reasons the results of parapsychological research are still not widely known. The phenomena on which they are based and the ability which permits them to occur are hidden behind the senses and the muscles. Every normal person uses the senses and muscles constantly to know about and affect the world around him, and is more or less aware of doing so. The extrasensory signals, however, are weak. The person is not conscious of them. They seldom break through to be noticed.

Another reason why such signals go unnoticed and the ability stays hidden is because it is unexpected. In order ever to get noticed the ability almost has to have some quite unusual aspect, so that it stands out as different from the common run of everyday experience. The times when it does get noticed, or at least suspected, are usually either instances when a person seems to "know something" that he had no ordinary way of knowing, something that stands out so sharply that he cannot convince himself that it was just a coincidence (as in the examples in Chapter 1); or experiences that stood out because they had some striking form that the person could not explain away.

A doctor in Pennsylvania, for instance, could not believe that an experience of his own one day was just a coincidence. He was on his way to see a sciatica patient who lived some distance from the office. As the doctor was driving there, suddenly, he said, he "had a terrific urge and *certain knowledge"* that another patient of his, a Mrs. A., who lived in the opposite direction, needed him at once.

Mrs. A. was pregnant, but the baby was not yet due. However, the doctor's urge was so strong that he turned around and drove as fast as possible to Mrs. A.'s house. He found her in the first stage of labor, and he was just in time to get her to the hospital for the birth of her premature baby.

Another experience, one that stood out and was noticed as probably psychic because of the unusual form it took, concerned a sixteen-year-old girl, Lois, in San Francisco. She was restlessly moping around the house one day soon after her sister, Alicia, had married and gone with her navy husband to San Diego. Home was uninteresting now that the wedding was over. Lois had seen and heard and felt it all so often. She was lonely for Alicia, dull and bored as only a teenager can be. Nowhere to go. Nothing to do. The four walls shut her in. They seemed almost smothering!

What, she wondered, was Alicia doing by now? She shut her eyes and tried to imagine where the young couple might be. She conjured up a restaurant scene. At a corner table she saw them ordering dinner . . .

But why be foolish? It was just imagination, even the clothes she saw her sister wearing—oh-hum—nothing interesting anywhere.

Fifteen minutes later the phone rang; long distance from San Diego. It was her sister, frantic. "Lois, what's the matter? We were here in the restaurant just ordering dinner, when I felt a tap on my shoulder and you leaned over and said, 'Hi!' Whatever did it mean?" (Yes, a corner table. Yes, the very clothes!)

Well, what did it mean? For the two girls it certainly was an unexpected discovery, a discovery that somehow they had communicated. At least, if the account that Lois sent the Parapsychology Laboratory at Duke some years later was true, it was a kind of communication and was recognized only because Alicia's experience was a very uncommon one (see Chapter 20). It was also a good illustration of the difference between sensory experience, the four walls of Lois' home, and extrasensory experience, the kind that does not obey the laws of space and time.

Such occasional experiences as Alicia's or even those more like the doctor's are, after all, not very common. Many a wife, many a parent has tried and tried to transcend space, to see, to know about some distant loved one only to find the atmosphere opaque, the four walls of sense experience smothering, no opening in them anywhere.

The fact is that the majority of us most of the time depend entirely on the senses for what we learn about the world around us. The senses do such a good job in general and we are so satisfied with them, that we never think of ourselves as needing any other way of knowing about the world. We do not expect to see things hundreds of miles away, or even wish to hear sounds that are not caused by air waves that strike the ear, and we never consider the possibility of actually knowing ahead of time the unexpected event that may happen tomorrow. In short, we are so satisfied with the way our senses serve us that we do not expect an extrasensory ability.

Because the psi ability is hidden and unexpected, it not only took a long time to be discovered, but also kept the news of its discovery from being quickly spread around! It was not like color television, for instance, something which had a long buildup so that the world was waiting for it. Also it does not yet have any easy commercial value to help it along. Television, for that matter, did not have commercial value until it advanced far enough to "work." The understanding of psi is not yet advanced far enough to be used in a practical way; for it is an unconscious ability and not under conscious control. This is an important point, and one that should not be overlooked.

The discovery of psi ability was the result of many carefully controlled experiments by many different people over a number of years. But the difficulty even today in getting information about it arises not only because the field of experimental parapsychology is still young compared to physics, chemistry, and biology, but even more because it has had a great initial prejudice to overcome before it could be taken seriously by scholars in other fields, a prejudice that only slowly is being overcome. Gradually, some scientists in other fields are beginning to recognize parapsychology. Even a few courses on the topic are appearing here and there on college campuses.

However, a new danger has appeared on the scene, or at least a threat posed by an old danger is suddenly increasing. It could well cancel out entirely the gains toward the recognition of parapsychology from whatever sources. The threat is posed by the rise of a new wave of superstition. The main idea of the research in parapsychology, of course, is to get away from untested superstition and to find out the truth about happenings of a psychic nature. That truth can be discovered only by proper investigation which could show whether such claims as the occurrence of telepathy, prophecy, ghosts, haunted houses, communication with the dead, etc., have any validity.

Parapsychology seeks to test the basis of these old claims before either believing or disbelieving them. Just as in medicine, for instance, proper research has given us "modern miracles" in place of old-fashioned charms to drive out evil spirits, in parapsychology by controlled experiments much has already been learned to show the dividing line between the truth and shadowy old occult beliefs. Those untested beliefs, however, still hang like a cloud, a fringe, around the field. This poses a danger for it, namely, that these loose, sensational, and often well-advertised approaches to psychic mysteries could well eclipse the slow, careful, and factual method of experimental parapsychology. Can persons stimulated by the uncritical beliefs of popular superstition really come to appreciate the more sober facts that research shows to be underlying?

This danger that the fringe, with its ancient untested claims, may tend to smother the reliable findings of the field, arises because many adults are credulous rather than skeptical in their attitude toward them, and many schoolchildren are still unaware of the experimental approach to psychic phenomena. Curiosity alone leads many of the young to do what they may think of as experimenting in these mysterious areas. Automatic writing, the Ouija, table-tipping in darkroom seances, etc., fascinate schoolchildren as well as their elders. They have little idea of the unusual mental processes they may stir up or how to handle or interpret them.

Even more threatening may be the rise of modern superstition among young adults. Reviving old discredited beliefs of the nonscientific past—necromancy, spiritism, witchcraft, astrology—with no attempt to find out if they have a basis, these people seem not to *want* to know the truth, but only to find something spectacular and exciting.

Still, one must believe that these credulous groups just *look* that way. They are intelligent, and surely no intelligent person actually wants to be fooled. These people are apparently so eager for answers that they are impatient with the necessarily slow ways of science, and in their impatience they simply believe too much too easily. *They have not learned to ask for proof.* They do not realize that before a claim can be considered reliable it must be tested by actual experimentation which can show whether the answer is No or Yes. Science gives a method that substitutes proof for guesswork.

And yet it must be acknowledged that even overcredulous groups, if they did try to get information by which to distinguish real from unreal, or at least established from unestablished, psychic claims, would have found it difficult. Neither grownups nor schoolchildren can find an easy source of answers.

Possibly the extent to which this wave of modern superstition will obscure the established facts of parapsychology will depend on the availability of proper answers, for the present public attitude is one that calls for instant information before the next sensational item blows the current one off the scene. But back of all the stir and fluctuation of popular interest the old bedrock human question remains.

"What is a human being?" and "What is his full capacity?" No one could really want less than the complete truth on that one. And the advances in the field of parapsychology are real advances toward that truth. But before going into the account of those advances, some discussion about "proof" itself is needed: how to recognize it and how to find it.

3. The Fringe

My name is Angela. I did a science fair project on ESP at school. For Christmas I got a Ouija board. Yesterday my Ouija's name was Dexi from Athens. Today I asked if anyone was there . . . no answer. Then I found that Dexi had gone to heaven, and my new spirit's name was Gavin. I asked him if he had ever contacted J. B. Rhine at Duke University. He said, "Yes." "How?" I asked. "Ouija," he said. He said he was born in heaven. "How can you be born in Heaven?" "Spiritually," he said. "Do you mean that your soul formed before birth?" "Yes." (He also said) "A baby was born in 1959 in Nazareth to lead the world. . . ."

Would you check on these details? Also, do you believe that spirits can contact us through the Ouija? Do you use the Ouija in your experiments at Duke about ESP?

No, no, no, Angela, the answer to all your questions is no. But it is well you asked about this gadget. It is a real fooler. How could you ever tell if it was really a spirit? The idea is just a guess, a fantasy, though it is one that has often been made. (For the real explanation see Chapter 13.)

Many old beliefs that still cling like a fringe around the parapsychological area are based on the idea of spirits—invisible entities hovering all around. Long ago people believed that spirits inhabited—or even were—the heavenly bodies; that they controlled volcanoes, earthquakes and practically everything that was clearly beyond the control of the people themselves. Those ideas are outdated now and no longer needed for explanation. But even yet the idea of spirits pops up with little provocation. Not only schoolgirls like Angela can easily convince themselves that a spirit speaks through the Ouija board, but many more educated and older persons too, with or without the use of the Ouija, believe in spirits and spirit influences much too easily; which means, without any proof.

This easy belief, this remnant from earlier times, shows up in the response so quickly given by much of the general public to the claims of popular prophets and mediums, especially if the person writes a book about it or appears on television. Then, in spite of common sense and the total lack of real proof, the idea that a spirit was involved catches on like wildfire. And if a medium, probably in trance, tells what a future spirit life is like, the words are taken seriously. She must know because she was in trance!

Nonsense! But otherwise intelligent people are often no better in this area than six-year-old Chris one night when he tossed around, sleepless, long after being put to bed. Finally his mother came in and asked him what the trouble was.

"I'm scared, Mama."

"Why, Chris? There's nothing to frighten you."

"I'm scared of vampires."

"Oh, Chris, you know there are no such things! I'm surprised at you."

"Yes, I know there aren't any, Mama, but I'm scared of them anyway."

Part of the problem is, then, the lingering old idea of spirits. Like Chris's fear of vampires, it still can have an effect, whether the person actually believes it or not. The remedy, however slowly it becomes effective, certainly lies in the fact that all scientific and intellectual advances tend to give other explanations for phenomena once ascribed to spirits, and all parapsychological advance does the same.

Of course, Angela could not tell about the Ouija for sure, though she did question it. How, for that matter, can anyone tell the fringe from the real, the unreliable claims from those that are reliably established?

It is a matter of proof, of course. But how does anyone find the proof, or recognize it if he does find it? How can anyone judge all the fads, cults, and unorthodox claims from astrology to witchcraft that today clamor for his attention from friends, from television and radio programs, and even from the pages of supposedly reputable magazines?

If it is a new cult or claim, go slowly. Be openminded, but do not decide anything hastily. It is just as easy to say, "I don't know," as "I believe," or "I don't believe," and very much wiser. There could be *something* in the Ouija, even if not spirits.

Angela was wise, for she tried to get information. In regard to any such far-out idea that sounds mysterious when not fully understood, one should try to get something of its history, its origin and, most important, to find out whether the claim is based on authority, someone's idea only, or on careful observation and research.

If the idea goes back to an authority, is it new or old? Old ones are likely to depend on blind faith in some sort of "ancient wisdom," originating with wise men of long ago. If so, it is well to remember that they thought that the sun goes around the earth; they never heard of bacteria; they did not know about the steam engine, to say nothing of the automobile, or radio or television, or the conscious and unconscious parts of the mind. However wise they were in their own day, could they be expected to tell anything reliable today on, for instance, the effect of the moon and stars on man?

Right here might be the place to say, regarding the idea that people are affected by the position of the heavenly bodies at the time of birth, and all the rest of the astrological claims (which, as already mentioned, do not even come in the field of parapsychology), that these claims are perhaps the most widely advertised of their kind today, and on the most completely unresearched or inadequately researched basis. Of course, it is not that no reliable research has been done to show that the heavenly bodies have effects on the earth, but no basic research has been done to show that the personality can be affected by the position of the planets at the time of birth. As a matter of fact, the occurrence of such an effect is contradicted by much research in biology and genetics, which has long since proved to be sound and reliable. Yet the astrological myth today is netting its practitioners the most handsome fortune of any of those that take the public for the suckers that too many of them show themselves to be.

If the idea is one that did not originate so long ago, if it was an impression or belief that originated in the early years of psychical research, for instance, then too, treat it as the product of its time, and not necessarily of parapsychology today. For instance, careful research was made on mediums with results that sometimes appeared to mean that a deceased person had communicated. But the psychic ability in living people like the medium herself, which could also explain the results, was not then known. Therefore, it is necessary to remember that in this field, too, changes do come, even if slowly. As later chapters show, even though research well done fifty and more years ago, seemed to mean one thing, the light thrown on it by new discoveries may change the interpretation. Old ideas must give way to new ones if the real meaning of life and the real nature of man are ever to be discovered.

If the authority is a new wise man, a guru, a self-proclaimed prophet or sensitive, look up his credentials. Try to get his *complete* record, not just what he publishes. And when that proves impossible, as it will for all those who have so far appeared, then observe the rule above, which if good for the Ouija, is good here too. Just say, "I don't know," and do not decide.

If the new idea is the result of scientific research, its chances of being valid are much better because it means that careful methods of making sure of the facts have been used instead of just guessing at them. But even so, its results are not necessarily perfect. Scientific method is not easily evaluated by nonscientists, and scientists can make mistakes. Usually other scientists nose the mistaken ones out, and sooner or later, if the finding is a sound one, it is confirmed, and then can be considered as established.

It is true that recently criticisms of science have been quite widely published: it is too cold, too impersonal, and takes no account of the effect of its discoveries on human welfare. This kind of criticism is based on a misunderstanding of just what the scientific method really is. After all, it is simply a method of making sure. Whether its results help or hurt people depends on the way they are used. Even knives, forks, pins, and needles can hurt people, but if they do, it is the fault of those who misuse them. It is just the same with scientific method.

Techniques vary with different sciences, but several cardinal points are the same in practically all of those in which experiments can be made. The plan of the experiment must include a control to show what would have happened anyway. Then, if the result depends on a judgment of any kind, say, for instance, that one of two experimental results is larger than the other, it must be evaluated "blind," so that the experimenter's preference will not be able to affect his judgment. Other lesser requirements too not necessary to detail here must be fulfilled in order that the result can be true and reliable, and not, instead, a form of pseudo-science resulting from the misuse of scientific method.

The formula for telling how to judge a new idea is fairly simple, a little like that for crossing a railroad track: "Stop, look, and listen," then proceed with caution and try to get the facts about it. Remember too that "I believe" or "I don't believe" is an unnecessary end point. What seems to be a proper decision today may change again when the light of tomorrow gives a different outlook. Newton seemed correct in his own time, but Einstein gave a new view of the universe, and now the physicists of today are already changing the Einsteinian universe.

The person today who does not want to be fooled must look for evidence that a new idea has been carefully investigated before he tries to judge it. The most careful method is the experimental one that can show if the idea is or is not correct. That method is necessarily slow, but it can bring the most reliable results of any so far devised.

The acceptance of quick, sensational, publicized claims about psychical matters is evidence really of a general need to know the answer to "What am I?" and to know it now. Like a cancer victim, the general public wants a cure and quickly without waiting for the slow, painstaking way of science. But the same impatience leads to quack cancer cures in medicine and to the occult fringe of parapsychology.

The careful person must therefore beware of unproven claims, even while he keeps an openminded attitude toward new ideas which may seem impossible, but are as yet untested.

the material body of the dead or dying person was not present. The communication would have to have been from his mind to that of the living person. Communication from one living mind to another, an idea which had been named "telepathy," had often been reported, but no one knew whether or not the reports meant what they seemed to mean. But to the people in the Psychical Research Society, the question whether or not telepathy actually occurs became an important one.

Some of the members began to collect all the accounts they could find of experiences that might have involved telepathy to see how strong a case they would make. A very wide range of "unexplainable" experiences, then as now, were often suspected of being psychic, but in order to have as firm a basis as possible for their collection, these psychical researchers included only those that had a truth-telling or veridical aspect, one in which the experience seemed to be related to some real event.

This was a lucky requirement, for it meant that emphasis would be concentrated on the simpler idea of telepathy, the obtaining of information without the senses rather than more complicated ones like, perhaps, haunted houses or poltergeist effects. It meant that reliable insight would be obtained that would eventually shed light on the more complicated kinds of psychic phenomena, too.

Even the research on telepathy, however, followed a zigzag path rather than a straight one which might well have saved a half century. For no one at first realized that some experiences that were taken as instances of telepathy did not necessarily involve it at all, and that a bigger job than even they expected lay ahead before it would be possible to say whether telepathy could really happen. The research that finally did straighten out the tangle came in parts, separate but connected, and at first did not actually count directly for telepathy. And then even telepathy did not count in just the expected way.

After the members of the society had collected a large number of reports of experiences which they thought might be evidence of telepathy, several hundred of the strongest cases were selected and in 1886 a book about them, *Phantasms of the*

Living (1),* was published by three of the leaders, E. Gurney, F.W.H. Myers, and F. Podmore. It showed that many people seemed to have received ideas about other people's thoughts and about other events too, that their senses did not bring them.

This book, however, did not prove telepathy, although it surely made it seem more familiar and reasonable. But already by the end of the century scholars were getting harder to convince of ideas that went against common sense, as this did. To convince them was going to necessitate an experimental approach.

The reason the evidence of individual experiences was not good enough to convince the more careful thinkers of the day was partly because of the same old counter-explanation that in any single instance it was "just a coincidence." And so all the cases in the book, *might* have been just chance occurrences and not actually the result of thought transference at all.

It was fortunate, however, as it later turned out, that some people began to make experiments too. While these did not at once prove that telepathy occurs, they were on the right track. Experiments needed the development of proper techniques and safeguards against mistake, including particularly a way to measure results of tests to see whether or not they were "just coincidence."

In the experiments that were made at first, one person would try to receive a thought that another tried to send him. The two thus came to be called "receiver" and "sender," the sender the one who had the thought, the receiver the one who got it. It was taken rather for granted in these experiments that the receiver got the message when he did because the other *sent* it to him. Of course, experiences like Alicia's in Chap 2, in which Lois was thinking so earnestly of her sister also suggested this. The idea, however, was actually a mistake because in many other telepathy cases the thought is not sent at all, but no one noticed that then. This mistake in the way such a mental process might work was one of the reasons why telepathy, rather than clairvoyance, was studied first, and for a long time seemed the more important of the two.

*Figures in parentheses refer to references at the back of the book, which are numbered by chapter.

In these early tests, the sender had an idea in mind to be communicated. It may have been a number, a symbol, but in the first tests it was usually a picture or drawing that the sender picked out and would look at as he concentrated and, without giving any sign, tried to send to the receiver. Sometimes, to avoid all possibility of giving a sensory sign, the sender was not even in the same room as the receiver.

Sometimes the receiver guessed the thought correctly, and did it often enough that the result appeared to be well beyond chance. And so, in experiments carried out in England and America, in the latter nineteenth and early twentieth centuries, it often seemed that telepathy must have occurred, but no way had been developed to know for sure that the experiments were conducted carefully enough. Many persons were skeptical and still said these results were due to chance or carelessness.

They could say that the results were only due to chance because there was no control in the experiments to tell what would have happened anyway. For instance, if the sender drew a sketch of a tree and then if the receiver also drew something that had any resemblance to the target drawing, it could be claimed as a hit by one person, or a miss by another who could say the subject could have just drawn his similar picture by chance. Or if the picture had been a complicated scene, and the receiver drew only a little part of it, the believer could emphasize the similarity and the disbeliever the dissimilarity. The judging was not blind. The method was not good enough to lead to a reliable conclusion.

Right here one of the curious little quirks of history comes in. Just across the English channel one of the greatest scholars in France at the time, Dr. Charles Richet (3), a physiologist, and Nobel Prize winner, made some careful experiments that showed that sometimes one person could draw a picture that matched another hidden in an opaque envelope *that no one knew*. This could not be telepathy. He called it a sixth sense. It was the effect that today would be called "clairvoyance."

Clairvoyance would be the kind of mental process involved, for instance, in the case of the woman in Chapter 1 who found the lost watch, if indeed it was more than a coincidence. It would have been involved also in the dream of a six-year-old girl in Arizona. In it she saw a particular spot in a vacant field across the road from her home, and knew that if she dug there she would find some pennies. Next morning she rushed over to that spot, and digging with her hands and a little stick she found twenty-eight pennies. Her excitement at the dream and the discovery was great enough that she still remembered it clearly twenty and more years later. Of course, the awareness in the dream of objects, pennies, was the fact that would have made it an instance of clairvoyance.

Richet told the English Society about his clairvoyance tests but apparently they did not take him very seriously. It was telepathy, not clairvoyance, in which they were mainly interested, and so the evidence for clairvoyance was discounted for the time.

Then, as it happened, in the 1920s one of the members of the English Society, Miss Ina Jephson, also made an experiment that did not fit in with regard to telepathy (2). Instead, it helped to cause a detour on the trail to telepathy that made it a much longer one than could have been foreseen.

Miss Jephson noticed that, when playing cards, she sometimes knew what a given card was before she saw it. Intrigued by this, which she recognized could not be telepathy, because no one else knew what card it was, she began to keep records, and as she went on she was more and more certain that her hits were too frequent to be "just chance." But in the early 1920s few people knew the way to tell for sure just how much better such results were than chance alone could give. This was just the beginning of the use of modern scientific method in such cases. That method depends very much on the statistical value of the results. Such values serve like yardsticks to tell whether a result like Miss Jephson's is better than expected by chance, and if so, how much better. In other words, the statistical value tells the odds against chance.

Miss Jephson did go to a famous mathematician in England, Dr. R. A. Fisher, and he helped her to figure out the odds. They were such that she was encouraged to believe that she was getting something more than chance results. If so, she must have evidence of clairvoyance. These results, even though they were not very high, did look like something more than chance, especially because she often hit the first or second of the five cards, but missed the last one or two. It seemed that if it were all chance, the hits would be no more frequent on one trial than another.

Miss Jephson had the true spirit of a scientific investigator, for she did not stop when she felt only fairly certain. She was not satisfied, but wanted other people to try tests like hers too. Then through the society, she succeeded in having hundreds of people in a number of different countries do so. The result was that many got most of their hits on the first or second of their five trials, just as she had done.

Miss Jephson then tried still another experiment with a number of subjects, but this was a disappointment. The results were just about what chance alone would give. Although of course she did not know it, she was experiencing then one of the frustrations that make parapsychological research slow and difficult. The second time around with a given test can never be exactly the same as the first, because the attitudes and feelings of the people change, and this affects the way they score. It means that in this field results often cannot be confirmed directly, as is possible in chemistry and physics. Other ways must be found and today, after many years, researchers are learning how to do this. But at the time, while Miss Jephson's experiments certainly made clairvoyance seem a possibility, they did not completely prove it.

It is a good question whether in 1928, the time when Miss Jephson's work was published in England, anyone really appreciated the difference it would make in regard to the nature of the mind, if clairvoyance as well as telepathy occurs. To most of those interested, the possibility of clairvoyance more than likely seemed just a curious oddity of no great importance, while the supposition about telepathy was that it would mean that some kind of hidden "brain waves" were involved. But for a mind to "know" about an object, like a card, did not seem so interesting or so credible a possibility.

In the next few years a few other tests for telepathy by other researchers were reported. However, no persistent efforts to settle the question about its occurrence were made until after J. B. Rhine (JBR) and I, in 1927, came to Duke University and the search for telepathy became the first objective.

5. Roadblock: Clairvoyance Discovered

The road that was to lead to an adequate test of telepathy when JBR first started on it about 1927 at Duke University looked clearer than it turned out to be. It seemed then just a Yes-or-No question which could be decided by a simple test, but quite soon the first roadblock came in sight. Usually roadblocks are nuisances because they keep one from getting where he is going as quickly as he would like. But they can have uses too. They can make him explore new country. This one did. It was the claim of clairvoyance, as touched on in Chapter 4. The detour around it led to the exploration of territory much greater and more significant than that of telepathy alone. And this, JBR, newly out of graduate school and by this time at the Psychology Department of Duke University, found out in the years following his initial attempt to see whether or not telepathy occurs.

The reason we had come to Duke University was because one of the leading English psychical researchers, a prominent psychologist, formerly at Oxford, and then at Harvard, had just gone to Duke University to be head of the Psychology Department. This man was Dr. William McDougall, and by his writings he showed that he was interested in the question of telepathy raised by experiences that suggested communication from the dead. As a psychologist he particularly wanted to know what the whole nature of man is. Is he just an intricate arrangement of physical and chemical components of the body, which lasts for a while and then dissolves again when the body dies, or is there another part, too? The part that in religion is called the soul? That part supposedly does not depend entirely on the body and presumably may even be separable from it. This, of course, was the survival question, and it was the one that had interested JBR and me, too, and had brought us to Duke University to study with Dr. McDougall.

The physical side of human beings, the actual body, of course, was the only one that gave scientists something tangible to work on. They could study topics like digestion, the circulation of the blood, anatomy, and the functions of the brain. But no one could see the soul or find any actual objective evidence of it, so that most scientists had come to believe it to be a myth. However, nearly all of them had ignored those reports that seemed to show that the dead had communicated with the living. They did not believe the occurrences could possibly have such a meaning, but were instead just the result of wishful thinking or some other kind of mistake. Only a few persons, like those in Psychical Research societies, thought this claim deserved a closer look.

Very few psychologists anywhere were concerned with the question, however, and very few graduate students were either. The question was not generally recognized, much less investigated in science. It was usually classed as a religious question, and the general policy, if not actually stated, was not to mix science and religion in college classrooms.

Professor McDougall thought differently, and so did we. We all thought it was tremendously important that the subject of survival be investigated. We agreed that it could never be settled except by scientific methods, and although the Psychical Research Society had used careful methods, science now had newer, more advanced techniques than had been available earlier. The obvious starting point was telepathy and JBR very soon began to plan experiments.

He was given an instructorship in the Psychology Department at the university, and he then could use students from his classes in tests. Since it had been reported that in some European experiments on hypnosis, telepathy had apparently occurred, it seemed that perhaps the quickest way to find a "good subject," if such indeed existed, might be to hypnotize the students before testing them for telepathy (1).

One of the professors in the psychology department, Dr. Helge Lundholm, was a hypnotist, and so he and JBR collaborated, one doing the hypnotizing and the other giving the tests. For tests, JBR would think of a number between 0 and 9 and Dr. Lundholm would assure the subject after being hypnotized, that now he could tell what the number was even if it was hidden. In the meantime, as a control, similar tests were made with subjects who were not hypnotized.

The results turned out to be only a little better than chance, the hypnotized subjects being hardly any better than the others. Therefore, since the hypnotizing was slow and took considerable time, it was given up and further tests were made without it.

The work of Miss Jephson, recently published, then came to attention, and although it did not bear directly on telepathy, it did suggest that the mind must have an ability to get information without the senses. If so, that would be an important finding on the way to discovering the whole nature of the mind.

One of the easiest ways to test subjects to see if they could get information without the senses was the one Miss Jephson had used, which was to have them guess the symbols on cards that were carefully hidden so the subjects had no sensory way of knowing them. In the tests JBR had made up to this time, the experimenter had always had a target number in mind, so that the result could be evidence of telepathy . . . but now the idea was to rule out that possibility and see if the subject could guess the card when no one knew it.

In order to make the testing easier it was decided not to use the standard playing-card deck, but to make one especially for this research. It had only twenty-five cards, with five different symbols: star, cross, circle, square, and wavy lines. By chance alone, with this deck, five hits would be the expected average per run.

One fortunate development for JBR and for the field of parapsychology was that now statisticians had come up with a "yardstick" to measure the results of tests like these (2). An experimenter no longer had to guess when his results were high enough to show that something more than chance had caused them. Now it was like the difference between just guessing that one is a little over five feet tall, and measuring with a yardstick and being able to say "I'm five feet, three inches tall." The difference here was made by a formula that showed what could

With this attitude the fringe beliefs will not smother the good research as it slowly separates the true from the false. And some of those fringe beliefs may have in them elements of truth that will be needed before the entire secret is revealed.

SECTION TWO

Discovering psi ability: clairvoyance, precognition, telepathy, psychokinesis. Who has it?

4. Starting on the Trail: Clairvoyance Suspected

New ideas, like paths in the wilderness, seldom spring up out of nothing. Usually they can be traced back as far as one cares to go. So it is with the idea of psi ability. Proof of its existence was not obtained as one big, single discovery, like finding a gold mine. Instead it came slowly and in parts stretched out over the last hundred years or so; but since this account must start somewhere, let it be in England about 1882, when a small group of scholars organized the Society for Psychical Research for the study of certain psychic occurrences.

One of the main interests of this group was the question whether the spirit survives death. Some reports of psychic phenomena suggested it because they seemed to mean that a deceased person had communicated with a living one. Many of these accounts were of apparitions that were seen at the time of a death. Similar ones are still reported today.

For instance, a North Carolina woman whose brother was in the army in France during World War II was sure one day she heard him call, "Sister." She ran to the door, but he was not there. Her father was on the porch at the time and he saw his son come up the walk, smiling and fully dressed in his uniform. The father extended his hand, but the figure faded away, and then the father said he *knew* his son was dead. Later reports confirmed the death and as near as could be determined, it was the time of these experiences in North Carolina.

Such reports of apparitions and of ghosts, even of haunted houses, raised the question whether the spirits of deceased persons actually do survive and are able to communicate. If so, of course, it would not be in the ordinary way, because be expected by chance in the experiment so that it was easy to measure the results of the experiment against chance. The actual formula is not important here, but it was very important for parapsychology then. It made it possible for JBR, his students, and all those who have come since to know practically for sure when their results were "better than chance" and when they were enough better to be "significant."

Scientific method, it might be emphasized here, consists of finding a way to be certain of a point, instead of just speculating, or in other words, of taking the guesswork out of measurements and making them exact and therefore reliable. This use of the formula was the beginning of modern parapsychology. More and more researchers in the field came to use it and other methods still more efficient that were developed later.

In making the tests for clairvoyance, the experimenter usually sat across the table from the subject and laid a well-shuffled deck of ESP cards on the table between them, but behind an opaque screen that kept the subject from actually seeing the cards. Sometimes the experimenter would pick up the top one and, without looking at it, lay it face down beside the deck. Then the subject would record on a record sheet his guess as to which symbol was on that card. In a different technique, the subject would just write his guesses for the entire deck in a column. Whichever method was used, at the end of the twenty-five-card run, the subject's calls were checked against the target deck. Since the total number of hits to be expected by chance was five, if the subject's guesses were more or less than that on the average, the formula could tell how unlikely it was that chance alone would account for them.

After a great many trials with students whose scores on the average were slightly better than chance, two special subjects stood out. They were not perfect by any means, but again and again their averages were considerably better than chance and better than the averages of the other subjects. These two special subjects were just what the experimenters had been looking for, but the fact that many of the others also had scores that were somewhat better than chance suggested that special subjects are not the only ones who may have extrasensory ability; others may have at least a little of it too.

All together, further work with both of the special subjects and the others was carried on for several school years. Soon it was quite clear that these subjects somehow "knew" what some of the cards were when their senses could not tell them. In other words, it was shown that clairvoyance was a fact, just as Richet in France and Miss Jephson in England had thought it must be. For JBR and Dr. McDougall, it meant just as clearly as if it had been telepathy instead of clairvoyance, that the mind does have an extrasensory way of knowing. It did not answer the survival question, but it made a lot of difference in the idea of the nature of the mind.

The discovery of clairvoyance also made a difference in the way telepathy experiments would have to be made. The experimenter would have to devise a test procedure that would be strictly from mind to mind. Therefore, he could not use cards as objects on which to concentrate when a subject was trying to read his thought. If he had an object like a card, then the card could be "read" by clairvoyance. However, the target in a test for "pure" telepathy would still have to be selected at random so the statistical formula could be used to evaluate the results. It would have to be done in some way that did not leave a material record.

Before such a test was devised, however, another detour was made, this time, however, not with frustration, but eagerness because now the experimenters realized more fully the extent of the new territory that was opening up. For the time, they almost forgot about telepathy because the new territory, precognition, offered an even greater challenge.

6. Detour: Precognition

Not satisfied to tackle just the unpopular and unorthodox question of the occurrence of telepathy, another even more "impossible" project came up next at what was to be the Parapsychology Laboratory of Duke University. In 1934 before the telepathy question was settled one way or the other, a detour on the trail was made to find out if precognition could occur.

"Precognition" was just another word for prophecy. Everyone knew of the prophets in the Bible, and practically everyone believed that they correctly foretold events that happened years, even centuries, later. Many people, too, no doubt knew that some persons claimed to have had dreams that came true, but this they were less likely to take seriously. Prophets in the Bible no doubt had special God-given powers, but hardly someone like a Mrs. L. in Pennsylvania. She said that she dreamed the night before her usual Bingo game that she hit a jackpot on 68 for three hundred dollars. She even said she dreamed just the exact number of ones, fives, and tens the usher paid her. But who would want to say that Mrs. L. had prophetic ability because of that?

Or, a boy in Georgia, one of many who have written to the Institute for Parapsychology to tell about dreams that came true? This is the Georgia boy's letter:

I am a boy of 14. My name is Robert G. A few months ago I dreamed I saw a boy and girl dancing the mumbo. She was wearing black tights and he a calypso shirt and pants.

A few weeks after, at an Industrial Arts gathering, the dream came true. After the judging of the exhibits they had a beauty contest and talent show.

When the talent show began I heard the mumbo music I had

dreamed about. And the boy and girl began to dance, dressed in the same clothes I mentioned. This happened inside a gym. In the dream I remembered looking down at them. In reality I was in the balcony and looking down at them.

I thought I was really cracking up.

If the letter had come before 1933, the answer that boy would have received would probably have been that even though the dream and the reality seemed so much alike, there could not have been any connection between the two, for if so it would mean that the dream scene occurred before its cause. Everybody knows that an event cannot happen until after its cause. Then the boy probably would have been reminded of the great number of dreams each person has and that of course, once in a while, one of them may resemble a real event. Add to that the tricks of memory and the whole thing then could be explained away.

Until 1933 no one had ever made scientific tests to find out if the future can be foreseen. Probably few, if any, researchers had ever thought the possibility that it could occur great enough to be worth a test. No one tests for something he does not suspect can occur, and no one suspected that ordinary people may have a precognitive ability.

Robert's letter, and also Mrs. L.'s, came in the 1960s, however. So by that time they could be reassured and Robert could be told that he was not cracking up just because his dream came true. He could be told that many careful experiments had now been made to show that people do have the ability to foresee future events at least a little. Of course, the fact does not fit in with the way people have been looking at the world of space and time, but that just means that the old view cannot be perfect and needs to be revised.

Precognition experiments were first undertaken by JBR at Duke University soon after it was realized when making tests for clairvoyance that it did not matter whether the cards were just across the table from the person trying to guess them, or in another room, or in a different building (1). The distance between the person and the cards did not seem to matter. The question was, "How did he do it?"

Did the cards put out some kind of radiation, for instance,

that the subject could pick up? If so, then the farther from them he was the less clairvoyance he should show, for radiation falls off rapidly with distance.

Tests of clairvoyance at longer and longer distances then were made, in separate rooms, buildings across the campus, and finally with a subject in Yugoslavia, some four thousand miles away. Of course, none of these subjects got perfect scores even when they were only across the table from the cards, and those they got at a longer distance were about the same as those at shorter ones. It looked as if clairvoyance was not affected by distance, and certainly not in the way that would be expected if it was any known kind of physical radiation.

After this was realized, it was only natural to wonder whether clairvoyance was unaffected by time too. At this point the target deck of cards had always been prepared before the subject made his calls. What if the deck were shuffled after the calls had been made, and the subject told that their order *then* would be the target order.

The idea was tried out. A subject mentally aimed his guesses at the order of the cards as it would be *after* they were shuffled. Some of the same persons who had been getting above chance scoring in clairvoyance tests soon found that if they wrote their twenty-five guesses in a column knowing that the experimenter would shuffle the deck before checking up, they could get about the same number of hits as before. This began to look like evidence for precognition, but it was far from the end of the story, for the trail to precognition had a number of roadblocks and detours of its own.

The first of the detours was caused when two of the researchers at the laboratory found that they could shuffle a deck of cards and by ESP make the order somewhat like that of another deck, when they used that other deck as the target while they were shuffling. Ordinarily, two shuffled ESP card decks, if matched against each other, will show an average of only five similarities or hits. But these researchers had been able to do better than that by shuffling until they had the impulse to stop. Some of their results were nearly as high as those they had made on precognition tests. They called this process the "psychic shuffle."

Of course, if the persons who had shuffled the cards in the

precognition tests had used the psychic shuffle, then their results would not prove precognition at all. Even though those persons had not tried to make their shuffled decks match the subject's calls, no one could be sure they might not have done so unintentionally.

This meant that before precognition could be proved to occur, some way would have to be found to get a target list that could not possibly be similar to the list of calls for any reason but precognition. This difficulty in getting a truly random target list threw up one roadblock after another, but after a lot of trying over several years and in many different ways to prepare chance target lists, a method was finally developed which beyond reasonable doubt answers the purpose. It involves a complicated mathematical procedure which must be carried out on a calculating machine, because presumably no one can do it in his head. That procedure gives a figure which tells which page in a book of random numbers should be used to get the target list. The details of this method are not important to anyone unless he needs to make the target list for a precognitive experiment. But like the statistical formula for evaluating ESP results, it was very important in the research that such a formula was worked out, so that if the results were high enough to show that something other than chance was involved, they could only be evidence of precognition.

Over many years and numberless trials, the results have shown that subjects can to a significant extent foresee before shuffling what the order of the deck will be *after* it has been shuffled. Today the evidence for it is too strong for reasonable doubt. Besides this experimental evidence are all the true dreams that are reported, and also cases when a person seems to glimpse a future event even when awake. A girl in the eighth grade in a school in New Mexico, for instance, was listening to the teacher read a poem one day, when her attention wandered and she saw herself in nurse's uniform and in a hospital ward with other nurses. She remembered one nurse particularly, for the glimpse had been brief but vivid.

Four years later the girl entered nurse's training. She was "speechless" with surprise, as she reported, for it was the scene exactly. And yes, the charge nurse who admitted her was the person of her dream.

Surprisingly, even though the possibility of knowing beforehand is not yet generally recognized, half at least of all the experiences people report because they suspect them to be psychic are of the precognitive type. They seem to indicate that ordinary people have at least a trace of precognitive ability.

Sometimes, too, it appears that they may have more than just a trace, at least if the detail shown in many reported experiences is any indication. For instance, a woman in North Carolina said she dreamed one night that she heard shrieks and shouting in her yard and rushed to the door. There she saw her own and some neighbor children and her dog and cat being chased around the yard by a monkey. She thought she opened the door just in time to herd the children in before the monkey got there and threw himself against the screen. Then he turned and chased the cat, which escaped, up a tree.

The dream was so fantastic that she told the family about it. None of them knew of a monkey in town, but that very afternoon *it all happened, just as in the dream.* They learned later that a man who lived nearby had brought a monkey home for a pet the night before, and it had escaped from its pen that afternoon.

After the precognition experiments had fairly well shown that ESP can go into the future, it was realized that precognition and clairvoyance were really just the same except that one told what the target was in the present, the other, what it would be at a later time—only a few minutes later in most of the tests, but some of the tests covered a longer time.

The longest time interval covered in a test up to the present involved a Duke University student who had taken some ESP tests in the laboratory and got better than chance results. Then she went to France for a year of study. While there she did some more tests and sent her records of guesses back to the laboratory to be kept for one year before being checked.

When the year was up, the target list was made at the laboratory, and then the year-old records that had been made in Paris were checked against the new list. The results were good enough to show that ESP had operated in them too. It looked as if a year of time does not prevent ESP from working. And as for spontaneous experiences, some of them appeared to be covering even longer time intervals, as in the case of the girl who became a nurse four years after she "saw" herself in the hospital ward.

But now, what about telepathy? At the Duke Laboratory that question had been waiting all this time for someone to see if an experimental answer could be obtained.

7. Telepathy at Last—Or Was It?

One afternoon a young man stopped at a Howard Johnson's to get a cup of coffee. As he was drinking it he noticed two chocolate-covered doughnuts in a case with a lot of other pastries, and thought he would like to have them. The waitress was facing away from him, but then she turned, picked up a plate, went to the pastry case, picked the two doughnuts from the assortment and set them in front of him. The man was "flabbergasted."

The waitress laughed and said, "This is what you want, isn't it?"

A schoolteacher in Texas was busy marshaling her line of children from their second-floor classroom downstairs to the cafeteria which was in a separate building at the back and without a telephone. Just then she knew with strong conviction that she should stay near a phone. A call was coming which she must not miss. The principal's rule, however, was that she must stay with the children. This time she did not do it. She went back upstairs. In minutes the call came. It was her older sister calling to say that their younger sister was at the point of death. She must come home at once.

The first was an unimportant happening, the second a very serious one. But either experience could raise the question of telepathy, on which, ever since the 1870s in Europe and America, an occasional experiment had been made. Often these experiments had given encouraging results. It was not until the first year or two of research by JBR at Duke University that the realization was clear, however, that none of those earlier tests could have proved "pure" telepathy even when the results were significantly above chance because the experimenters always had their targets written out or printed, and so the possibility of clairvoyance had not been ruled out.

About 1935 when the Parapsychology Laboratory at Duke University was set up under Dr. William McDougall, with JBR the director, it was separate from the Psychology Department. Although JBR had been following the trail to telepathy, the detours already outlined—clairvoyance and precognition—had slowed down the advance toward the old original objective.

Then too, after the results of the clairvoyance tests were published in 1934, a new reason for hesitating in regard to telepathy emerged. Many people, particularly scientists in other fields, did not accept the report about the discovery of clairvoyance. They believed it impossible to "know" something like a symbol on a hidden card, and so they claimed that the results were either just chance and the formula used wrong, or that mistakes of some other kind had been made, or even that the reports of the tests were just plain lies.

Luckily the charges could be refuted because the formula was not wrong, and all of the results of the more conclusive clairvoyance tests had been carefully checked. In many of the researches they had been checked by two different persons, independently, so that they did not depend on one person's word alone. Even though two persons could both be liars, this double-checking made it less likely, and it also safeguarded against unintentional mistakes.

This need for double-checking made the clairvoyance test results more certain and reliable, but at the same time it made testing for telepathy more difficult. This was because it was not easy to perform a test and avoid having objective targets and records and yet be able to have the results checked by two persons independently. Specifically, in a "pure" telepathy test, the experimenter could not use a written target list against which to check the subject's calls, for that would make clairvoyance possible. He had to have a random target list so the formula could be properly used, but it could be only of an idea in his head. But then how could two people check the result? Because of the difficulty in finding a technique which would solve this problem, the test had been continually postponed.

TELEPATHY AT LAST—OR WAS IT?

Finally, however, a way was found. Two research assistants at the laboratory, both named Betty as it happened, managed it (1). They could do so because they knew each other well and had many memories in common.

One of the two, Betty Mc., was the experimenter, the other served as the second checker. Betty Mc.'s first step was to do a coding job. For this she memorized a number from one to five for each of the ESP card symbols. Then she took a well-shuffled ESP deck, and using her set of code numbers instead of the actual symbols, recorded them in a column of 25. She did this with four decks of cards for each of the subjects she meant to use, and with the understanding that her code would never be recorded in any way so it could become a target for clairvoyance or precognition.

Then in the test the subject was in one room and the experimenter in another down the hall with only an electric-light system connecting them. When the experimenter was ready she thought of the ESP symbol that the first number in the column meant to her, and kept that symbol in mind as she pressed the button that turned on the light in the subject's room. Then when the subject had recorded the guess, he pressed the button turning off the light. They repeated this for each of the four runs of twenty-five calls that each subject made. When a run was finished, Betty Mc. went to the subject's room with her list of numbers and mentally checked the subject's list of calls, but without indicating which ones were hits because that might have revealed the code to the subject and spoiled the experiment. She could tell the subject how many hits he had made but not which ones they were.

After a series was completed the lists were checked and double checked. For this the other Betty, Betty H., played her part. Although Betty Mc. could not repeat or write the code, she could let Betty H. know what it was because of their common memories. For instance, suppose her number one had stood for a star (of course no one knows to this day whether it did or not), she could say number one stands for something we saw last night when we were looking at the moon.

Then when Betty H. knew and had memorized the code, but without ever speaking it, she could take the subject's records and check them against Betty Mc.'s list of numbers. But neither of the checkers could even make a check mark by a hit on the record sheet because marks might have made targets for clairvoyance.

After a large number of tests like this had been made and double-checked, the excess number of hits was measured by the same formula used in the clairvoyance and precognition tests. It was great enough to show that something besides chance was involved. That something could be considered to be "pure" telepathy, since no clairvoyance was possible, and even precognition could be ruled out if neither of the Bettys ever revealed the code. This was in 1945, and so far as is known, they never have revealed it. Beyond much doubt, by now they have both forgotten it.

Whether it is actually "pure," however, depends on a still unsolved riddle about the nature of the mind. Is it an "entity" in itself, or only the shadowy result of brain processes? If it actually is the latter, then the target the subject perceived could have been just the physical effect in the experimenter's brain when he was thinking of the symbol. If so, then the telepathy effect would actually be a clairvoyant one, after all, for it would depend on a physical brain process and not a thought as such.

This uncertainty about the relation of brain and mind makes the actual telepathy situation unclear. Until the psychologists get an answer worked out, parapsychologists can speak of telepathy as the awareness of the thought of another person without committing themselves to either view of the brain-mind relation.

This test in which all possibility of clairvoyance was eliminated (except the possibility that it was involved in the brain action itself) was considerable trouble to make, and it has seldom been repeated. On that account the evidence for telepathy "pure" at least to this extent is slight as measured by the actual number of tests, compared to clairvoyance, but it is strong enough that it can be reasonably accurate to say that pure telepathy as the awareness of another person's thought occurs.

However, in tests in which an experimenter does look at cards or other objective targets when the subject is trying to guess them, the results very often are higher than when only clairvoyance is possible, though this is not always true. It could be that ESP is easier when the target is both a thought and a thing, a situation that is called General ESP (GESP), or it could be that it is not actually easier, but simply more interesting for the subject and on that account he may score higher than with clairvoyance alone.

At any rate, most of the experiences people report are such that either pure clairvoyance or pure telepathy could be involved because in most life situations, thoughts and things are so intertwined that no one can be sure whether one or the other or both was the actual target. And more than that, in real life no one cares too much which it was, though often they prefer to think it was the thought they got.

For instance, a young engaged couple were separated while the girl was away teaching school and the young man off with a camping party. One lovely autumn night the girl could not sleep, and got up and sat by the window, enjoying the moonlight and wondering about her boy friend and if he was asleep and wishing she could send him a message. A few days later she had a letter from him telling about the vivid dream he had had of her that night in which he saw her sitting by the window. Of course, they felt certain it was a case of telepathy. It would not have meant half as much to them if they had realized that it could just as easily have been a case of clairvoyance, since it was not the girl's thought but her image that the young man saw in his dream.

It was important for the sake of science, however, to get reasonably strong evidence that a person can know another person's thought just as well as a symbol that no person knows. Even though the controversy about brain vs. mind is still unsettled the range of possible targets for ESP was widened by the telepathy tests from things in the present and in the future to other person's thoughts as well. The three are widely different and between them cover about every kind of target imaginable, so that now it is possible to say that extrasensory perception is simply another way of knowing about the world. The familiar one is by the senses, and it tells us about the part of the world that is close enough for seeing and hearing, at least when no barriers like walls or other physical objects are in the way. And of course, to be seen or heard, the object or event must be existing right then. Seeing and hearing do not tell directly about what occurred before or will occur later.

But the extrasensory way of knowing is not interfered with by walls or physical barriers, nor even by time itself. Clairvoyance, telepathy, and precognition bring information about different aspects of the world, but the method by which they do so is the same for each. It is a mental ability, the ESP ability.

The discovery of the ESP ability gives a quite different answer to the original question, whether telepathy occurs, than had been expected. It calls for a different kind of explanation from any that were imagined when the question whether telepathy occurs first came up.

As already mentioned, the idea that telepathy might be real had suggested that, if so, it must mean that some kind of radiation or brain-wave process accounts for it. After telegraphy was invented, and later radio, it was natural to begin to look for similar kinds of explanations for a mental mystery like telepathy if it should prove to be a true effect and have to be explained. But now extrasensory perception of more types than just telepathy had been shown to occur. Clairvoyance and precognition were found to be mental abilities too. They extended the range of extrasensory perception enormously. The explanation must be even more difficult than any earlier supposition about telepathy alone could have been.

What then did this discovery of ESP ability mean for the question of survival that had been in the minds of Dr. McDougall and JBR in the beginning? That is a separate story for later chapters (see Section 5). The next one is the discovery of another aspect of the mind that may well be the one least suspected beforehand of all.

8. Moving Dice, Not Mountains: Psychokinesis, or PK

The Bible says that by faith man can move mountains. No one has yet seen it done, however. But then, no one can say that anyone who tried to move a mountain by that method had the high level of faith such a task would call for. Perhaps the situations have been more on the level of this one:

> My son, Jerry, has learned to control objects if he thinks it is necessary. For instance, he is a student and athletics do not interest him, but during his grammar school days, he felt left out because he simply could not make a basket or hit a ball. One day he determined to make an experiment. The result was his first home run and excellent results at the basket. He said he simply first visualized the ball hitting the bat as it left the pitcher's hand, or visualized the basketball falling into the hoop. It worked. The boys began to choose him to play. He had achieved "social success."

That boy's mother, who lives in Iowa, believed, as the rest of her letter to the Parapsychology Laboratory shows, that her son somehow influenced the situation and, by mental attitude, changed the course of the balls. His changed attitude perhaps could have been a little like the biblical "faith." But even so, probably few people would agree with his mother. They would say that perhaps the reason Jerry did poorly in these sports was he was too tense and nervous, but that when he tried to visualize the ball, it diverted his attention and so changed his mental attitude that the anxiety that usually affected his muscular coordination was removed. In a situation like Jerry's, certainly no one could tell whether anything more had been involved. In fact, the reason Jerry's mother even suspected it may have been was because she had heard about research on psychokinesis (PK) that was going on at the Parapsychology Laboratory.

The PK research had begun not long after that on precognition. As if the still unsettled question of the occurrence of telepathy and then precognition were not a sufficient number of "impossibles" to engage the developing Parapsychology Laboratory, the question whether the mind can affect matter directly was also taken up.

Psychokinesis was an idea that few people outside of parapsychology had ever taken seriously, but it was one that had long been suggested in psychical research. However, it had never been tested experimentally. No satisfactory way to do so had ever been worked out, but now it was realized that the common technique of throwing dice, essentially as used in gambling, could be adapted to the experimental situation. By this method a mental effect on a physical object could be measured, as it could not be in life situations.

The way to do it would be to have subjects throw dice for specified faces. By chance alone, on the average, each die face has one chance in six of falling uppermost each time. This would give the necessary basis against which an excess of target faces, if they should be secured, could be measured. It could then be determined by a statistical formula if the excess was great enough to be significant.

Perhaps the best way to describe this PK technique would be to give directions for performing a simple experiment. To do this experiment, procure six ordinary dice and a small container in which they can be easily and thoroughly shaken. A cylindrical quart ice cream carton will do. Have a paper and pencil handy. Shake the dice well with one hand over the top of the box, and then vigorously toss them into a corner (on the floor or on a table) while willing the ones to come up. Count and record the actual number of ones obtained. By chance alone, with six dice thrown, one target face on the average should come up on each throw. Repeat three times for one run (four throws, twenty-four die falls in all) and the number of hits by chance would be four.

Then make similar runs of four throws each for the two face, the three face, and so on around the die for one set. The number expected by chance per set will be twenty-four. Then repeat for six sets and chance should give 144 (6 × 24). But most persons will have more hits than this.

If the total score for the set had been twenty-eight instead of twenty-four, and six such sets were made, the number of hits would be 168 (6 × 28). Then the excess twenty-four (168 − 144), according to the statistical formula, would mean that the odds are about a hundred to one that something more than chance was involved. (See Appendix) If the test were properly done (without tricky throwing, and all die faces used as targets equally), that something would be PK.

Thousands of tests were made by this method with controls against biased dice and tricky throwing (2). Over the years different experimenters and many different subjects at different places were involved, and the overall results showed that something had certainly disturbed the laws of chance. In experiment after experiment, the number of hits significantly exceeded that obtained when no human will was involved. The effect had to be recognized as one of mind over matter. The evidence for it, by this method and others developed later, is now so strong that no one actually has to prove again that PK occurs.

In a case like Jerry's it is not impossible that he might have exercised a PK effect, but if so, certainly no one could prove it. It is even possible that in many unrecognized and unrecorded instances the proper attitude—or faith?—may have called out the same ability. Such effects may very well have lain behind the biblical statement about the mountains, but whether so or not, nothing but controlled experiments, in which the chance factor could be estimated, would ever have proven that an ability like PK exists.

The fact is that in ordinary life situations, if PK does occur, it is masked by the expected and much more obvious effect of the muscles, just as ESP is masked by the expected and obvious effect of the senses. Because of this, it is still difficult to believe that PK is real, for almost no one ever sees it happen in ordinary life.

One could try forever—it would seem—to move even a ball just by looking at it and wishing it to move, and—no movement, unless an air current or vibration helped out. Such is everyday and commonsense experience. Few people are easily convinced of anything that goes against common sense. That is the reason it took people a long time to believe that the world is not flat, even though hints were given all along from the beginning of the world to show that the earth's surface is curved, as for instance the way ships disappear on the horizon, bottoms first.

Similarly, hints of PK have always existed, but remained hidden, and few people noticed them or took them seriously. For instance, over many ages people occasionally have noticed after a death or injury in the family that a clock or watch stopped at the critical time. For instance, on a certain Sunday, in Queensland, Australia, a man noticed that his watch had stopped at 10 minutes to 10. It was not run down, and was a usually dependable little timepiece. He could find no ordinary reason why it should have stopped. He learned soon after, however, that at that time a hundred miles away, his mother was struck and knocked down by a speeding motor bike. She died thirteen hours later. He noticed the coincidence, thought it unusual, but until PK had been experimentally proven no possible explanation except coincidence could be advanced.

Not only clocks, but other effects, like pictures falling from the wall, dishes breaking, electric lights coming on or going off —all, of course, for no reason that could be found, were reported from time to time.

For instance, a girl living away from home was in bed and nearly asleep one night when suddenly the light overhead went on, frightening her badly because she was the only person in the room, and she knew she had not turned it on. For some reason, perhaps because she had heard that such things were "signs" of distant crises, she said she "knew" that something was wrong at home. In the morning she got word that her father, a miner on the late shift, had been critically, but not fatally, injured when a motor fell on him and crushed his pelvis.

More common a hundred years or so ago, than such experiences, were reports of objects that moved in seance rooms. Special persons or mediums were said to produce them. But the seance rooms were usually darkened, and objects could be seen to move only because they had been marked with luminous paint. Under such conditions a number of tricks were possible. If the person in charge was dishonest and could gain his ends by so tricking the audience into thinking they were seeing miracles, nothing could prevent it. If, on the other hand, the medium was quite honest and objects did actually move, no one could be certain of that either.

Over the years many researchers tried to find out in seance rooms whether the mediums who produced physical effects were honest. But their attempts were never successful enough to impress the more critical. Even demonstrations made in lighted rooms did not either, for even a lighted room in which a number of persons are present is not necessarily a good place in which to make a scientific experiment.

The accounts of clocks stopping and other kinds of effects that happened at the time of a death or other crisis, were in one way less questionable than the phenomena reported from seance rooms. At least the people who reported them had no motive for faking the case. But even so, such occurrences could be passed over as just a "coincidence," "one of those things." No one could prove by personal experiences that a strange force like PK exists.

In addition to these cases, poltergeists were reported. (see Chapter 26). In them sometimes stones and dishes were said to be thrown around very strangely. But these too sometimes were shown to have been tricks when some "bad" boy or girl had fooled his elders, and so they could be dismissed without being considered to mean a special force like PK. Nevertheless, reports of these kinds actually could mean that an unknown force must exist to explain them. The old saying "Where there is smoke, there's fire" was probably coined for just such situations as this.

This situation in regard to the possibility of a psychokinetic force was in the background in 1934 when JBR instituted the PK research. Naturally he was impressed by the fact that the ESP research had shown that extrasensory perception, at least of the clairvoyant type, was a reality. It made the possibility of an "extramotor" force seem more reasonable, and so the time for this particular research had come, even though precognition and telepathy were still not fully settled.

In fact, the beginning of the PK research overlapped that on precognition sufficiently that it caused a major correction in the method of selecting a proper random target for precognition tests. Before the PK force had been suspected, one method of getting the target had made use of a throw of dice to provide a number at which to enter a random number table for the required sequence of targets. But as soon as it was realized that the dice just possibly could be influenced by the person throwing them, they were eliminated and other randomizing procedures used.

For a number of years after 1934, the PK experiments were made mainly with dice in tests much like the one described above. Then the experiment was changed, and a different kind of PK test was introduced. In it the subject tried to make the dice go to a specific *place*, rather than trying to cause a specific face to come up.

For this test it was necessary to release the cubes from a stationary container to roll down a sloping runway onto a flat surface divided down the middle into left and right sides. The subjects would try to influence the falling dice to one side in half the trials and to the other side in the other half, thus equalizing any bias that might exist if the table were not perfectly level.

Of course, by chance alone half of the dice should fall on each side of the line. If a sufficiently greater number fell on the target sides, then PK could be considered to be involved. This endeavor succeeded in a number of experiments carried out by different investigators. In general these "placement" tests yielded results comparable to those for die faces, both in level of significance and in the conditions under which they did or did not succeed. They provided the first experimental data to show that the PK ability can operate under more than one circumstance.

However, both the tests for face and for place involved objects already in motion. The mental effort had been to try to divert them from the path that natural causes would dictate. At the same time, it was well recognized that the effect suggested by seance room reports and certain spontaneous cases were made on objects at rest like dishes and pictures. But direct attempts to move or affect static objects in the laboratory had never been successful, though those on moving dice had been ones like the attitude toward the test, but also internal ones that might have an unconscious effect. It made the experimenter's part in the test more important than had been realized, and it also made it seem likely that everybody has inherent ESP, but that unconscious conditions may keep them from showing it.

When PK testing began, the same effect was found. The subject had to have the proper spirit. He had to be interested, determined, and confident, but even so, he could not always succeed. He might have unconscious reasons why he could not, for PK too was clearly an unconscious process, and the subjects did not know how they did it.

Another similarity between ESP and PK is the one already hinted at above, the tendency for the scores sometimes to go below chance, as those of the goats often did. Sometimes the scores would go so far below, even when the subject was trying hard, that they were not the result of chance, an effect that came to be known as psi-missing, missing so often that it took ESP or PK to do it. The same formula that could measure positive scoring could measure this negative scoring too. It was another aspect in which ESP and PK were alike. This all led to the idea that PK was as much a mental ability as ESP was, and for all anyone knew it could be part of the same one. Or perhaps it would be better to say that ESP and PK may well be just two different ways in which a single general ability operates.

However, no one could be expected to explain such an ability as this so soon after its discovery, or to be sure just where it fits in with what is known. An English psychologist, Dr. Robert Thouless, asked after he himself had obtained evidence of both ESP and PK, why not give the ability the name of a Greek letter, *psi*, which will not even give a hint of its nature? (2) And so it came to be called the psi ability. Of course it could just as easily have been psy, for psychic.

But who then actually does have the psi ability? Are the persons who show it only a special few who are gifted with psychic powers? Or does everyone have it, but because it operates unconsciously, it only breaks through a little now and then like flecks of sunshine on a rainy day?

As everyone knows, the old idea before the discovery of either ESP or PK was that prophets, mediums, even fortunetellers and clairvoyants, had special gifts that accounted for the times when they seemed to know things that ordinary folks had no way of knowing. As the research in parapsychology went on, this question about whether ESP is a special gift of a few persons was slowly answered.

10. Who Has Psi Ability?

I am a young girl of thirteen. I was ten years old when my father died. This is the story. My father kissed us goodbye and left to see my mother who was suffering from a nervous breakdown at the hospital. Usually I did not kiss him goodbye, but for some unknown reason that time I did.

We washed the dishes and went to bed, two younger boys and my sister who was fourteen. My father had said. "I'll be home late tonight." We all bunked down in the living room.

About 4 A.M. I heard sirens. I woke my sister and said, "I hear sirens." She listened for a moment and told me she heard nothing. I woke up later and told her that the sirens were for Dad, meaning that he had had an accident. She scoffed at me and told me to go back to sleep.

I dreamed on, and suddenly I saw it. My father's car overturned on the boulevard near the house. We woke up the following morning with policemen in the house and the neighbors cooking breakfast. They told us Dad was dead.

Can one person be more susceptible to ESP thoughts than another?

This touching reminder that tragedy can come to young as well as older persons shows, too, that even sisters can be very different in their susceptibility to "ESP thoughts." One of these two slept only fitfully, apparently disturbed and even awakened by an ESP "message" about her father's accident. The other one gave no sign of premonition. But did only one "have ESP"? Or was the situation for the other somehow simply not quite right for the message to come through?

It took many years of study of parapsychological effects before an answer could be given to the question of who has psi ability. And when it could, it was not what people had always expected. When research began at what later became the Duke

Parapsychology Laboratory, the main idea was to find a person who had this ability and study him to find out what the power was and what made that person different.

With all this in mind at Duke University in the early 1930s, a number of student volunteers were tested to see how many cards from a concealed deck they could guess correctly. JBR and a colleague tested their psychology classes to see if someone could be found who could guess an especially high number of cards correctly. The majority of those tested, like the sister who slept the night her father was killed, gave little or no sign of psi ability. Their scores were practically at chance. A few were even lower, but a dozen or so out of many were higher. These were singled out for more experiments. Out of this group, two persons already mentioned (Hubert Pearce and Adam Linzmayer), did much better than any of the others. From their records, it looked as though they might have been the "gifted subjects" for whom the search was being made.

It seemed probable that these two and perhaps some of the next best were somehow different from the others. But how? They seemed like normal college students, with no special characteristics to set them off from others. Nor did they seem to be alike in any noticeable way. Still, perhaps some unusual trait of personality that other students did not have was hidden in them.

In the following years, the personality of subjects who took ESP tests was studied to try to find a clue. It seemed possible that a *type* of personality would be found that permitted more than the usual expression of psi. All through history occasional persons have been reported who seemed to be especially psychic, and in repeated tests all subjects were found to vary considerably in the level of results they achieved.

But psychologists trying to construct tests to separate people according to their common traits have not had an easy job because humans are so very individual. No two are exactly alike, or even very much alike, except identical twins—and even they are not entirely the same. It would take a page or more to list the differences we all see every time we are in a group of people or even with the family around the dinner table.

Nevertheless, psychologists have managed to classify persons into groups according to some of their most outstanding differences. Usually it is done by making a list of questions by which those who answer Yes are separated from those who answer No, but a study made in 1946 by Dr. Betty Humphrey at the Duke Parapsychology Laboratory was based on the kind of freehand drawings a subject might make (6).

A psychologist, Dr. P. Elkisch, in working with children, had noticed that they showed different personality patterns that were reflected in the kinds of drawings they made. For example, she found that the lively, spontaneous children, if asked to draw a house, would make a big, free and easy drawing, and perhaps use most of the sheet of paper for it. She called this kind "expansive." At the same time, the shy, quiet, reserved children would usually draw a tight little outline up in the corner of the sheet for their house. She called them "compressive."

Dr. Humphrey then tried this expansive-compressive test with a number of ESP subjects. First she took the ESP results of the subjects who had been given clairvoyance tests and asked each one to make a freehand drawing. (The clairvoyance test, it will be recalled, is one in which the subjects guess the order of cards in a hidden deck when no one looks at the cards.)

It would have been just fine if all the high scores had been in either the expansive or compressive group, but it did not turn out that way. The subjects did show a significant difference in their scores. The expansives had scored above the average that chance would give. The scores of the compressives, however, fell below the chance level just about as much as those of expansives were above it. It was the psi-missing effect mentioned in the preceding chapter. Both groups had shown ESP, but in opposite directions!

Then the same subjects were given a GESP test. In these, the experimenter looked at each card while the subjects tried to guess it, so that either clairvoyance or telepathy could operate. Again, the subjects made freehand drawings, and each group got scores significantly different from chance. But—they were reversed! The expansives had scored below chance and the compressives above!

The tests, then, did not show that expansive or compressive tendencies mean that a person does or does not have ESP. They did show that, depending on the kind of test, the two groups tend to score in different directions. But it did not show that either kind of personality has more ESP ability than the other, only that they react differently even to such slight variations as whether or not the experimenter looks at the cards during an ESP test.

Also, while still an undergraduate before coming to the Parapsychology Laboratory, Humphrey had used the Bernreuter personality test then in vogue in an attempt to divide ESP subjects according to whether they were of the more outgoing type or tended to be inhibited and reserved. (1)

Later, in 1951, although the Bernreuter test was no longer in much use in psychology experiments, Humphrey found that when applied to ESP subjects, as high as 74% of the extraverts gave positive ESP scores while 71% of the introverts scored below chance.

These results did not really mean that the extraverts had ESP and the introverts did not, because some extraverts scored lower than some of the introverts. The occurrence of ESP thus did not appear to be exclusively linked with either kind of personality, but rather, if anything, with the *direction* in which their ability would be expressed.

Over the years, a number of other personality tests which have included the many ways in which people differ, have been given to ESP subjects. Even the original observation of Schmeidler that belief or disbelief in ESP (the sheep-goat difference) affected scoring tendencies is not an "all-or-none" fact. When the group labeled sheep was broken down into well adjusted or poorly adjusted, the former obtained higher average scores in ESP tests than the latter.

In 1971, two experimenters from India, Miss Kanthamani and K. Ramakrishna Rao, published the first of four studies on the personality characteristics of ESP subjects. The third of these included the extraversion vs. introversion difference, and they found, as had earlier experimenters, that psi hitting was correlated with the former (extraversion) and psi missing with the latter (introversion) (2).

Another factor which Kanthamani and Rao studied was that of neuroticism, of which anxiety is one of the components (3).

The study showed that <u>less anxious groups scored higher</u> than anxious ones. They reasoned that the less anxious subjects adjusted more easily to the test situation, were consequently more at ease, and therefore more likely to score positively. The experimenters concluded that the way the subject adapts to the novel ESP test situation can determine whether he will hit or miss the target.

Thus it is that, to date, personality studies have fairly conclusively shown that the *direction* <u>of scoring is affected very much by the way different</u> personalities react to test situations, but in none is it <u>shown that all signs of ESP are found in one personality group and none in the other.</u> All subjects seem to have the possibility of showing ESP, but the slightest change in the situation can make a great deal of difference in whether it will be expressed in an above chance or below chance direction.

Sometimes in real life people have experiences that seem to indicate that something keeps ESP from operating until all at once, just like sunshine from behind the clouds, there it is. Somewhat like the watch case in Chapter 1, a man in Ohio lost a tiny leather purse in which he carried a small but valuable gauge which he used in his work in an experimental laboratory. There were also twenty-eight tightly folded dollar bills in the purse. He hunted the house over and posted a notice on the bulletin board at work. He thought if someone had found the purse, he might at least return the gauge, but there was no response. His wife, who was away on a visit at the time, returned home. She too hunted all over the house but could not find the purse.

Months went by and the incident was forgotten. Then one night, after hours of sound sleep, the wife woke up as if someone had called her saying, "Go look in the big chair." She thought of the big, overstuffed chair in the living room, but she had looked under the cushion there and cleaned under it many a time. She tried to go back to sleep but could not.

Finally she slipped quietly out of bed into the living room in the dark so as not to waken her husband. She slipped her hand under the cushion. Nothing. But then she slid her hand along the side and came upon a small hole. Slipping her fingers down into it she felt a small leather case, the lost purse. She could not wait, but woke her husband, and both of them marvelled not only that she had dreamed where the purse was, but that she had done it so long after it was lost. Why then, rather than at the time they were so actively hunting it?

Such experiences show, just as the personality tests do, that somehow little changes in the obstructing conditions must occur before psi can break through. Possibly in this case, the necessary mental state did not come until the strain and tension of the loss had worn off.

Both from experiments and many spontaneous experiences, then, it seems that psi appears to be a possibility for everyone. But in some people, ordinary circumstances may let it happen freely; in others, these are not enough. For these, it apparently takes a strong emotional crisis, such as a death or accident.

For instance, one woman had her only psi experience the fourth night after her acutely ill father had been taken to the hospital. The doctor thought her father had a fifty-fifty chance of recovery, and she herself felt that he would recover because he was comparatively young and fighting very hard.

That night the woman dreamed she was floating upward toward a pale blue mat. She knew her father was on the mat although she could not see him. A light fog was all around her, but higher up around the mat the air was clear and beautiful. She thought, so this is what heaven looks like. Then the ringing of the telephone awakened her. It was the hospital calling; her father had just died.

For that person, if her dream actually did involve ESP, one could at least guess that the obstructions that prevent psi are thick, and only such a crisis as her father's death could break through them. For many others, life may never provide the necessary combination of factors to permit a recognizable psi occurrence. But on the other hand, for a favored few it seems that ordinary life situations do. In recent parapsychological literature two personalities stand out as especially gifted ESP subjects: Mr. Lalsingh Harribance (L.H.) and Bill Delmore (B.D.).

L.H., a native of Trinidad in the West Indies, had become well known there because of the "readings" he gave. At the Psychical Research Foundation, Durham, N.C., a number of experimental studies were made with him in which his results were high enough to bear out his reputation as a special subject, though not an infallible one. In two sessions his brain wave patterns were recorded while he was taking ESP tests, and high-scoring ESP runs showed more percent time alpha (see Chap. 13) than chance scoring runs (5).

B.D., a law student, had a strong interest in his own psi ability. He reported many spontaneous psi experiences and was noted for the "tricks" (which did not seem like legerdemain) he displayed with cards. He came to the Institute for Parapsychology and underwent a series of tests mainly by Dr. Ed Kelly and Dr. Kanthamani (4). He did not like formal card tests, but preferred situations in which he could respond more spontaneously. However, in 20 standard ESP card runs, he averaged 8.2 hits per run, a CR of 7.16.

Tested with other devices, including a PK machine, his results often were phenomenally high, but his personal temperament and general impatience made him far from an easy subject with whom to work under acceptably tight conditions. He did, however, display a high level of results in a range of different kinds of tests, although the experimenters were not able to subject him to standard personality tests. Certainly the casual observer would see little personal similarity between B.D. (white) and L.H. (black), the one quick, voluble, spontaneous and impatient; the other, calm and self-contained, almost phlegmatic.

Quite obviously the basic personality qualities that mark the specially gifted ESP subject are just as obscure as those of the run-of-the-mill subject whose ESP abilities are more modest.

From all these signs, then, and too many more to mention here, it seems that everyone has psi ability, but like the ability to sing, though every normal person can do it, some do it better and easier than others. Singing, however, can be improved by proper teaching, but for psi no teachers yet know the rules. It is a spontaneous, natural gift, much like humor. Any rules for how to tell a joke can only help a little. It is something a few people "just know" and others never learn.

It is perhaps a bit like the discovery of the first trace of radium. That probably did not look so important then either.

Probably many persons when they first heard of it thought ... so what? It is nice to know, of course, but it could never be of real importance, if only because there is so little of it.

But one of the thrilling stories of chemistry is that of the Curies processing tons and tons of ore to get an ounce of radium. Its value was soon discovered and it affects very greatly the world in which we live. The value of psi may be somewhat the same. It has been discovered. Now it will take much more research to complete the story. Some of it has already taken the story farther (Section Three, Chapters 11–17), and some of it helps to show how psi fits in with the rest of the person. It may not be linked up closely with any special kind of personality as delineated in the personality tests of the present time, but it does have close links with the rest of the mental processes that we all use every day. And now that its reality has been established and enough about its nature discovered, it is no longer to be considered just a curiosity, but a significant element of mental life. It means that human beings have much greater powers than they have realized—how great they really are is still part of the mystery.

In chapters four to ten, the main finding of parapsychology has been outlined, and each of the parts that compose it has been discussed. Perhaps it should be emphasized again that the facts that make up the parts of this finding are the result of much careful experimentation by many different people at different places. However, though these people have confirmed the results over and over, others have tried and some have not succeeded in confirming them. Also, as already mentioned, some experimenters as well as some subjects succeeded at one time and later failed.

These failures seem to mean that when testing for such an unknown process as psi, attempts to secure evidence of the elusive phenomena are for a long time something of a hit-or-miss affair. No one at first knows all the rules for finding evidence of them and those who by pure luck or by special insight happen to do it properly get results, but others miss some necessary point and fail. In this case, since some did succeed, the failures only show that for them the conditions were not right. Such failures do not cancel successes any more than failures of certain "poor" teachers cancel the successes of the "good" ones.

The main finding of parapsychology, the fact that probably everyone has the psi ability, comes to most people at first as a far from convincing idea. However, more recent experimental work (Section Three, Chapters 11–17) which has been based on it adds its weight of confirmation.

SECTION THREE

Advances in psi research: in the schoolroom, in dreams, in various mental states. PK on static systems, on lower organisms, in the healing of disease, and ESP and PK in animals.

11. ESP in School

I am a high school senior. As every other student, I've had problem subjects. The one that most upset me was Latin. I struggled through Latin I. When I reached Latin II, I fell into the "Slough of Despond" and I began to give up. So I decided that I would repair to God for help. So I prayed. After about two hours a calm fell upon me, and I went to bed.

I felt I was spinning. Then I saw, as clear as day, my Latin teacher making out a "pop" test for the next day. I saw every question and her answers. I dreamed I took the test the next day. I saw the mistakes I would make.

When I entered Latin the next morning I nearly fainted when the teacher said we were going to have a "pop" test. I was even more amazed when the questions were the same I'd dreamed of. I remembered the correct answers and made my first 100. Every night thereafter I had dreams about Latin. My grades went up and I passed.

There is no way of proving I dreamed this, but I know I did. I sometimes have dreams of forewarning too. You may consider me a little off—or you may receive many letters like mine.

Betsy A.

Dear Betsy: Not many, but some. Few from students who prayed so long, or who prayed at all, and few who were able to answer all the questions correctly. At the least you obviously got into a very good mental state for ESP to function.

No, I don't consider you a little "off" for this, but quite a little unusual and quite a lot to be congratulated. I have heard of boys who managed to pry open a window at school at night and get a copy of the teacher's questions. They too "passed" the test, but failed the real one. You passed them both.

Could ESP function like that? Could the girl read the questions by clairvoyance in her dream, or by a combination of telepathy and clairvoyance? Why not, given the necessary motivation and receptive state of mind? It would be unusual, but no one can say it would be impossible.

The question of the possibility of ESP in the schoolroom has now been studied at some length. At least enough research has been done to show that the schoolroom is quite a fertile field for ESP and accordingly, its investigation. However, until the actual experiments were made, it was perhaps something that only an occasional "good" teacher guessed might happen. But it was because of such guessing that actual experiments were undertaken.

Only a few years after the results of the ESP tests at the Parapsychology Laboratory were first reported, a grade school teacher in Florida, Miss Esther Bond, later Mrs. Arthur Foster, noted the report and was curious to see if she could get evidence of ESP in her class (2). She had twenty-two pupils. As it happened they were mostly retardates and at the fourth and fifth grade level. She interested the children by telling them that she wanted to see if guessing numbers would be a fair way to choose pupils for special tasks like passing out materials or running errands. Consequently, they became very interested, just as she was, so that they all seemed to enjoy the test. After all, it was quite game-like.

The night before the test, the teacher would prepare a randomized list of numbers from 1 to 10. At the appointed time the next day, she would stand before (sometimes behind) the class and think of the first, then the second, etc. number on the list for about four or five seconds each while the children wrote down their guesses.

The results were quite surprising to Miss Bond, and she wrote to the Parapsychology Laboratory reporting them. She had made 2870 trials in all in this experiment, in which the number of hits to be expected by chance is only one in ten. But the total number of correct responses was 371, or an excess of 86. That gave a CR of 5.2 which is the next to the highest score ever reported in a schoolroom test. But it also was one in which both teacher and children were highly interested. However, the fact that the children were retarded apparently had little if anything to do with it, for although their degree of retardation varied considerably, no correlation was found between their level of intelligence and their scoring in the tests.

It was 1953 before another classroom test for ESP was reported, and when it was it came from Holland. School systems there are organized a bit differently than in the U.S. An inspector of schools, somewhat like a superintendent, has overall responsibility for schools situated over a considerable territory. One inspector, Mr. J.G. Van Busschbach, wondered about possible telepathy between teachers and students, and he proceeded to try to find out if he could get evidence of it (11). He interested the teachers in his district in the question and began with the fifth and sixth grade children of 10 to 12 years.

He had lists of targets prepared beforehand, and also a large cardboard screen behind which the teacher who would act as a sender would sit at the back of the room and out of sight of the children. He himself would observe the experiment, but have no actual part in it.

The teacher would look at the first target, and the children at the signal "ready" would write their guesses. Like Miss Bond's, it was a typical test of general ESP. It was tried in a hundred different classrooms—and it worked, not perfectly or in every class, but often enough to be considered successful, even though the scores were not nearly so high as Miss Bond's. But, of course, in these the teachers could hardly have been as involved as she had been. Van Busschbach, in a few cases, tried having a pupil instead of the teacher be the sender, but the results were not so good. Also his tests with higher-grade students were not so successful as with the fifth and sixth graders.

After he published his account of the tests, Van Busschbach was invited to the Duke Parapsychology Laboratory in the United States to see if he could repeat his experiment in American schools. At the laboratory then was a former teacher, Miss Margaret Anderson, and a colleague, Miss Rhea White, both of whom were also interested in ESP in the schoolroom. With their help, Mr. Van Busschbach tested 23 fifth and sixth grade classes and 17 seventh and eighth grade classes in two American cities.

The results on the fifth and sixth grades were about as good as those in Holland, but those of the higher grades were close to chance, just as those at that level in the Dutch schools had been. It seemed possible that the students of the lower grades had been more interested than the older ones in the particular type of test that was used. Later on Miss Anderson and Miss White gave tests to higher grades too, and they adapted them so as to make them more interesting to the students of these higher grades. They then obtained significant evidence of ESP in them too (1).

When Mr. Van Busschbach had to return to Holland, the two American testers continued with classroom experiments, making changes to adapt the tests to the age and the stage of the students. Back in Holland, meanwhile, Mr. Van Busschbach tried out some first and second grade classes, with a technique made especially for them (12). It included no writing of their answers, but simply crossing out on a special record sheet the target they chose for each call. Again, he got significant results. On the whole he felt convinced that some ESP at least goes on in classrooms.

Meanwhile in the United States, the Anderson-White team expanded the schoolroom experiments in a number of ways, including a large number of classes and conditions. They did much of their testing in high schools, but also some in elementary grades in two North Carolina cities.

In general, they used tests of clairvoyance in which a target sheet was made up for each student; it contained 125 symbols, that is 5 columns of 25 each. The sheet was enclosed in an opaque envelope. A record sheet was stapled on the outside just over the target sheet inside. The students were given these envelopes and told to fill in, in the spaces of the record sheet, the symbols they guessed were on the target sheet underneath. In some tests, however, a precognitive technique was used. In this the students filled out their record sheet first, trying to match the target record that would be made *later*.

These variations in type of ESP test both yielded positive results at about the same level. The precognition tests thus added evidence for precognition which was only then beginning to be used in tests like this.

In all the experiments the amount of interest aroused in the students was found to be important. For example, the more enthusiastic the teacher was, the better the results, probably partly because she then passed her enthusiasm on to the children. Another element that helped was in adapting the test to the special interests of the students, at their grade level and there by getting them to feel involved in it.

One innovation the testing team introduced yielded perhaps the most meaningful finding of all; meaningful, that is, for teachers and parents, in fact for the teaching profession especially. The new finding was the relationship between the ESP scores and the personal liking of the student for the teacher and of the teacher for the student. In order to test this relationship, the teachers were asked to rate the way they felt about each student. Then the students were asked to rate how well they liked the teacher. Their ratings were sealed and mailed to Anderson and White so the children could be sure their responses would not be seen by the teacher.

These ratings produced four groups of relationships among the students: 1. those who liked the teacher and were liked by her; 2. those who disliked the teacher and were disliked by her; 3. and 4. groups that combined like-dislike attitudes. The results were that ESP scores were highest in the mutual likers (1), and lowest in the mutual dislikers, (2). These last were so far below the chance level that they were "psi-missers" (see Chapters 9 and 10), which meant that they *avoided* the targets more than they could have done by chance alone.

Later Anderson and White correlated the ESP scores with the students' attitudes toward the teacher and with their class grades. In general this showed that the higher the student's grades, the higher his ESP score too. Of course, the attitude of the teacher to a pupil probably affected his grade, but the ESP score was an independent measure.

Most interesting of all was the fact that the children who received low class grades and whom the teacher did not like had ESP scores regularly below chance. It looked as though the student-teacher attitude, which of course was linked with the class grades, was disclosed in the ESP test itself. Thus, the ESP result could serve, in a way, as an indicator of teacher-student relations.

In the decade and more since Anderson and White finished their research, several attempts to replicate their research have been made, but none have yielded significant results (9). Some were in the expected direction but not significantly high; others were at chance. The difference in outcome could have been because Anderson and White were highly interested in their projects and inspired the teachers (who were mostly friends of theirs) with whom they worked with their own enthusiasm. On the other hand, those that tried the repetition could hardly be supposed to have had the same high level of interest and enthusiasm the original experimenters had, and this is a factor that apparently is as important as the record sheet on which the results are recorded.

Soon after the first report of Van Busschbach's tests in schoolrooms was published, a primary school teacher in Amiens, France, decided to see if she could show the importance of strong rapport between teacher and pupils in her class of first grade children (13).

She was Madame Christiane Vasse, the wife of a physician, who was teaching because she wanted to and because she liked children, trying to develop strong, personal friendships with them. But she realized that her rapport with them only developed gradually as the school year progressed. Her idea, therefore, was to test for ESP at the beginning and again at the end of the school year.

The French school system prohibits a teacher from introducing during school hours an outside project like an ESP test. She therefore worked only with children who wanted to play "the ESP game" at recess.

Three groups of tests were made using similar clairvoyance techniques in all but adapted to first grade level. In the spring of 1955, the first group of tests was made with fifteen children taking part. By that time the rapport between the children and herself was strong. The results were nearly as high as Miss Bond's had been.

In the fall of 1955 with a new class, only five children volunteered. Two scored positively and three negatively. The difference between them was significant, showing that ESP was probably present, but with no definite overall trend. But in the spring of that school year, when the third group of tests was given, the same five children all scored positively and their scores, along with six more children who by then wanted to join in "the game," was the highest that has so far been reported. Madame Vasse could feel that she had made her point, that the demonstration of ESP in school children depends very much on the pupil-teacher relationship.

Another test with school children, these even younger than Madame Vasse's, but also suggested by the work of Van Busschbach although quite independent of him, was later reported from the Netherlands (8). This was conducted by Miss N.G. Louwrens.*

This experiment was made with preschool children (4 to 6 1/2 years) instead of the older ones tested by Van Busschbach. The details of the method were complicated, but in general, groups of twelve children at a time were given colored pictures of toys. As the teacher told a fairy tale, she (behind a screen) looked at one of a similar collection of pictures of toys selected in random order. As she did so, at breaks in the story, she asked the children to pick out the toy that they thought she had in mind and lay it aside in a pile. The order of the pictures in the pile each child made was recorded at the end of each story and served as the basis of the later check-up.

The experiment yielded overall significantly high scores, this in spite of the fact that in ten of the groups Miss Louwrens herself took the place of the teacher, and none of these ten yielded above chance results. This, of course, is more evidence on the point made by Madame Vasse, for Miss Louwrens was not a familiar figure to the children and no doubt the necessary rapport was lacking.

One observation on Miss Louwrens' experiment was that in a number of her groups, though not in all, the girls had scored significantly above chance but the boys did not. This suggestion of a sex difference in ESP scoring was followed up through a number of different test projects over a number of years by Dr. John Freeman, then at the Parapsychology Laboratory.

In 1963 Freeman reported a study made under his direction

---

* Under the direction of Prof. W.H.C. Tenhaeff at the Parapsychology Institute of the State University at Utrecht, the Netherlands.

by a teacher of mentally retarded children (4). This and all of the succeeding ones reported by Freeman involved a precognitive technique. It was a game-like test involving mimeographed picture booklets which Freeman had designed and which could be returned to him at the Parapsychology Laboratory. There he could secure random target lists against which the children's responses could be checked. The advantage of this precognitive technique in tests sent out to teachers or students when the conditions cannot be controlled with certainty is obvious, since in any event the check-up is controlled. Each successful project thus gives added evidence of precognition as well as for the specific purpose of the test.

On each page of the booklets used in this test with the class of retarded children were five rows of five pictures each. The teacher told a story to the pupils and at appropriate places paused and called for the selection by each child of the "right" (the one she was thinking of according to a randomized order) one of the pictures on a given page of the child's booklet. When he had selected it, he marked it with an X.

To Freeman's surprise, the boys scored above chance, the girls below. The difference between the two trends was significant. Then before the teacher was told the results, she was asked to rank the pupils according to her feeling for them. She put all the boys first, the girls last. She did not like girls! Here again, as in the Anderson-White experiment, was evidence of the "underground" working of ESP, apparently according to psychological influences which are not too deeply buried to be recognized.

Following this tip as to the possible obscure effects of the sex difference in ESP responses in schoolchildren, Freeman then varied the details of his technique in repeated schoolroom tests. From his first report he had found indications that above or below chance scoring marked the overall scoring tendencies of the sexes. They tended to score differently under similar conditions not only because of the teacher's attitudes, but probably because innate and other tendencies also were different.

Still using the idea of booklets, Freeman rearranged and amplified the target material in different ways in different projects over several years. In the course of them, he tested schoolroom groups at various grade levels from kindergarten to high school, always finding what appeared to be sex-linked differences in response trends, even though the reason for them was not easy to see (as for instance when boys and girls scored in opposite directions from chance depending on whether the pictures in the rows on the booklet pages were the same or different).

However, when he tested seventh grade children and applied sub-tests from the psychological personality test of Primary Mental Abilities along with the booklet ESP tests, the situation was somewhat clarified. He first used two sub-tests, one measuring verbal reasoning ability, the other spatial relations.

On each of these, psychologists have found sex differences in ability to be particularly pronounced, for this early adolescent stage is a critical one in the development of the higher mental abilities. For instance, at this stage girls are markedly better than boys in the verbal tests, boys better than girls on spatial relations. The ESP tests followed the same pattern of difference.

A third test was then administered to the pupils at the end of the seventh grade year, a test of reasoning ability (5). In this, the girls who had a higher spatial IQ than verbal (a minority) and were also high on the reasoning test scored in the same direction as the boys on the ESP booklet test. The boys who had the reverse results (also a minority) and were low on the reasoning tests, performed on the booklets like girls. The difference between the two was significant, and it appeared to be the result of varying stages of mental development rather than the sex difference.

While these tests have not as yet been independently confirmed, they suggest that the apparent boy-girl difference in ESP may not be directly sex-linked but is rather connected to certain more or less obscure mental characteristics which do tend to be sex-linked. Such a view makes a degree of sense. It needs to be confirmed however, and if it is, followed up in greater detail.

One other test, mammoth in size if not in scope, also suggests a fundamental difference between the sexes in the manner of response to ESP tests. It was reported by Robert M. Brier, then at the Institute for Parapsychology (3). The experiment resulted from an article in the junior high school magazine *Read* which included a sample record sheet for a test of precognition. The student was invited to fill it out and send it in to the Institute for checking. There an individual target list would be made out for each sheet in order to avoid a statistical complication known as the stacking effect which results when a common target is used for a group of subjects.

The result of the *Read* test was an unexpectedly large response. Over 100,000 boys and girls in roughly even numbers sent in responses. The job of providing individual lists for each and checking them was probably the largest of its kind to date.

As expected, the overall results were at chance, expected because in no group of responses in which subjects are undifferentiated in any way has significant evidence of ESP ever been found. As is now known, the conflicting tendencies of individuals, some who are psi hitters, others psi missers, cancel out and only chance averages result. This may be one of the reasons why historically ESP was for so long unsuspected.

But internal evidence of ESP was found in this mass of data, and it was in connection with the only differentiation possible, that of boys vs. girls. The score distributions of the girls were significantly different from chance, but those of the boys were not. But in 22 out of the 31 classes represented, a certain fluctuation of hits within the run was significantly different from chance for boys while that for girls was not. These differences were obscure and perhaps only to be noted in a large mass of data. But they suggest again that psi probably is present "underground," whether or not circumstances reveal it.

Some recent experiments go farther than any of these earlier ones to demonstrate this. These were carried out by a husband and wife team, the Drs. Hans and Shulamith Kreitler of the Psychology Department of the University of Tel Aviv, Israel (6). They wanted to see if ESP could influence the outcome of a psychology test, when both the experimenter and the student subjects were unaware that an ESP aspect was hidden in it.

In the Kreitler experiment, it was arranged that, unknown to both the student subjects and the experimenter who carried it out, a number of persons, strangers to the subjects, were stationed in other rooms. These were instructed to act as "senders" and to try to convey answers to the subjects taking tests. The details of the setup varied in the four different experiments reported and the details of the results varied accordingly, but in general a statistically significant effect was registered. It was slight in individual cases, but cumulative over the number of subjects who took the tests. The result indicated that unknowingly the subjects had been influenced somewhat by the thinking of the hidden senders.

An unexpected aspect of the result was that the ESP effect was not distributed evenly among the answers to the test questions. When the questions were separated according to those to which the subjects "almost" knew the answers and those to which they did not know the answer at all, a difference was shown. The ESP effect occurred almost entirely on the latter. Contrary to expectation, it seemed that rather than reinforcing and completing an "almost" response, the weak ESP signal could only have an effect if the person had no other source on which to draw.

In a later set of experiments by the same investigators, a number of variations on the same theme were tested (7). In one of them, some of the senders were instructed not to try to send answers to the student recipients but only to keep the answers in mind.

The result as before showed the strongest ESP effect on the questions to which the subjects did not know the answers or in which the information they had beforehand was wrong and thus conflicted with that which the senders had in mind. Further, the responses roughly corresponded to those made when the senders were actively trying to send.

All of these tests with senders were essentially GESP tests. As already mentioned (see Chap. 7), it has been noticed that when GESP and clairvoyance tests are compared in an experiment the subjects often but not always seem to score higher on the GESP test. When everything else is equal, this appears to mean that the fact that a sender is involved serves to *enhance* the target—to make it stand out and thus be more likely to be a hit. It does not necessarily mean that the sending was essential to the telepathy process as such, for as will be shown in Section

Four, it often seems to occur in spontaneous experiences, particularly when the sender is not sending and even when he is entirely unaware of the percipient.

The details of these experiments need to be repeated and confirmed and already one confirmation was reported at the Parapsychological Convention of 1974 (still unpublished). No doubt others too will be, for their results could have a bearing even greater than that of the effect in the classroom. A recent review by Stanford (10) covers a number of other instances in which findings indicate that ESP effects occur when the subject is unaware that they could. After reviewing some relevant earlier work of his own, Stanford discusses not only the more recent Krietler work but also earlier experiments by various researchers in which the same feature was involved. In all of them some evidence was given that the subjects were affected, however slightly, by the hidden ESP targets.

Stanford notes that such "unconscious" ESP effects (psi-mediated instrumental response, or PMIR he calls it) could occur without making the person in any way aware of them. This again could mean that an ESP element could well be involved much more broadly than is usually suspected, as perhaps in many spontaneous experiences that have been regarded as only coincidence. He ends by urging that the possible implications of parapsychological findings be considered more seriously than has yet been done in connection with possible psychological and biological applications.

Toward this, the actual ESP tests in the school room can be considered as only an introductory step, of value first in their educational bearing, but leading on to a wider application in many life situations.

12. Experimental Dreams and ESP

A woman in Wisconsin, sleepless one night, picked up a new book by her bedside. However, it turned out to be a disturbing kind of story, and when she came to an episode in which a bunch of hoodlums attacked a girl and dragged her to a garage, she put it down and tried again to compose herself for sleep.

Just then her teenage daughter came out of her adjoining bedroom, upset, she said, by a terrible nightmare. She had dreamed that she was attacked by a bunch of hoodlums who had dragged her into a garage to rape her. The dream seemed almost a copy of the scene about which her mother had been reading.

Such experiences in which one person seemed to get the thought of another were of course the kind that led to the experiments to show whether telepathy occurs. But in the early days of psychical research, people were impressed more by experiences that came when the person was awake than they were by dreams. Dreams then were not considered to be of very much value as evidence of anything more than erratic and unguided thought processes. Not until after the work of Freud showed that they may have great psychological significance were dreams taken with some seriousness.

In parapsychology, even though many spontaneous experiences that seemed to involve ESP come as dreams, the subjects used in experiments were generally awake. The use of dream material seemed inconvenient and cumbersome. Of course, no one knows even yet whether a larger number of persons would succeed in ESP tests if it were possible for them to dream their responses instead of having to give them when wide awake. In the spontaneous experiences that people report (discussed in

Section Four) both waking and dream forms occur in roughly equal numbers.

Only fairly recently have parapsychological studies been made on dreams, and, as it happens, on one type especially, that of telepathic dreams. However this type of dream was probably not selected because telepathic dreams are the most common kind, for they appear to be rarer than other types. Only a few of the ESP dreams that are reported seem to involve only telepathy. Even in a case like the one above, the girl could have taken the theme of her dream from the page her mother was reading (clairvoyantly) rather than from her mother's thought. Or it could have come from the two together. At any rate, the choice of telepathic dreams for study was apparently made because this type had excited the interest of psychiatrists especially, or more correctly, of certain psychiatrists. And this was because sometimes a patient, when told to report his dreams, obviously had some that were true and that involved the psychiatrist himself. If this occurred often enough, and if the psychiatrist was sufficiently openminded to recognize such cases for what they were—evidence of an extrasensory way of knowing—then telepathy at least whether "pure" or not, became a reality for him.

Dr. Montague Ullman, a psychiatrist in New York, was one to whom this happened (1, 2). In 1953 he made a preliminary study with Mrs. Laura Dale of the American Society for Psychical Research to see if they could induce telepathic dreams. They had enough success to be encouraging. But it was about ten years later, after a new technique for dream study in general had been developed, that he began on a larger scale.

The new technique for the study of dreams had followed on the discovery in brain research with a device for recording brain waves (the electroencephalograph, EEG) that when dreaming, the sleeper's eyeballs moved rapidly under the closed lids. By attaching electrodes properly, these movements could be recorded on tape. They were shown to come in bursts, with quiet intervals in between. This meant that now an experimenter could tell when his sleeping subject was dreaming. By the Rapid Eye Movement (REM) technique, he could waken the subject and ask him to tell his dream, when formerly he could only guess when a dream was in progress.

At the Maimonides Hospital in Brooklyn, a center for dream research was set up. (1, 2) In 1964 Dr. Ullman and several others undertook to try to induce telepathic dreams. In the years since, they have made a large number of experiments with considerable success. But the procedure is necessarily slow and costly in comparison to the ease of experimenting with subjects when awake. The objective here, however, was not to prove telepathy, but to show experimentally that dream content can be affected by the thought of a sender (or at least by a GESP target which this was).

In the technique that was used the object of the experiment was explained to the subject: he was to try to dream about the target a sender would have in mind. He was put to bed in a darkened room at the laboratory, the proper electrodes attached to record general brain activity and the periods of REM sleep.

In an adjoining room the experimenter was located with the EEG machine and an intercom system to the subject and the agent who was located in a room still farther away from the subject. The agent had been provided with a target randomly selected from a dozen others all in opaque envelopes. The targets usually were art prints chosen to be as different in detail and general tone as possible.

No one knew which print was in the envelope chosen by the agent at a given time. He opened it after he was alone in his room and for the first half hour concentrated on and recorded it and the associations it called up in his mind.

While this concentration may have made it more likely that the dreamer would pick up the idea of the target, it was not actually necessary that the agent try to send his thought, although, as mentioned earlier, often people think that telepathy occurs because a thought is "sent" by the agent. But the mother in the case above did not send the idea of the scene she was reading about to her daughter. The girl got it because of her ESP ability; that is by a mental process that is the same whether the target is a thought or a thing or a combination of the two. The experimental dream situation was similar.

When the experimenter could see that an REM period was

finished he woke the subject over the intercom and asked him to tell his dream. The subject's report was recorded on tape. He was then told to go back to sleep. The same target was kept for the night, so that several REM periods might be related to it.

The data for each night's session thus consisted of the target picture plus the agent's associations with it and the records of the subject's dreams. The question then was whether the dreams did truly reflect the target. This was a judgment not so simple to make as when in an ordinary ESP test a list of call symbols is checked against a target list, for the dream imagery seldom reproduces the target picture exactly. If any of these dreams are ESP dreams, they are of the unrealistic rather than the realistic type (see Chapters 18, 21, 22) and the same question applies: does this imagery refer to the target or not?

Often there were suggestions of similarities between the two that were far from exact, and then the question was whether the test response should be counted as a hit. For instance, in one case the target picture showed a group of Mexican revolutionaries and clouds and mountains in the background. A subject's dream protocol went like this:

A storm, rainstorm. It reminds me of traveling . . . approaching a rainstorm, thundercloud, rainy . . . a very distant scene . . . for some reason I get a feeling of memory now, of New Mexico . . . etc.

Thus, to judge material of this kind is not a simple matter. On that account it was necessary that it be done "blind" and preferably by several different judges. The first judge used in the above tests was the subject himself. When this session ended, the experimenter removed the electrodes and gave him the twelve pictures that had made up the target pool, and he was told to rank them from one to twelve as he thought they may have been the subject of his dream.

Copies of all the material were then sent to three other judges who were asked to rank the dreams to the target pictures, from one to twelve just as the subject himself had done. These judges were people who had studied dreams and also parapsychology. Then a fourth judge was also chosen to decide in the opposite way, which protocol was like which picture. From the results of all the judgments of the judges, it could be determined whether the dreams were or were not significantly like the targets. Over a considerable number of experiments using different agents and different subjects, sometimes significant and sometimes nonsignificant results were obtained. It looked as if success was better with some combinations of subject and agent than with others. Also, the subjects varied in the amount of correspondence their dreams showed to the targets. In one outstanding experiment a male psychologist was the subject, and when he ranked the targets with his dream record, all twelve of them were correct.

A study of hits in this series of dreams showed that some elements of the targets were taken over realistically in the dreams and others were "distorted" or transformed, apparently by suggestion, into something else, like Atlantic Ocean into Atlantic City.

The total impression that the dream experiments had given Dr. Ullman by 1970 was that they had shown that ESP does occur in the dreaming state. While this can scarcely be said to be news, in view of all the reports of psi dreams, it is at least news that the fact has now been confirmed by controlled experiments.

The dream research, with the techniques that were developed in connection with it, also served as a stepping stone to the study of other aspects of the relationship of brain processes and psi. Most of this study, however, is still far from finished. Even the basic brain research is constantly leading to new concepts. In fact it appears that this field of dream and brain research is now just fairly opened. The next ten years or so should tell much that is still unknown today about the relationship of brain, and mind, and psi.

13. Psi and Various Mental States

An archeologist and his wife were staying at a hotel in a small Greek village. The archeologist had to make an extended visit to a museum at some distance. One morning during his absence, his wife decided to visit the excavation where he had been working. It was about two miles over a mountain trail. It was a hot, sunny morning in early autumn when she set out, accompanied by her little Greek dog.

The mountain, covered with loose rocks and boulders, was practically treeless. After walking a ways she became quite warm and noticed a single tree ahead on the trail. It was a gnarled old olive tree. Gratefully she sat down upon a stone beneath it and smoked a cigarette. She noticed that the little dog did not come and sit beside her as usual, but had stopped on the trail and when called, did not come but ran off, nose to the ground, in the opposite direction.

When the cigarette was finished, the woman started on down the trail. She called the dog and it came bounding up, licking her hands as if overjoyed to see her. The dog's actions seemed a little strange. They walked on to the excavation. It was nearly lunchtime when they started back.

The return trip was hotter than ever and she looked forward to the shade of the old olive tree, where she could rest a bit. But the tree was not there! She could not find a single tree anywhere on the trail. Puzzled and a little disturbed, she returned to the hotel. She mentioned her strange experience to the woman who ran the hotel. The woman shrugged and said: "That's the way it is here. They come and they go."

The next morning she set out over the trail again, determined to find the tree. It still was not there. When her husband returned they together followed the trail, but could find no sign of the tree. Her husband laughingly suggested she must have been sitting in "another dimension" which would explain the dog's curious action that day too.

The story ends here. If someone could prove that such a tree with such a stone beneath it had once upon a time been in that place on that trail, the experience could at least be called a possible instance of ESP. Without that information, it does not fulfill the definition necessary for the classification ESP because it may not have been actual information. What kind of experience could one call it then? It will have to remain nameless here, for it does not fit into any category, even though no reason exists to think that the woman who reported it did not believe it really happened.

The husband suggested, probably only half-seriously, that she might have been sitting in "another dimension." But what would that mean? People, especially philosophers, speak of dimensions when hard up for a reasonable explanation. But the term is only a figure of speech and explains nothing, although as used here, it would refer to a dreamlike state of consciousness, different from the ordinary one of full alertness.

For different reasons it has often been thought that parapsychological effects are linked with unusual mental states. In some cases it is easier today than it once was to see that no real connection exists. In others more investigation is still necessary. In instances like that of the missing tree, nothing can be decided because too much necessary information is lacking. One cannot tell if the woman was in an unusual mental state or whether the tree had been or ever would be at the place she thought.

Another kind of occurrence which has been considered to be related to parapsychology is the so-called out-of-the-body experience (7). It has interested parapsychologists because of the meaning that, at least on the surface, it seems to have.

For instance, a girl from New York, in normal health and sound asleep one night, felt a "tugging" and then found herself outside her body looking down at it as she slept. Then, "as if by a magnetic force," she said, she felt she was drawn up a long flight of stairs toward a bright light at the top. She came at length to the top and passed through a gate into a land of sunshine and warmth.

There she met her deceased relatives and friends and had a happy visit until someone blew a long note on a trumpet and she was told to hurry back so she would not be lost between two worlds. The experience was a great consolation to her and helped her to cease grieving for her loved ones.

However, in a case like that, although information seemed to have been given, it cannot be checked. It could have been pure dream fantasy, and the girl's feeling that she was out of her body just as unreal as the presumed glimpse of heaven. And so again, the experience does not necessarily have anything to do with parapsychology.

A somewhat different kind of out-of-the-body experience was reported by another woman, as it happens also from New York. She was in fairly good health, though she had been having minor medical problems for which the doctor had just given her a prescription. She meant to have it filled the next morning.

The doctor, a woman, was also a personal friend.

The next morning the patient overslept and when she awoke or thought she did, it was 9 A.M. Although she knew she was in her own bed, she somehow consciously felt that she was halfway up the stairs at the doctor's office. The office, however, she knew was downstairs, the living quarters, upstairs.

She had never been upstairs before because the doctor's father lived there too, and he kept the radio so loud that they could not talk there. But this time she knew he was in a room on the right. She could hear his radio and knew that he was listening to the news. She continued on down the hall to the doctor's bedroom, turning out for something as she did so. The doctor was propped up on pillows in bed, fully clothed, smoking a cigarette and running her fingers down the pages of a book. The patient felt happy to be there. She knelt by the side of the bed thinking that the doctor wanted to tell her something and waiting to hear what. The doctor just then *reached through her* and picked up the telephone.

The sound did it. She then came back to full consciousness in her own bed hearing the telephone ringing downstairs. She raced to answer it. It was the doctor, who explained that the prescription the patient had was the wrong one. Would she bring it back and get the proper one?

She did so and told the doctor about the unusual "visit." It was exactly correct in every detail. The book was the telephone book from which the doctor was getting the patient's number. The something she turned out for was a bureau that did not quite fit in the corner of the hall. Also, the doctor's father was in a room on the right, listening to the 9 A.M. news.

In this instance the information could be checked and it was true. The details given could, of course, have been perceived by clairvoyance. The experience then could be considered as parapsychological, but only because it brought information extrasensorially, not because the person thought she was out of her body and had travelled to the scene she visualized.

The main reason parapsychologists have had an interest in out-of-the-body experiences, however, has been because of the suggestion such experiences give that the mind (spirit) can separate itself from the body and operate without it. If that idea could be proven, it would be extremely important; it would tell us a great deal about man's nature. Even though religions, as discussed in Chapter 5, have taught that man is both body and spirit and that the spirit can exist independently when the body dies, science has not found any evidence of the independent existence of the spirit. Out-of-the-body experiences, on first thought, however, have seemed to offer such evidence. New projects for their study are occasionally reported (7, 8).

The argument about experiences of this kind, however, has a weak spot, so that it is not clear that research on them could have the desired bearing. No matter how free the person may feel when he thinks he has left his body, it is still living. There is no evidence that the connection between mind and brain is actually broken. The situation is not comparable with that of death after all.

Of course, it is always possible in science that research may unearth some new and meaningful result. Apparently that is the hope behind the recent research projects on the phenomenon. But unless some evidence is produced that complete separation does occur, this effect may not show that the investigation even belongs in the field of parapsychology. The out-of-the-body effect may simply be, whether or not an ESP element is involved, an instance of the creation of imagery necessary to make the person feel that he traveled to another place. In other words, it may be an *imaginary trip*.

Experiences like the one about the tree and the out-of-the-body kind are both comparatively uncommon, and certainly not everyone has them. But everyone does experience different states of consciousness, one of the most common of which is drowsiness. Then the mental state is certainly "altered," while in actual deep sleep ordinary consciousness lapses entirely.

Another kind of mental effect, automatic muscular action, also involves a mental change, even though of a somewhat different kind. When the pointer of an Ouija board seems to move "by itself" or when a person writes "automatically," unconscious muscular action is involved.

To understand something of the origin of the various automatisms, the way ordinary physical habits are formed should be considered. In these, after sufficient repetition, muscular movements come to occur without conscious attention being concentrated on them. For instance, such gestures as switching on a light when going into a darkened room can soon become practically automatic, as also is the case when one finds his way home along an accustomed route. He no longer needs to decide when to turn left or right but does it practically automatically. Habits like these are multiplied as, let us say, one learns the touch system of typing or piano playing. Soon the muscular movements become so automatic that the less attention paid them the better. They have become unconscious, and to notice and follow them consciously is even likely to "make all one's fingers thumbs" again.

This very ordinary experience of making muscular movements by habit can go on and on, and some of its more complicated effects have puzzled, mystified, and confused many people. This was particularly true before it was realized that the mind has an unconscious level. Now it is easy to understand that in forming a habit, one is really allowing the controlling of the muscular movements to drop below the level of consciousness. Nothing is strange about this.

However, when movement drops out of consciousness, it can do so because the mind allows itself to separate a bit, to dissociate, as psychologists say. If it is just the habit of pushing a light button, no one thinks about it. But suppose such dissociation occurs not because of habit, but for some other reason, as it also may do, and does in operating an Ouija board, or in automatic writing. Many people, and especially mediums, have produced volumes of material by these methods. The automatic effects so produced have puzzled many people in the past and may still be misinterpreted today. For instance, the Ouija board message that confused Angela (see Chapter 3) showed only that she could dissociate sufficiently to receive a message that made a kind of sense, even though it had no real significance at all.

The outstanding instance of the use of the Ouija is probably the one that began in 1913 in St. Louis, when a housewife, Mrs. John Curran, found that she could get intelligent responses using it. The messages purported to come from the spirit of a seventeenth century Englishwoman who called herself Patience Worth. The claim, however, has never been satisfactorally validated although the language used was of that place and time.

The volume and kinds of material received, novels, plays, poetry (some by the Ouija, and later by other automatic methods,) and its high literary quality have created an unending puzzle to scholars ever since. The story of Mrs. Curran and her amazing production has been completely and interestingly retold by Irving Litvag, in the book *Singer in the Shadows* (Macmillan, 1972). Litvag poses afresh the question of the identity of Patience Worth. Until that is settled, and unless it can be shown that Patience Worth ever lived, the case cannot be counted as actually falling into the field of parapsychology, although it will remain an outstanding literary accomplishment in any event.

Occasionally an Ouija message tells something that can be checked as true, and that is unknown to the person operating the board. For instance, a young woman and her roomates had occasionally "played around" with an Ouija and had great fun with the messages they got but did not take seriously. Then one day, alone at home and in bed recovering from the flu, the young woman suddenly found the pointer racing around spelling out a message about a charming young man she had met at a party.

The message she got was almost unbelievable. In fact, she

took it as a joke, for it told her, in effect, that the young man was a convict, that he was on parole, and that he was going to be involved in a shooting and a robbery.

He called her on the phone later in the day, and she kidded him about being dangerous because of his criminal past. But the joke was received with strained silence, and it was, she thought, a "sixth sense" that prompted her to ask him not to call her again.

Several days later, the young man's picture was on the front page of the newspaper with an account of his attempt to rob a warehouse. He had been shot by the police.

The Ouija message in that instance seemed to be also an ESP experience, a precognitive one, even though it came *as if* from an outside intelligence. That intelligence, however, was her own, as this person realized, for she did not think, as some might have, that it was a spirit. She quite rightly said, "This time ESP somehow came through, using the Ouija board as the means of communication."

As already indicated, the same explanation applies to automatic writing, a practice that was fairly commonly used by many mediums long ago, when people tried to learn to do it by sitting with a pencil in hand, while trying to divert their attention to something else. Eventually many succeeded in getting some meaningful material, even occasionally something that seemed to be significant. Usually the person not understanding unconscious mental action was convinced the material did not come from his own mind. And if he asked a question, he did not stop to think that the answer would be certain to sound as if coming from another intelligence.

Occasionally, an individual succeeded and found his hand had indeed written something of which he had no direct awareness. Such persons presumably are those in whom the necessary dissociation can occur. The messages so received, like most of those via the Ouija, may have no particular meaning. They at least have none for parapsychology unless, as in the case about the convict, they tell something true that the person holding the pencil did not know. In this event they become possible ESP experiences.

Many such automatic messages, like the out-of-the-body trip

to heaven, have seemed to give information about life after death, etc. But as already indicated, such material cannot be counted as significant because it cannot be checked for accuracy.

Other kinds of automatisms occur too. Some of them are like automatic writing, produced by one individual alone. One of these involves a free-swinging pendulum, and by holding this over a chart, or perhaps deciding beforehand which movement would indicate yes or no, fortunes are said to be told by the way it swings in answer to a question.

Still another form of motor automatism comes in the use of the dowsing rod, a device that appears to turn by itself in the dowser's hands when he walks over an underground stream of water (6). In this case, if the effect actually does show where the water will be found, and if other explanations do not apply (it is usually impossible in the field to be certain that they do not), then the effect would be one of clairvoyance expressed automatically by the dowsing rod.

A still different automatic effect is involved in the ancient practice of table-tipping. In this usually a group of people (or at least more than one) seated around a table with hands lightly on the tabletop ask the table to answer a given question.

If the table tips sufficiently to tap a leg on the floor, sometimes an intelligent response is received by using a prearranged code. It may be by numbers of taps for yes and no or by spelling words by stopping at appropriate letters of the alphabet.

In this procedure, if movement is obtained, the operators may not be aware that in their slight contact with the table, usually a finger or two at least, they can unconsciously exert sufficient pressure to cause the movement. Of course, PK could possibly be involved as well as automatic muscular action. If so, however, the two would be indistinguishable and whichever it might be, the significance of the answer so received would depend on its meaning, not the method of its reception. It could only be considered a psi experience if it fulfilled the definition: information received without the senses. The automatism as such would not in itself be significant.

Before ESP was recognized, automatisms seemed mysterious and sometimes were taken as psychic manifestations, the answers so received as coming from sources outside the individual involved. But now any intelligent response can be taken as coming unconsciously from the minds of the persons involved. Some automatisms, if carried to extremes or indulged in by persons of high suggestibility, could even have an unhealthy effect, such as encouraging extreme mental dissociation and the consequent release of abnormal psychological responses.

Ever since psi was recognized as originating in unconscious mental levels, it has seemed likely that the greatest barrier to its free operation is the difficulty of converting unconscious knowledge into conscious form. In Chapters 18 and 19 it will be shown that, when the person is awake, ESP information from the unconscious seems to be hindered by the difficulty of crossing the conscious threshold. This will be shown especially by incomplete, fragmentary, or otherwise imperfect intuitive experiences. In experimental tests too it appears that ESP is manifested only when it manages to break through the overlying layer of consciousness. Consequently, one objective in parapsychology has been to find an easier situation for the inducing of ESP than the ordinary one of trying to get evidence of it when the person is wide-awake and in full possession of his conscious faculties. Consequently, a renewed attempt has developed in psi research to find an "altered" mental state that would permit unconscious material to break through more easily (See review by Honorton [3]).

The research on ESP and dreams was in a way a venture into experimenting with an altered state of consciousness. But even before that, much research had been done on ESP and PK with the aid of hypnosis, which is considered by some to be an altered state.

Well over a hundred years ago, when hypnosis was first brought to public attention and before experimental work on ESP had begun, some of the persons who were studying hypnosis had strong evidence of extrasensory perception, and for a time it was thought that the two were connected (2). Even at the time when JBR began testing for ESP at Duke, as already mentioned, tests were tried with hypnotized subjects to see if they would give more evidence of ESP in the hypnotic state of mind than otherwise. However, not much improvement was found.

At various times since then the question whether or not hypnosis might help in demonstrating ESP has come up and experiments to test it made. The question seemed valid because in hypnosis the effect of the conscious part of the mind seems to be controlled, so that one might expect that material from deeper-lying unconscious levels could more easily break through. However, results have not been as decisive as expected. Consequently, even today it is not possible to say just what the effect of hypnosis on the occurrence of psi really is.

For one thing, research on hypnosis itself has hardly begun, and authorities do not always agree as to just what mental processes are involved. For another, the ways of inducing hypnosis are not entirely standardized, so that different hypnotists may use different methods. In addition, it is not easy to be certain of the depth of the hypnotic "trance," as it is called—if, as it seems, it actually is a distinct mental state. All of these difficulties along with the fact that each person has his own way of reacting to hypnosis, makes the hypnotic state a somewhat unpredictable one. Because hypnosis itself is an uncertain quantity, it is not too surprising that research on its relation to psi has not yielded very uniform or definite results.

However, in some instances ESP scores have been significantly better with hypnosis than without, even though still far from perfect. It is not certain, however, whether the improvement was the result of the hypnosis itself or because in inducing it the experimenter gave the subject so much special treatment that he did better on that account. One of the bothersome aspects of many psi tests is that a new technique in which either the experimenter or subject or both are especially interested is likely to yield better results, at least for a time, just because of the novelty and emphasis.

As mentioned in Chapter 12, the development of an apparatus for recording brain waves (the electroencephalograph) has facilitated research on ESP in dreams. It also made possible other important insights into brain activity.

This apparatus records on tape the electrical pulses or waves that the brain gives off. It has shown how they differ in different mental states, of which sleep is only one.

One of the mental states that everyone sometimes experiences is that of a certain quiet and relaxed condition that produces on the electroencephalograph a particular kind of wave known as "alpha." Of course, ordinarily no one knows at any time what kind of brain wave he is producing, but we all know that we have different mental states and that they feel different. For instance, think of the differences in feeling when one is almost dozing in comparison to when one is trying very hard to solve a difficult problem in math, or when petting a dog, or when fighting a bully, or when scared just before a car wreck.

A few years ago a psychologist, Dr. Joe Kamiya of San Francisco State College, put EEG electrodes on a subject's head and by giving him a sign, taught him how to recognize some of the mental states that produced special waves (4). The alpha wave was one which he controlled especially. The machinery was arranged so that when a subject fell into the mental state that produced the alpha waves, a certain tone was sounded. This was "feedback" to tell the subject that he was in the designated mental state. In time, some of the subjects learned to recognize and enter it.

The alpha state—calm, relaxed, but still alert—seemed so much like the one that has long been recognized as the optimum for ESP tests that parapsychologists began to experiment to see if ESP scores would be especially high when subjects were in it (1).

Again as with hypnosis, the results were not a simple Yes or No. The situation is too complex for an easy answer. More recently, Honorton, Stanford, and Lewis and Schmeidler in experiments differing in certain ways but all involving the EEG recording of brain waves during ESP tests did not confirm each other specifically. However, all of them did find a relationship of one kind or another between ESP scoring and the alpha state (5). In general, while the presence of alpha did not necessarily mean that elevated ESP scores would be produced, some of the highest positive scoring occurred when alpha was high or shifting from low to high, while it seemed that psi missing was related to the reverse alpha shift. Other interesting variations were suggested but all await further confirmation. In general they support the idea that the mental state that produces alpha and the ideal one for ESP are similar. Obviously mental state alone is not the only factor that influences ESP scoring in tests.

However, the greater insight into the relation of the alpha state and the production of ESP that further research should permit cannot help but add to the understanding and control of the psi process.

Recently a wave of interest in still another altered mental state has arisen. This is the one induced in meditation mainly by using ancient practices from India, such as the various meditation techniques of Yoga and Zen. Attempts to examine their effects on psi have been reported. Here too, some encouraging but not final results have been obtained. None of them so far has proved to be an "Open Sesame" that can fully unlock the gates of psi, but these mental states too need more basic brain research before it will be clear just what they mean or where they fit in.

When the brain itself is more fully understood, then surely psi will be. Exciting developments thus may lie just ahead.

14. PK on Static Systems

A woman in Maine, alone at home one cold winter evening, was watching television. It was a Walt Disney feature that ran from 7:30 to 8:30. She knew that her parents, who lived in a New York town, were in poor health, but she was not thinking of them specifically as she watched the program.

About halfway through the feature a sudden rush of frigid air seemed to come from the area of the outside kitchen door. Startled, she leaned forward to look into the kitchen to see if the door had blown open. But she saw that not only was it shut, but it was locked and bolted as well.

Two hours later she received word that her mother had died at eight o'clock that evening. (Her interpretation was that her mother had managed to come to her as she died. For a discussion of interpretations such as this see Chapter 24.)

Reports of "cold drafts" felt at significant times as in this case come up occasionally in spontaneous experiences and frequently over many years in reports from mediumistic seances. But no factual basis for phenomena of this kind nor any experiments to test them were reported until 1973. This claim, like many other "old wives' tales" was left unverified for, after all, perhaps the effects were purely psychological, i.e. hallucinatory, imaginary, the result of suggestion, fear, tension or other emotional influence.

However, if actual temperature changes could be caused by PK, they would be effects on a static system in distinction to those on moving objects like dice. The movement of the molecules would be initiated by PK. However, as mentioned in Chapter 8, direct attempts in the laboratory to affect static objects by PK had never been successful. In fact, none (excepting the possible effect of that on photographic film) had ever been sufficiently encouraging to merit even a preliminary scientific report.

The experiment reported in 1973 was carried out by Dr. Gertrude Schmeidler (3). It was suggested to her by Mr. Ingo Swann, whose spontaneous experiences had led him to think he could cause changes in temperature.

To test the idea, a thermistor (a kind of electric thermometer whose changes could be read on a Dynograph in another room) was sealed into each of four thermos bottles. These were placed at varying distances from the subject and in each test trial, one of the devices was designated as the target.

Test periods were forty-five seconds long. At the start of each, the experimenter asked the subject to "make it hotter" or "make it colder," according to a prepared balanced list. The recordings showed some success in heating the bottles. While some of the changes were highly significant, on the average they were relatively slight. Only one was greater than one degree, and the average was only about half a degree. Still, the experiment indicated that this subject at least had caused some significant temperature changes on the thermos-enclosed thermistors.

It was noticed that the non-target thermistors which were at a distance from the target tended to register in the opposite direction from it. This raised the interesting suggestion that possibly the energy used in the target thermistor's change was drawn from the adjacent area. The idea, of course, needs to be tested further as does the entire experiment, both in order to put a reliable basis under the possibility of an actual "cold effect" in spontaneous situations and to add to the known areas in which PK can function.

Dr. Schmeidler also briefly tested two other subjects. They were both graduate students and although one of them secured only chance results, the other produced a significant score. This is encouraging to others to repeat the experiment until it can be stated with confidence that PK can effect temperature changes.

While the account of completed and fully published laboratory experiments on PK on stable systems ends here (summer 1974), in recent years reports of demonstrations of apparent success in moving static objects have come from Russia. As remarked earlier, demonstrations are never quite on the same level of reliability as well-controlled and repeated experiments, but these demonstrations have been made to a number of non-Russian observers, some of them parapsychologists.

In spite of the restrictions and limitations that at times have been placed on investigators in Russia, a subject, Nina Kulagina, has been reported as able to move small, stationary objects by PK.

Two parapsychologists, Dr. J.G. Pratt and Dr. H.H.J. Keil arrived at the subject's flat unannounced and unexpectedly and brought with them several small objects of their own, intending to leave them with Kulagina until the time of the test they expected to make on her later (1). But she at once made an attempt to move the objects placed on the table before her. Both men saw the objects move, while neither one saw any evidence of fraud or trickery. The hoped-for experimental test to come, however, was forbidden by the authorities.

The observations possible of this subject have thus been limited, but they encourage the idea that if Kulagina can exert a PK effect on static objects, it probably is an ability that other human beings have. If so, in time subjects may be found and tested in areas more amenable to experimental control.

In fact, at the present time several other claimants to the ability to influence static objects or systems by PK are appearing on the horizon, and not only in the popular media. Some reports of two of these claimants were made at the scientific meeting of the Parapsychological Association in 1973. The investigation of neither of them, however, can yet be considered to have passed definitely from the demonstration stage to that of thoroughly controlled and repeated experimentation.

The most widely publicized of these claimants is Uri Geller, a young Israeli. Because of his TV exposure he has become widely known in the U.S.A., Europe, and Japan for his alleged ability to bend metal, spoons, forks, and keys merely by touching or stroking them. Although some reports of fraudulent manipulations by this subject have been made in the popular press, no method has been advanced by which metal could be bent normally under the conditions as alleged. Two researchers, Harold Puthoff and Russell Targ at the Stanford Research Institute, investigated Geller. However, their report to the Parapsychological Association Convention (1973) did not cover the bending of metal (2). They did testify that Geller was able to exert a force on a laboratory balance shielded from ordinary physical influences. The experimenters reported that the displacement shown on the chart recorder represented forces of one to one and a half gram. The same experimenters also reported that Geller apparently succeeded in generating a magnetic field as recorded by a magnetometer. Both experiments were repeated several times.

At the 1974 Parapsychological Association Convention, Mr. Edward Cox reported a test made with Geller which perhaps approached an actual experiment as closely as any so far reported (report awaiting publication). In a session alone with Geller, Cox presented the medium with two keys which he had brought with him. One, a safe-deposit box type too hard to bend by hand, was laid on a glass coffee table where Cox testified that it was perfectly flat. Cox then placed his finger lightly on the larger end so that there could have been no substitution. Geller then gently stroked the key with his finger, and as Cox watched, the key slowly began to bend upward to an angle of 12°.

The second key, one of the ordinary 3-inch skeleton variety made of softer metal was subsequently bent with Cox's finger on it until it reached an angle of 36°.

In addition, since one of the feats Geller had been reported to accomplish in popular, not test, situations was to make stopped watches start again, Cox brought along his Hamilton pocket watch. He had prepared it in advance by inserting a strip of tin foil about an inch long and 1/16 inch wide upon the balance wheel bridge, but beneath the speed regulator arm, extending 1/4 inch over the balance wheel with the arm set at F. Before the interview, Cox depressed the shorter portion of the strip into the spokes of the wheel and thereby stopped the watch.

Cox handed the watch (with chain) to Geller. Geller said he was uncertain if he could start it, held it to his ear, did not shake it unduly nor take it out of Cox's sight. Then Geller listened again and ejaculated, "It's ticking! It's ticking!" as indeed it was.

On opening the back, including the second cover which was difficult to open, the regulator arm had been moved to S pulling the shorter end of foil with it up out of the wheel. The remaining foil had itself been moved 1/2 inch away from the F-S section. The regulator arm had moved a total of 40°.

The demonstration on the keys and the watch especially, was such that Cox could conceive of no possible deception. He is convinced that increased research on Geller is warranted, although the performer's interest in entertainment and publicity make it difficult.

If Geller's ability is genuine as it now seems to Cox that it is, the gap between this accomplishment and the relatively minor ones so far secured in laboratory experiments is so great that even parapsychologists are scarcely prepared for it. Also, it makes all the greater the need to understand more fully just what may be involved.

In their 1973 presentation, Puthoff and Targ also reported work with the subject Ingo Swann, the man who was used in Schmeidler's experiment with temperature effects. For these experiments, Swann as well as Geller succeeded in generating an electrical field as measured by the magnetometer. Naturally, each new subject who proves able to accomplish such feats encourages the hope that a sufficient number of such gifted persons will become available for research so that the nature of their ability and its scope and limitations can eventually be understood. The availability of suitable subjects will no doubt be a necessary first step in this research.

Of course, no one can predict when such subjects will appear or when a breakthrough on a topic so unexpected and revolutionary as PK will come. No one can gauge the rate of scientific advance even in an orthodox and popular field, and certainly no one can do so in an area as obscure as that of PK. However, experiments on living organisms are yielding significant and encouraging results, as following chapters testify.

15. The PK Effect on Lower Organisms

Madame Christiane Vasse, the young wife of a physician in Amiens, France, and the primary school teacher, mentioned in Chap. 11, was a person with a restless and inquiring mind. She began to wonder if human thought could affect the growth of plants—make them grow faster, for instance. And so she planned an experiment to see, and she interested her husband in it too (5).

Madame Vasse planted barley seeds in two sets of little dishes on the windowsill: one set for her husband, and one for herself. She marked each dish in halves. The seeds in one of the halves were to be willed to grow faster than those in the other.

In a few days Madame Vasse's dishes began to show a difference, but the doctor's did not. By the time they decided to end the experiment the difference between the sides in Madame's dishes was so noticeable that she photographed them, and sent copies to JBR at the Parapsychology Laboratory because she thought he would be interested.

He was, not only because the plants on the sides of the dishes willed to grow faster were clearly larger, but also because the doctor's dishes showed no special difference. But of course though the pictures suggested that perhaps Madame's thought had had an effect, it was quite possible that the heat or light or water had been uneven. The conditions would have to be controlled more strictly than had been possible for the Vasses' before anyone could decide anything. But if the plants had really grown better because of Madame's thought, then it apparently would have been a case of PK on living tissue.

While the Vasses had done very well even to try such an experiment and to get results that were at least suggestive, they did not have the apparatus that would be necessary to be sure that all of the seedlings had just the same amount of heat, light, water, etc. They therefore had to turn to a different kind of experiment. It was no longer one involving living matter, but in a way it did have a bearing on their plant experiment.

This was in the early 1950s, and at the Parapsychology Laboratory, testing for PK with dice was still being carried on, and more work on it needed. JBR therefore suggested that the Vasses make some dice tests. They could make them at home and they would show if Madame really had PK ability, and if so, how her results would contrast with her husband's.

The Vasses took the suggestion. They made tests with dice and, sure enough, the results were similar to those with the barley seeds. Madame got scores that were highly significant. She apparently had considerable PK ability. But her husband's scores were only slightly positive and could have been the result of chance. And so, in an indirect way, the dice tests seemed to confirm the plant tests. At least the Vasses' work gave a good suggestion to later experimenters who tried to see if PK can actually affect living tissue just as it can affect moving objects like falling dice. But it was over fifteen years (1968) before another experimenter carried out an experiment that in some ways was fairly comparable to that of the Vasses and which will be described later.

Meanwhile in England, about the same time the Vasses were experimenting with plants, Mr. Nigel Richmond was also experimenting on the effect of thought on living organisms (4). But Richmond did not use plants. Instead he chose paramecia for his experiment.

Paramecia are tiny single-celled animals that live by the millions in pond water. They are so small that a low-powered microscope is necessary to see them. Richmond wondered if he could affect the direction in which they moved by concentrating on them and willing them in given directions.

He would put a drop of water on a slide under a microscope and center one animal under the cross-hairs, and then will it to move forward or back according to a random selection of targets. He did a large number of such tests, and his results showed that the animals had responded in a manner that strongly suggested that his thought had affected them.

Richmond's experiment was suggestive, but several other people who have tried to repeat it have not succeeded, whether because some necessary condition was lacking or whether Richmond's results were wrong, no one can say. However, the former seems more likely, especially because another experimenter has reported positive results in a somewhat similar experiment, but with a different kind of animal.

This experimenter, also in England, was Mr. John Randall, a teacher in a boys' school (3). He was impressed by Richmond's experiment. He was one of those who then tried to repeat it but did not succeed in getting above-chance results. He then devised an experiment in which he could get some of his students to act as subjects. He decided to use woodlice for his experimental animal. They are commonly found in dark crevices and under rocks in dark damp places.

In the test a woodlouse was placed in a small petri dish with the only light in the room, a single electric bulb, directly above the dish. The animal would at once try to get out of the lighted dish. The dish was placed over the center of a large cardboard diagram divided like a pie into five equal sectors, each one marked by one of the five ESP symbols. The subject then tried to will the animal to crawl out onto whichever sector of the diagram was chosen as the target. The targets were chosen by taking the symbols in order as they appeared one after the other in a well-shuffled deck of ESP cards. If, for example, the top card was a cross, then the subject willed the animal to crawl out onto the sector marked cross.

The result was that the animals went to the target sector, rather than to any of the others, a marginally significant number of times. Just as in Richmond's test with the paramecia, it suggested that the human subjects had had an effect on the animals.

One other observation of Randall's experiment was that the various students had varying degrees of success. The subject who got the most hits had a very significant score if taken by himself, and the one who had the least, had an almost significant negative one. But of course it would break a statistical rule to pick these scores out and think of them separately, except just to note in passing that differences like these, just like the one between Madame and Doctor Vasse, suggest personal differences in the PK ability to influence living organisms. Understandably, Richmond could have been an exceptional subject.

Another attempt to influence a lower organism was reported from France in 1972. The experimenter in this case was Louis Metta (pseudonym), a teacher of zoology at the Sorbonne (2). He used young caterpillars (*Lepidoptera* larvae) about three to twelve millimeters long.

As in Randall's experiment, the animal was dropped into the center of a petri dish under which was a paper, in this instance marked into twelve equal radiating sections. The attempt was to see if subjects could influence the sector onto which the larva crawled.

In alternation, half of the sections were designated "good" and half "wrong." The subject tried to influence the larvae to go to the "good" sectors in one session and then the dish was rotated so that the area that had been "good" was now "wrong."

The test period was one minute long. At the end of it the record was taken. If the caterpillar was not then definitely in or out of a target sector the attempt was labeled a mistrial and repeated.

Two subjects made eighty trials each. One scored at chance, the other had a significant negative deviation. A third subject acted as a control and attempted in his eighty trials to prevent the animals from scoring either positively or negatively and his results were at chance.

This experiment again, while being far from conclusive, suggested that individual subjects may vary a great deal in their ability to succeed in a task like this. Considering the known variability of subjects in ESP and PK tests, this would be no surprise. But until tests of this kind have been repeated and confirmed they are only preliminary and suggestive, not in any way final.

The 1968 experiment that somewhat confirmed the Vasse experiment on the growth of barley seeds was also carried out in France. It was made by a physician, Dr. Jean Barry (1). He was fortunate in having the help of the staff and equipment of the Institute of Agronomy at Bordeaux, so that his conditions were strictly controlled and the whole experiment was done according to established biological techniques.

Because he was a medical man, Dr. Barry was interested to learn if the growth of harmful organisms like certain disease-causing fungi could be slowed down by human thought. If so, it would be something the world needed to know. It might be one of the reasons people have believed in such phenomena as "spiritual healing" (the healing effect of prayer on disease), medicine men, witch doctors, and "healers" of all kinds who have been said to cure illnesses without doctors and medicine.

In Barry's experiment, he arranged sets of petri dishes uniformly containing a suitable nutrient medium for the growth of the organism. Then each of his ten subjects was assigned five experimental dishes and five control dishes. All of the dishes were then inoculated with a disease-causing fungus and put in an incubator to control the heat and assure that it was the same for all the dishes. (The lack of such equipment had made the Vasse's experiment inconclusive.)

At each subject's session all ten of that subject's dishes were brought out and put before him, and for fifteen minutes he willed to slow down the growth of the fungus in his experimental plates, but he was to pay no attention to the control dishes. In judging the results, it was necessary to decide if the fungus growth was greater or less in the control dishes than in the experimental ones.

At the end of the experimental period which had included nine sessions for most of the subjects, the average growth for each person's five experimental dishes was compared to the growth in his five control dishes. If it was less, the subject had scored a hit for his experiment.

Of course, by chance alone the results should have been about half hits and half misses, but instead, in the thirty-nine tests that were completed, thirty-three were hits and only three were misses, and three were ties. And so the results were very strongly in the direction the subjects had willed. It looked as if these subjects had indeed slowed down the growth of this fungus just by will power. The Vasses' experiment suggested that Madame Vasse's thought could *increase* growth; and the fact that Dr. Barry's subjects under well-controlled conditions seemed to *inhibit* growth was in a way a confirmation of the

Vasse experiment. But, of course, until similar experiments have confirmed these findings on a wider range of organisms, the experimental evidence on the topic is not complete. The indications, however, are very encouraging and suggest that the human mind—or some human minds—may indeed be able to exert an effect on living tissue. If so, it would seem very necessary to find out as quickly as possible how this can occur and the extent to which PK can help in the control and cure of disease.

16. PK and the Healing of Disease

In Iceland a man whom we will call Sigurd K. had long been famous for his horsemanship. He was often called a wizard for his skill in breaking and training horses. However, in the late 1960s, when he was over sixty years old, he began to have a pain in his back. First he tried to ignore it, thinking it was just rheumatism from all the jars and jolts of a lifetime on horseback.

In time, unfortunately, the pain became so bad that, reluctantly, he went to the hospital for examination. All sorts of tests were made and a bone sample sent to Reykjavik. The diagnosis was a malignant and rapidly spreading bone tumor.

The tumor was inoperable, and he was given X-ray treatment. It did not help. He could still walk a little, so the doctors advised him to stay home and have sedative treatment from his local doctor, until finally he would have to return to the hospital.

Somehow, during this bleak time, when he slowly became paralyzed from the waist down and was in constant pain, he heard of a "healer" in England who was said to have helped people recover from all sorts of ailments. Sigurd K. got in touch with her and a schedule was worked out under which he would write her every month and describe his condition. She would reply and tell him to pray at certain times.

Sometime after the schedule started it began to look as if Sigurd's disease was arrested. Even though he did not actually improve, he did not get worse either. The doctor still prescribed sedatives, but Sigurd tried to do without them as much as he could. He believed wholeheartedly in the healer, prayed when she told him to, etc.

Her letters to him were mostly the same: "Have faith." "Hold fast to me," etc. They were hardly the kind an outsider might think inspiring. His to her were mainly a list of pains and aches, but both went on regularly for over two years, with Sigurd never doubting the healer, and she telling him over and over to hold fast to her.

She charged him only a small fee, about $2.50 per month. It covered her time and the postage.

Finally, in 1971, the pain began to subside. Then he could move one toe. Little by little he got back the use of his legs. Then he could walk with crutches. Finally the healer advised him to go to a rehabilitation center for massage and that sort of treatment.

By 1972 Sigurd was riding horses again. He still needed a little help in mounting, but once in the saddle, he was his old self once more.

Doctors can make mistakes, of course, and a number of doctors were involved in this case. All of them said the same thing: Stay at home and take the sedatives as long as you can but eventually the disease will get worse and you will have to come back to the hospital.

Sigurd's case is only one of the many that are from time to time reported from all over the world, in which a person suffering from some disease or ailment that seems beyond the reach of ordinary medicine is helped or even cured by so-called unorthodox methods. Such methods usually involve a "healer" and a cure that seems unexplainable by any ordinary rules. Sometimes the original diagnosis can be questioned but Sigurd's diagnosis was more certain than many because it was made by a number of medical authorities. It therefore should have been reliable. Also a rapidly spreading malignant bone tumor would ordinarily be considered incurable, and Sigurd's physicians obviously so considered this case, since they gave him no reason for hope.

It is true that medical people do occasionally report surprise remissions, even of cancer. This means that sometimes, though rarely, the body somehow heals itself. But in this case in Iceland, and in many reputed "faith" or "spiritual" healings, the very element for which they are named does enter in. It adds an ingredient that thus far orthodox medicine fails to consider seriously. In a case like that of Sigurd's, what could the healer's thought, from across an ocean, have done to the man's body? And what could his own faith, hope, and will power have done to the tumor? Was it a one-in-a-million coincidence that this was "uncaused" remission, or was the cure a caused one after all, even though the means of cure was not yet a recognized medical one?

Questions like these are unanswerable today. Unorthodox healing goes on to a certain extent in all cultures. Cases of it, like this one, seem undeniably to occur. But explanations must wait for basic research, even for answers to the initial question, which in a case like this (granting it was more than coincidence), is whether the healer or Sigurd himself "did it." But whichever one was responsible, or if both together played a part, then mind affected matter: PK on living tissue was involved.

Of course, even the reality of PK itself is still too newly discovered to have yet been widely accepted by a skeptical and conservative world, or by a medical world perhaps even more skeptical and conservative of new claims regarding disease and therapy than scientists in general. Researches on PK on living tissues have been encouraging (see Chapter 15), but they are still in a preliminary stage.

It is true that reports of faith healings have been made in all ages, and those ascribed to supernatural or religious influences, as at Lourdes in France, have been studied for years. Also probably in all ages certain persons have felt and claimed to have healing powers. These claims of individuals more than anything else have at last led to specific research to find out if such healing "without medicine" (i.e., unorthodox healing) does occur. In parapsychology, the possibility of a PK effect in the healing process is beginning to be investigated.

The earliest published research report on the effect of a healer came from Canada in 1961 (1). At McGill University an experiment on the effect of a healer, a Mr. E., was made by a biochemist, Mr. Bernard Grad, and colleagues. The experiment was set up to show whether any positive effect obtained could be ascribed to the power of the healer rather than to suggestion on the part of the individual whom he treated. Partly on that account, mice instead of humans were used as the experimental organisms.

In Grad's experiment three hundred mice were used, and each one was wounded by snipping out the same-sized piece of skin from the back. Then one hundred were assigned for treatment to Mr. E.; one hundred to another person who made no claim to have healing power; and the third hundred were controls and were treated by no one. The objective, of course, was to see if the treatment by the humans had any measurable effect, or at least if that by Mr. E. did.

The method of treatment was an approach to Mr. E.'s idea that he healed by the "laying-on-of-hands." But instead of touching each mouse, the animals were left in their cages, and he held the cages between his hands for two fifteen-minute periods each day. The cages were enveloped in paper sacks so that he couldn't see the animals, but he could put his hands inside and touch the cages. The second person followed the same procedure.

At the end of the experiment, the results showed that healing in Mr. E.'s animals had been more rapid than in the others, but the effect was not sufficiently pronounced for the experimenters to think it conclusive. They wanted to repeat it, but circumstances changed and Grad made succeeding experiments with Mr. E. on the growth of plants instead of animals. In all of them Mr. E. continued to show a positive effect on the growth, so that his work with Grad argues strongly for a special PK ability in this healer at least.

Another experiment with Mr. E. has been reported by a different experimenter, Sister Justa Smith (2). It too is classifiable as basic research. She tested Mr. E.'s effect on the enzyme trypsin, which is involved in the digestion of protein. The healer was asked to hold a sample of the enzyme between his hands. At the same time the control sample was heated to the same temperature in a water bath. Sister Justa reported an effect on the experimental sample.

A third experiment on the effect of a healer (or healers) on living organisms is reported by Graham and Anita Watkins (1971) at the Institute for Parapsychology (3). In this one too the possible effect of suggestion has been eliminated by using mice instead of humans as the experimental animal.

This experiment was undertaken to test the idea of a young woman, K.G. (not a proclaimed healer like Mr. E.), that she had healing ability. The procedure decided upon was designed to avoid the necessity of wounding the animals. It was also one that could produce data much more rapidly than Grad's technique, which of course took considerable time before the rate of healing could be measured. For these reasons anesthesia itself, rather than a specific injury, was taken as the malady to be "cured." An experimental and a control mouse would be rendered unconscious by ether, and the healer would try to revive the former in less time than it took the control mouse to come back to consciousness naturally.

In preliminary tests the healer succeeded in resuscitating her mouse more quickly than the control frequently enough to justify more serious experimentation. In the course of it, then, conditions were increasingly tightened until they were felt to be strictly "blind" from all angles, including that of the experimenters themselves, who presumably, if they had known which of the pair of mice used in each test was the experimental animal, could have been biased in the judgment they had to make.

In the technique as finally perfected, two mice identical in sex and age were selected for each test and etherized. The time involved for each to become unconscious was recorded by the experimenters. The inert animals were then placed by the experimenters simultaneously in adjoining dishes separated by a screen so that each experimenter could observe and note the time of awakening of his own animal.

The healer, in an adjoining room, was assigned a list of targets, either the animal in the left or the right dish, which she could observe through a one-way mirror. She could thus concentrate on the assigned experimental animal without permitting the experimenters to see which it was. Her list of targets would be the record against which her hits and misses could later be checked. The timing records that the experimenters kept permitted the average times required for all of the animals to awaken to be reckoned. Twenty-four such individual trials were made as a run before a checkup was conducted.

In the course of the experiment not only K.G. was tested, but eleven other persons too, most of whom had no reason to think they had healing ability. And of the dozen, four stood out as "gifted" subjects, including K.G. as the "best" and another, L.H., who had a previous reputation as a sensitive, though he had not claimed to be a healer. The eight remaining subjects had varying results, but were mostly only at the chance level.

The results achieved by K.G. ranged from one perfect run, twenty-four hits, to fifteen out of twenty-four, with most at the rate of about nineteen. L.H.'s runs were mostly at the rate of nineteen per twenty-four too.

The experiment thus suggests strongly that the healers (the "gifted" subjects) did have an effect in hastening the return to activity of the anesthetized animals, and without any contact except that of sight. It showed too that individual differences in subjects were such that only a few could exert the effect to an appreciable extent. Probably the few "had something," but the many had little, so that the positive result depended upon special subjects—healers.

One comment made by the authors of this report is that the rate of scoring made by the "gifted" subjects in their experiment was exceptionally high as compared to the results of subjects in PK tests. As a matter of fact, the history of PK tests has shown very few subjects who were particularly high scorers. While in ESP tests, cases of perfect scores are on record, no perfect runs of PK have been reported. Along that line, if it could be so considered, K.G.'s perfect run in the resuscitation experiment would be the only one. The authors suggest, in partial explanation of the high results, that all the subjects in this experiment became very involved in it, all showing "strong empathy with the animal which they were trying to awaken."

As the experiment was continued, the attempt was made to seal off even more tightly than before any loopholes that could have existed in the "blind" conditions. Other experimenters were called in to see if, by following the procedure used by the Watkinses, they too could get the same kind of result. Although one pair has reported marginal results no really successful repetitions by other experimenters have yet been made. Therefore, any final conclusion cannot be drawn at present. It must await the outcome of repetitions, preferably those that may be performed at other places.

The implication of this pioneer work is, of course, that other physiological processes like those of healing may also be affected by human thought. Despite the obvious conservatism of orthodox medicine in cases like this, the results of the experiments already done seem like an invitation for much more general and widespread research in the future. If it could be established beyond any question that PK can operate within organisms, as this work on anesthesia in mice suggests, it could be a boon of untold value for mankind. Even though Sigurd's faith in his healer may well have contributed to his recovery, the possibility that the healer "had something," too, cannot be ruled out. It may well turn out to be another instance of "where there's smoke, there's fire."

17. ESP and PK in Animals

Sugar is perhaps the most famous cat outside of fairyland. Even though he's dead now, he left behind a record of what is among the most spectacular animal feats that have ever been recorded. It has also been exceptionally well documented (5).

The cat, a large, cream-colored male with "Persian emphasis," was raised from kittenhood by the family of Mr. S.W., a school principal in Anderson, California. When Sugar was well grown the family moved to Oklahoma. They intended to take him along, but when Mr. and Mrs. W. and their ten-year-old daughter set out on their long drive, Sugar, who was afraid of cars, leaped out of the window and could not be caught. They had to go on without him. The neighbors, who had his littermate, said they'd look after him.

Fourteen months later, at the new home of the W. family in Oklahoma, a cat leaped from an open window onto Mrs. W.'s shoulder as she was standing with her back to it in their cow barn. Startled, naturally, she brushed the animal off, but noticed that it looked like Sugar. Jokingly, she told the family that apparently Sugar had come to see them. But it was no longer a joke when, a few days later, after the cat had made itself quite at home, she was stroking it and felt a peculiar deformity on its left hip joint. Then they all recalled that Sugar had had this peculiar deformity. The bone extended far enough that it could easily be felt when stroked. Although they "couldn't believe it," the family was then convinced that this must really be Sugar.

A few months later the California neighbors who had volunteered to look after Sugar visited the W.'s in Oklahoma. No news about the cat had been exchanged, but when they saw this one they exclaimed at once and asked how Sugar got there. They remembered the bone deformity and also said that Sugar had disappeared a few weeks after the W.'s moved away. They had not told the W.'s at the time because they didn't want to worry them about it.

Strange stories of animals finding their way home or to human friends are not uncommon. Uncertainty is often felt about their authenticity, however, because of the impossibility of making certain that the animal that appears in the new place is really the same one that had been left behind. But in Sugar's case that uncertainty was practically removed because of the bone deformity. Just to be sure it wasn't imaginary, one parapsychologist, JBR, made a trip to Oklahoma to see for himself. After perhaps the longest trip on record of a man to see a cat, he confirmed the deformity, and consulted several veterinarians who assured him that protuberances like Sugar's were not common cat deformities.

And so it seemed reasonably certain that Sugar had traveled from California to Oklahoma in about fourteen months. If so, of course, it presumably would have been by foot and by foraging for food as best he could along the way, escaping dangers from traffic, dogs, and such; all of which would have made his chances for survival very slight. How he did it, crossing rivers, deserts, mountains, is of course a secret Sugar never told. The W.'s said, however, that he was a large and exceptionally strong cat, cunning enough too, that in Oklahoma sometimes he brought in a jack rabbit that he had caught. They also said that he was worn and thin when he first appeared there.

But the biggest question of all was how he found his way without a map or guide. Not even coincidence will explain a feat like this. Strong devotion to his family and strong ESP ability, however, could do it. The ESP would have had to be a steady, unwavering awareness of direction, to say the least. Altogether, it would seem to mean practically perfect clairvoyance.

As all animal lovers know, many kinds of unusual behavior that suggest ESP of one type or another are sometimes observed. However, among a large number of such reports collected at the Parapsychology Laboratory some years ago, perhaps those suggestive of clairvoyance were the most numerous, as they included many homing cases as well as those of trailing, like Sugar's. Another frequently reported kind that could be labeled "awareness of return of master" seemed also to suggest clairvoyance. Somewhat less frequent, but still fairly well represented were those under the label of "awareness of danger," and some of these suggested precognition.

A schoolboy in Wisconsin had a dog named Skippy who seemed to give evidence both of awareness of his master's return and of danger. Skippy was a beagle hound, but the odd one of his litter because he was black and white and looked more like a rat terrier than a beagle.

John, the high school boy, lived halfway down the block on an east-west street, and his school was four blocks away on a north-south street. The buildings were such that John, returning from school, could not be seen from home until after he turned onto his own street. The dog spent most of the day in the kitchen with John's mother or sleeping in the box in John's room. But just before John would come home, which might be soon after 4 P.M. or, when he remained for gym, anytime up till 6 P.M., Skippy would go to the window, paws on the sill, quivering with excitement. A few minutes later, John would round the corner.

Skippy also loved to hunt rabbits. When John's high school friends would come over with their guns, John would go get his shotgun, and Skippy would dance with delight. But one day the gang came with their guns and when she saw them coming she went in and lay down in her box. John called her. She looked at him and came out, then turned and went back to the box. He picked her up and carried her out to the car. She did a good job of hunting and brought a rabbit out of the cover, but just as she appeared, one near-sighted gunman, seeing the movement but not recognizing that it was Skippy with the rabbit she had caught, shot her.

John picked her up and held her in his arms. She feebly licked his face and then went limp.

Why did Skippy not want to go hunting that day?

Accounts of puzzling animal behavior go on and on. Partly because of them the question whether animals have ESP has been recognized and discussed. But especially since the discovery that human beings have it, other reasons for the question have been raised. Where does ESP come from? Is it hereditary? If so, does it go back to an evolutionary beginning? If it is inherent in human beings, then is it possibly the property of all living organisms?

Questions like these are easy to ask, but not easy to answer. Attempts to do so experimentally, however, have been made for quite some time. Not only have parapsychologists wondered whether ESP in man was an ability "going out" or "coming in" as organisms evolved, they have sometimes thought that, if animals do have ESP, it might possibly be easier to prove and to study in animals than in man. And so, for both reasons, attempts to show whether animals have psi ability (anpsi) began in parapsychology some years ago.

One of the first studies to yield fairly clear results was undertaken at the Parapsychology Laboratory by Dr. Karlis Osis, and reported in 1952 (2). The experiment was started with the objective only of showing that psi can occur between animals and humans. Osis was not concentrating particularly on the type that would be involved, if he got evidence of ESP. As it worked out, the situation he used would have involved either telepathy or clairvoyance or a combination of the two, or just possibly, though less likely, PK.

For several reasons cats were selected as the animal most convenient to use. Six different ones, all but one still kittens, five weeks to eight months old, were used in the course of Osis' rather extended experiments. In all cases, he petted the kittens as much as time permitted, trying, as he said, to establish friendly relations because he thought it might be easier to get evidence with pets especially if a "bond" existed, than with wild animals like mice or rats.

Osis decided to see if he could direct the animals by his thought or will power. He tried to do it by willing them to select a given one of two food dishes from which to eat, the target dish for each succeeding test being selected according to a list taken from a random number table. By having food in both of the dishes, the question of smell was not involved.

An apparatus was built consisting of long runways down which the animal could go to the food dishes placed at the end at the right and at the left, and equally distant. The animals could not see the experimenter, although he could see them.

After preliminary trials, in order to make the conditions blind, a second experimenter, who did not know which dish was the target, placed them and took the record. An animal having eaten from the dish on the right the first time, for instance, tended to turn to that one the next time, regardless of the target, and it was a difficult tendency to interrupt. It was a situation obviously in which any weak extrasensory signal from Osis was not likely to be noticed when the habit of going to a specific dish had been acquired. As a result, the first trials of different sessions yielded more hits than were expected by chance and the second ones fewer to such an extent that the difference between them was very significant.

Several other observations were made which supported the idea that ESP was involved in this great difference between the first and second trials of each session. When all the trials for the first chronological half of the test sessions were compared to those of the last half, more hits were made in the first trials of the first half than in the last. This difference, too, was very significant. It seemed to mean that for these kittens the ESP ability tended to decline in tests, just as it does in human beings.

Still another difference concerned the time of day. The kittens did better in the forenoon than in the afternoon. Also, some individuals did better than others. For instance, one kitten, Susie, became a star. Her scores were much higher than any of the others.

Osis felt that his tests had shown a psi effect between him and the cats, since no sensory cues were possible and the conditions were blind. But he did not attempt to decide how much of the result was due to man (by PK) and how much to the animal (by ESP).

More recently, anpsi experiments have been carried further, and more particularly on the question raised by Skippy: do animals have precognition? Of course, precognition is clairvoyance of the future, and since ESP is a unitary process and seems to operate regardless of time and distance, ESP tests of any type are in a sense tests of all types. And so, clairvoyance as shown in Sugar, in theory would be included in tests for precognition too.

These newer experiments were made in France, not on cats or dogs but on white mice. A professor who called himself Duval and his student, called Montredon, made an apparatus that permitted them to test for precognition and to record all of the experiment automatically (1).

Automatic recording, of course, does not necessarily mean that new discoveries are made because of it, but it usually does mean that records can be checked and rechecked more easily and quickly and mistakes eliminated. In this case, it had another special advantage. The experiment could be set up and the experimenter could leave it to run itself. In animal experiments like this a perennial question when interesting results are obtained is, did the animal cause them or was it the experimenter himself with his own psi ability who did it? This automatic recording that permitted the experimenter to leave the room and busy himself with some other activity seemed a step in the direction of showing that the effects secured were caused by the animals and not by the experimenters.

This French experiment was set up to test whether the mouse could precognize danger or discomfort by avoiding a slight electric stimulation. The animal was placed in a small cage that was divided down the middle into two parts by a low barrier, each part wired separately so the stimulation could be administered to whichever side was chosen as the target. If the mouse could precognize the danger, the supposition was that before each trial it would jump the low barrier and be in the safe side.

The essential mechanism was one that decided to which side of the cage the current would be directed. This mechanism (called a binary random number generator) controlled that timing and also left a record for later checking while another device (photocell) left a record of the side of the cage the mouse was in on each trial. The two records together would show whether or not the mouse had chosen the proper side.

The total results did not show a significant difference between the two sides. It was noticed that in most cases the animal behaved in an almost mechanical manner. When it was shocked on one side of the cage, it jumped to the other; and since the shocks, though in random order between the sides, were given an equal number of times to each, the total result, was slightly, but not significantly positive.

However, as the experimenters well knew, ESP gives only a weak signal compared to such natural responses as the tendency to leave an uncomfortable spot when an animal has just received a shock. It would hardly be expected that the weak stimulus would be obeyed in the face of the much stronger one.

However, the experimenters noticed that occasionally the animal did not behave so mechanically. Sometimes it remained on the side in which it had just been shocked; sometimes, it would jump from the side that had not been electrically stimulated to the other. In these instances, it seemed as if the animal was acting on some principle not so mechanical as usual, and if evidence of ESP was to be given it would be in these instances rather than in the more mechanical ones. The equipment made it possible to distinguish from the records whether trials were of the mechanical or the more random kind and therefore the number of each type could be evaluated.

Four mice were tested. Among them, they made 612 of the random behavior kind of trials. Each mouse had more hits than misses in these. The value of these random behavior trial hits (.001) was highly significant. The conclusion was that the animals must have used precognition in this kind of trial in order to avoid the shock.

Several years later (1971) an experiment was reported from Holland which had been undertaken to confirm that of Duval and Montredon in France. Although the objective of this Dutch experimenter, Sybo A. Schouten, was the same, to test for precognition in mice, he chose somewhat different conditions under which to do it (4).

One change was to motivate his animals by a positive instead of a negative reward. Schouten reasoned that a negative reward, like a shock when the animal missed, would cause it to become frustrated and that state would probably not be a good one for eliciting psi. Therefore, he decided instead to reward the animal for a correct response by giving it water, of which it had been deprived.

Another objective introduced in this experiment was an attempt to see whether evidence could be secured to show that a telepathic relationship exists between mice. Schouten first trained mice to touch a lever in one side of the cage, and thereby, as a buzzer sounded, to get a drop of water. When they had learned this performance, they were further trained in a cage divided equally into black and white sections. A white lever and a light bulb were placed in the white section, a black one and a bulb in the black, with the water delivery system in the middle of the back wall. When the buzzer sounded, one of the lights was switched on. The animals were trained to press the lever on the side where the light was shown, and a correct answer was rewarded by water, a wrong one by only turning off the light.

When the animals had learned this procedure, two test cages like the training cages were used. One, the target cage, contained the water-feeding system and the light in each of its two sections but no levers. The other, the response cage, contained the water-feeding system, a buzzer and in each section a lever. The two cages were kept several rooms apart. For a test, a mouse was put into each one. The mouse in the target cage could see which side, the black or the white, lit up and so it would know which was the target. But it of course had no lever to press. The mouse in the response cage could press one of the levers but did not know which, unless it could get the correct one by ESP (either telepathy or clairvoyance) from the other cage. However, if it selected the proper lever, both mice would get the water reward.

In order to determine whether any result that an experimental mouse might get was caused by telepathy from the second mouse or clairvoyance from the way the system itself was set up, half of the experiments were carried out with no mouse in the response cage.

Ten mice were tested in each condition, each one for six sessions performing twenty-five trials a day. The totals for sixteen of the twenty resulting scores per mouse were positive, four negative. This was a significant result, but it left the question of telepathy vs. clairvoyance somewhat unsettled, for three of the negative results occurred in the telepathic condition, only one in the clairvoyant. But that could mean possibly that some of the animals, like people, might have been showing psi missing in their negative scores.

But even though the experiment did not clearly show that mice can react telepathically to each other, the total experiment gave results in the same direction as that of the French finding that the test mice seemed to show precognition, but only in their random behavior trials.

Although these experiments do suggest that animals have ESP, further confirmatory work is needed before the conclusion can be considered as reliably established, but to some extent the expectation that it will be when more experiments have been carried out is justified because of the exploits of animals in real life like those of Skippy and Sugar. Also, if such spontaneous cases do involve ESP, then they are much more spectacular than any yet hinted at by the results of experiments. They suggest ESP on a level so high that even the most successful experiment would not approach it.

But still, it is only because the experiments have given evidence of ESP that everyday-life cases can be given weight. And in reverse, they can remind experimenters of the length they still have to go before they learn how to demonstrate ESP at its maximum either in people or in animals.

Even in the present experimental stage, the anpsi experiments have answered one question: is the ESP ability "coming in" or "going out"? Obviously, it's not coming in. Whether or not it is "going out," it exists, apparently far down the evolutionary tree.

And if that can be said for ESP, can it be repeated for PK? Does it even exist in animals?

In Seattle several years ago, a new kind of experiment was made. It was the first one of its kind (3). It was only a preliminary, almost accidental one. It was essentially simple, too, but especially unusual because it was designed to test the question just asked above. Do animals have PK ability?

The idea that humans have PK ability was still new enough that the world in general outside of parapsychology was either ignorant or at most skeptical of it. And even those in the field had scarcely gotten around to considering whether evidence of it could be found in animals.

Nothing that animals do had suggested that they have PK. It

was not like the situation in regard to ESP. Scarcely had that ability been demonstrated in human beings than people began to make remarks like, "My cat must be telepathic. She knows when I just *think* I'll go to the refrigerator and get her some food." And then, too, there were the reports of cats and dogs and pigeons that found their way home over long distances. For these reasons many people had often wondered if animals have ESP. But nothing comparable stirred up curiosity about PK.

Still, the question of PK in animals should have the same theoretical interest as that of ESP, because ESP and PK seem so much like aspects of the same ability.

In any event, the question of heredity and evolution is raised for PK just as much as for ESP. To test the question, then, was logical enough. But until the test in Seattle, that logic had not reached the do-something-about-it stage. One other ingredient of the experimental approach was lacking until then; the proper equipment for an experiment to test the question. This was supplied when the Seattle test took place.

Dr. Helmut Schmidt, a research physicist, then at the Boeing Aircraft Company in Seattle, (since at the Institute for Parapsychology) had a long-standing interest in parapsychology. He made an especially sensitive machine to test for PK. It was arranged so that a heat lamp would automatically be turned on or off each second, according to a random number generator. Without explaining how this operated, which only an engineer would understand, it is enough to say here that if nothing interfered, the heat lamp would be off as many seconds as it would be on. The off-on sequence, however, was random, and depended on a Geiger counter and the decay of a bit of strontium 90. The apparatus was equipped with electromechanical counters, and made a record of the "offs" and "ons."

Previously, Dr. Schmidt had tested subjects for ESP, using special sensitives who claimed to have it. Naturally, now, he felt that he needed individuals who claimed to have PK ability. However, he had no volunteer human subjects who made the claim. He did not then realize that many people may have psi ability of either type without knowing it.

A subject for this PK machine should be one that needed warmth, since the task was to get heat more than at the 50–50 rate at which the heat lamp operated when undisturbed. The Schmidts had a pet cat. Cats like warm places, and it was winter in Seattle. Why not try out the cat as subject?

An experiment was carried out accordingly. The cat was put inside a little unheated shack in the backyard in which the 200-watt heat lamp connected to the machine was housed. This was done for five half-hour sessions on consecutive afternoons. It was near-zero weather, and the cat seemed to appreciate the heat and settled down beside the lamp. With the automatic counter it could be left alone, and then the record read at the end of the half hour. When the cat was taken out of the shack and the record read, the generator was then left to run continuously so it could be checked each day to see if it was truly 50–50.

Since one number (either an off or an on) was generated every second, each one a trial, nine thousand in all had been generated at the end of the five sessions, and half (4,500) should have been on, half off. But 115 more of them had been on! This was an almost significant excess. It looked as if the cat had "turned up the thermostat," especially because between sessions the ons and offs were still 50–50.

Since the result was so encouraging, Schmidt intended to continue the test longer. But the cat did not agree. Until then, each of the five times when Schmidt had come to check at the end of the half hour, the cat had been sitting by the light bulb, but when he came back after the sixth trial, the cat was hiding in a corner and raced out when he opened the door. He tried four more times, and still the cat would not cooperate. It acted as if frightened of the flashing light, and would no longer go near it. Also the weather had turned warmer, and so the cat no longer needed the extra heat. In none of these later sessions was the light on for more than half of the trials. And so, Dr. Schmidt could not confirm his first results, but the five sessions had been so suggestive that he knew he would have to test further for PK in animals.

The cold weather was now past in Seattle, and the Schmidts that year transferred to the Institute for Parapsychology in North Carolina. There Schmidt's research on animals took a somewhat different turn. Or at least the animal species he decided to work with was quite different. Instead of a pet cat, he used a "beautiful" big kind of American cockroach. The choice was partly one of convenience. A stock of cockroaches was on hand from a previous experiment on another question.

In the cat experiment the stimulus had been warmth, which of course was a pleasant one for the animal. But in the cockroach experiment it was decided to use a very mild electric stimulus, presumably an unpleasant one. The insects would be placed in a plastic box with greased walls so they could not climb out, and with an electrified grid floor, connected to the random generator, just as the heat lamp in the cat experiment had been. The question now, of course, was whether the cockroaches could decrease the number of seconds in which the current was on, from its normal 50-50 times on and off.

Two cockroaches at a time were placed in the box, and a run consisted of sixty-four trials at the rate of one per second. The experimenter in this case watched the animals during the run in order to keep the current adjusted just so the roaches were stimulated to move, and also to turn them back on their feet if they flipped onto their backs as some had a tendency to do. Four runs a few minutes apart made a session, and usually three such sessions were held each day.

In an exploratory test of 6,400 trials to see if any increase would occur, the unexpected result was that instead of fewer, the number of stimulations had been so much *greater* than chance as to be statistically significant. It was a result contrary to expectation, but it could not be laid to chance, even though it did not seem likely that the cockroaches had found the stimulus a pleasant one.

With a tantalizing result like that, another experiment had to be undertaken. This was to be carried out as before and one hundred sessions were planned. In addition, this time the generated numbers were recorded on tape so they could be rechecked afterwards, and the machine was kept running all night between tests so that its randomness was constantly watched.

The result again was more stimulus periods than chance accounted for. Also, because the test was longer than the preliminary one, the result was still more significant. Two possible reasons were advanced for the result: first, since cockroaches never have experiences with electric stimulation naturally their reaction here might have been unnatural; second, since the experimenter had to watch the animals in this experiment, perhaps he "did it" and not the cockroaches. The experiment stopped at this point, and no matter whether man or cockroach was the subject, at least the result showed that somewhere along the line something, whether the random generator or the decay of strontium 90, had been affected by an influence outside the ordinary physical one. And that would be called PK.

The survey of front-line research on this question ends here. It is not complete, of course, and even if it were, the items in such a survey change tomorrow anyway. Other reports on other topics will come in. New ideas will get tested. Old ones will be retested, confirmed, rejected, amplified. But even those suggested by these chapters can well give food for thought, and hopefully, stimulus for new experimental research.

Experimental research, however, is not the only kind that can contribute to an understanding of psi. The study of experiences in which psi appears to occur spontaneously has certain advantages, particularly in giving suggestions about topics that have not yet been subjected to experimentation. As the next section will show, it also has the advantage of suggesting the way psi seems to fit into other mental processes, and even to operate according to certain well-known psychological principles.

SECTION FOUR

Psi in life situations. The forms it takes in consciousness, their psychological aspects.

18. The Forms of Psi Experience

If an experience brings a person true information he had no ordinary way of knowing, it could be a psi experience. It could be one, no matter in what way or form it came to him, or how much or little it told, or even whether he believed it or realized that it was a message for him. By definition it still could be a case of psi.

As examples, consider experiences like the five below, with their similarities and differences, and note how they fulfill the definition.

1. A girl in Minnesota had a date one night and was waiting for her boy friend to come and take her to a party. But this night he was late. She waited and waited. Finally in disappointment she walked to a friend's house nearby. There, chatting around the fire, she happened to glance into the open door of a darkened room, and for an instant she saw her boy friend, or so she thought.

Startled, she imagined he had somehow come and wanted to surprise her. The light was turned on. No one was in that room, nor even around outside. Soon a messenger came to tell the girl that her boy friend had had an accident, was in the hospital, and wanted to see her.

Let us say that the experience told the girl something she had no ordinary way of knowing, although too little to make immediate sense to her. If so it told her by a hallucinatory experience, a visual one, and it only told her who, not what, and so she did not know that it was a message.

2. A young woman in Chicago whose second child was just a few weeks old was getting around the house again and trying to care for both of the children. One morning, with the baby sleeping in the bedroom and the three-year-old playing in the

living room, she was working in the kitchen.

Suddenly she "just knew" the infant was choking on something the older child had put into its mouth. There had been no sound, nothing to suggest it, but she rushed in to find the baby looking normal, though waving its hands a little. She snatched it up anyway, held it upside down and with her finger dislodged a round piece of candy from its throat. The older child had intended to be good to her baby sister.

The experience told something that woman had no ordinary way of knowing. It told her by an intuition, and it told her just what had happened. She knew it was a message.

3. Jim and Kathy were engaged, but Jim was in the Air Force in Texas, and Kathy was at home in Oklahoma. One night Kathy woke from a frightening dream. In it she had seen Jim wedged in a tight place, grasping a heavy, round object, striving to push it away to keep it from crushing his chest. The scene had appeared in a flash. She could remember nothing more.

She wrote him in the morning and told him how silly she was because she could not get her dream out of her mind and go back to sleep again.

Two days after the dream, Jim was under an airplane working on the engine. Through some freak accident, the motor suddenly loosened and fell directly toward his chest. He caught it just in time.

Immediately afterward, he got her letter. "Kathy, how could you? You weren't just dreaming," he wrote her.

It brought her information that she had no ordinary way of knowing, not only of the danger to her fiance, but something about the kind of danger. It told her by a dream both realistic and true. But she did not quite believe or allow herself to believe that the dream was an actual message.

4. It was late Saturday morning in Indianapolis. Eight-year-old Edith was still sleeping when all at once she heard her father shouting, "Edith, get up right now," and then he pushed her out of bed so hard she hit the floor and woke.

Just then the sharp-edged plate that covered the flue above her bed fell off and cut into the bed just where her head had been.

She looked around for her father and mother, but no one was

there. Her mother was out in the yard hanging up clothes. Her father was mowing the lawn. They thought she was still asleep.

It told her something she had no ordinary way of knowing, that she was in danger. It told her by a dream, an unrealistic one, which still told the truth. She thought it must have been a message, but it was not the kind she thought. It was not from her father, but a dream fantasy which unconsciously she had herself "dreamed up."

5. During World War II, the elder son of a family in Philadelphia was in the army overseas. At six o'clock one night the family was just finishing supper when the clock on the mantle stopped. No reason could be found. At once the mother said, "Something has happened to Terry." It was some months before they heard that just at that time in Germany, Terry had nearly drowned as his company tried to cross the Rhine.

It told her something she had no ordinary way of knowing. It told her neither who nor what, but she knew who anyway. It told her by a physical effect, and she knew it was a message.

Those five experiences fulfill the elementary definition of psi experiences. But were they that? To decide about it, unfortunately, is not like discovering by experiments that ESP and PK are realities. The decision about spontaneous experiences can at best be a judgment made with many reservations. But still, careful judgments over a lot of cases have a reasonable degree of reliability, even though never the finality of experimental research.

In deciding about experiences like these five and all the others cited in this book, the first question to ask is the one asked by eleven-year-old Pamela. She read an article from the Parapsychological Laboratory in which cases similar to these were used. She wrote a letter to the Laboratory just to ask, *"Were they all completely true?"*

Of course no one can tell for sure if the people who reported experiences like these were telling the exact truth and nothing but the truth. They may have exaggerated. Or even more to the point, no one can tell whether they told *all* of the truth. Perhaps some little detail was omitted in some of the accounts, or never noticed in the first place, which would have made all the difference. It easily could be. That is one reason why such experiences could never prove that ESP or PK is real. But they did raise the question and, as already said, were the reason why experiments were started which could prove it. However, now that the experiments have been made and have shown that psi is a reality, instances of it in life are to be expected. They, of course, would have to be instances in which the person received a message without relying on the senses. They therefore have to be among the experiences that fulfill the definition. And they would show the way psi operates when it can do so naturally without the more or less restricted conditions that are necessary in laboratory experiments.

The answer to the question whether these examples are *completely true*, then, is that no one can say for sure in given cases, but whether or not all of them actually involve psi, at least experiences like them are the kind that would be expected when it does occur naturally. On this basis, in 1948 at the Parapsychology Laboratory, I undertook to study such experiences. It was first of all an inquiry to find out what experiences that could involve psi were like (1).

The psi ability by then was recognized as a reality at the laboratory, where much of the research establishing it had been carried out and where everyone was well informed about all that had been done at other places too. JBR thought it was time to look at psi in everyday life, and see what could be suggested, mainly for researchers, about the nature of the ability.

As mentioned earlier, hundreds, soon thousands, of such experiences were being reported to the laboratory by people who were puzzled about them and wanted to know what they meant. Their letters came from all over United States as well as from other countries. From these letters I collected for study all of the accounts of experiences that appeared to fulfill the definition given at the beginning of this chapter.

One of the first objectives was to classify the ways that experiences came to the person's conscious attention. It turned out that in spite of what at first seemed like endless differences, most of the variations were superficial, and that actually the cases took one of only about five different forms. Four of them involved ESP and the other PK.

These five forms were the same as those of the examples given above. Those five, in fact, were picked for illustration from many similar ones of each kind. No. 1, an instance of a hallucination (a visual one, but an auditory one could have been used just as well); No. 2, an intuition; No. 3, a realistic dream; No. 4, an unrealistic or fantasy dream; No. 5, the PK form.

A few experiences remained in which it seemed that the form was a "two-in-one." For instance, the two dream forms sometimes seem to be mixed together, as in the following instance:

A young woman during World War II had a brother in the army overseas. She dreamed of him only once, and that time she saw him clearly in a very white and clean hospital bed. She thought she was there and that he was in pain, and she rushed toward him to try to help him. But he stopped her, saying, "Rose, please don't touch my left leg. I've just had a bullet removed from it."

That same day word came from the Red Cross that her brother was wounded, and later they found that the night of her dream he was in a hospital bed, all in white, and in pain, having just had a bullet removed from his left leg.

The dream was realistic, although the part in which the sister was involved was a fantasy originating in her own mind, which nevertheless told her the truth about her brother's injury.

Since the two-in-one cases were not new forms, but only combinations of the others, it seemed safe to say that ESP in daily life comes in one or more of these four forms, and that PK may also be represented. But dreams and intuitions, which are sometimes called the "vehicles" of thought, are by no means limited to bringing information secured by ESP. Rather, as everyone knows, they are common forms of daily-life experiences and they generally have nothing to do with ESP. Even hallucinations are reported more often without ESP than with it, as for instance in alcoholic delirium and certain other hallucinogenic drug effects.

The result of this study, thus, was to emphasize for the first time the fact that *ESP has no special form of experience of its own.* Instead, it uses the normal, ordinary forms of mental action. This could have been expected, perhaps, if anyone had thought of it before it was pointed out by actual observations of many cases. But of course, until then the view was hazy and obscured by the many surface differences reported.

These surface differences help to make the accounts sound at first as if no two are the same. Phrases like, "I had a vision of . . .," "A voice told me . . .," or even, "I'm sure I wasn't asleep . . .," and many others can obscure the actual intuitive, hallucinatory, or dream forms that they represent. It did take a look beneath the surface of many such variations to ascertain the actual basic form of the experience. One necessity for that was to establish a rule regarding what could be taken as the distinction between sleep and wakefulness. If by the account the person was up and about at the time of the experience, he had to be considered awake, but if he was reclining or in bed, his wakefulness was questionable regardless of his conviction about it. With this in mind, the actual basic forms of the experiences were clearer.

The forms made sense in showing what goes on when psi occurs. It was already clear that it goes on unconsciously, and that somehow the unconscious part of the mind can "know" items of information concerning the external world directly without the help of the senses. This information, then, is relayed to consciousness by the same kinds of processes that are used for the information that does come by the senses.

The study thus emphasized the fact that information secured by ESP has to use the same forms or vehicles to get into consciousness that are used for sensory information, since it does not have a special form of its own. Once this point was recognized it explained why it is so difficult to be sure when an experience does bring a psi message. The form it comes in does not tell. Even the hallucinatory form does not by itself mean that the experience brings a true message any more than that snakes have anything to do with the hallucinations of delirium tremens. This is a far-reaching point that will come up again in the next two sections.

The experiences related above fulfilled the definition, but they did not very fully illustrate the fact that psi experiences may tell much or little. That is a point that will come up next in connection with a discussion of each of the five forms. The discussion will also show something of the way psi seems to operate in each. This of course, makes it possible to understand spontaneous experiences a little better in spite of the fact that each one has its individual characteristics.

19. Focus on Intuitive ESP Experiences

Elaine, a nineteen-year-old girl in California, was the only one in the family not so "tied up" that she could gracefully avoid the unpleasant duty of going to old Mrs. Black's funeral the next day. She scarcely knew Mrs. Black, the mother of her sister's girl friend. It was her sister's business to go to that funeral, but the sister could not leave her job. Elaine just had to go. It was her duty.

She awoke the next morning with an odd reluctant feeling. It got worse, and by afternoon, time to go to the cemetery, it was uncontrollable, and suddenly she knew why. It was because of her mother. She had to go to her mother, who, with her father and little sister, was down at the furniture store they had just bought. Ignoring the need to go to the cemetery, Elaine took a bus in the opposite direction, overwhelmed by an increasing urge to get to her mother quickly.

When she got there, everything seemed normal, and her parents were resting momentarily in chairs by the front window. They were surprised to see her, and she really had no explanation for being there. But she knew they should not be in that room. How to get them out? "I'm hungry, come back into the kitchen. Let's get something to eat," she improvised.

Scarcely had they reached the kitchen when a loud crash out front seemed to shake the building. It was a big black sedan with a large elderly woman at the wheel. She had driven at full speed right through the front window. The chairs Elaine's parents had been sitting on were smashed, just like the window glass.

In all the confusion, her mother fainted from the shock. Elaine was there to help her when everyone else was too preoccupied to do so.

What gave Elaine the strong compulsion that got her to the scene of the danger just in time? She never understood why she "just knew" she had to get there. She and her parents knew that it was an impulse that probably saved their lives, a compulsion that led her truly, if uncomprehendingly, to the proper place.

In probably half of all the reported experiences that could involve ESP in daily life, the person "just knows" something intuitively, without any reason he can recognize (1). One example of this was the mother in Chap. 18 who knew her baby was choking on a round object the older child had put into its mouth. She got a complete message, as Elaine did not.

Much more frequently in intuitive experiences, the person gets only an incomplete message, as did Elaine in the case above. Consequently he gets only a "sign," and it may not be enough to tell him what the actual message means. Cases like these, incomplete ones, give strong hints about the kind of mental action that goes on in psi experiences. Even though the individual experience only puzzles and worries the person who has it, the study of a collection of reports of such cases shows something more about the underlying process.

One morning in an Indiana town a woman had an unusual experience of which she could not at the time "make sense." It puzzled her all day until she learned the answer. It happened sometime after her husband had started off on the sixty-mile drive he and his neighbor made to work each day. She glanced at the clock. It was 7:15, time to get the children up and ready for school.

But just then she had a strange and overwhelming feeling that she should be thanking God for something. But she had no idea what for or why just then. She could not help but yield to it and dropped on her knees, saying over and over, "Thank you, God, thank you."

She felt almost lightheaded, as if something terribly dark and worrisome had lifted, though as she tried to think what, she realized that she really did not have a worry in the world.

That evening she had a phone call from her husband. He asked her to come and pick them up. He and his friend had had an accident that morning. The truck had rolled over three times, but somehow both men were unhurt and so they had gone on to work. He knew it was just 7:15 because he heard the factory whistle just as the truck came to a standstill.

The "sign" in that case was just a feeling of relief and thankfulness *as if* she had known about the wreck and its outcome. Sometimes the sign may be only a feeling that something is wrong, giving no hint of what or where.

For instance, a sixteen-year-old high school girl was getting ready to go to school one morning, when all at once she thought she should not go. Something was wrong, she had no idea what. She was not sick, however, and so she had no excuse to stay at home. She had not missed school that year, her mother could see no reason for her to stay home now, and so she had to go.

At school she was miserable, and wanted only to go home. At 10:00 A.M. she started to cry and could not stop. But still she had no excuse, and so she was not allowed to go home. When she got home that evening she found that at 10:00 A.M. the house had caught fire and her bedroom and all her clothes were burned.

In some cases, the person gets an incomplete message, as Elaine had, and is able to do something about it. For instance, in Miami an older woman had gone downtown shopping one morning. Her husband, who was well but somewhat feeble, was at home. She had prepared his lunch and left it on the breakfast table.

At noon she stopped at a cafeteria and started down the line. Like the sixteen-year-old girl in Chapter 1, suddenly she wanted to go home. No premonition, nothing, she just wanted to go home.

She left her tray, got her car, and drove quickly home. When she opened the door she knew the reason why. The house was filled with gas, but her husband was sitting in the breakfast room, oblivious.

She rushed first to open windows and doors and turn off the gas which was pouring out of the oven. Her husband had turned it on to warm the room a bit, but had forgotten to light the burner. He had lost his sense of smell some time before and was quite unaware of his danger.

Her reaction, merely a compulsion to go home, had no conscious reason, and she did not know what she had to do until she got there and her senses told her.

Another woman, this one in Oklahoma, knew what she had to do, but not a rational reason for it. She and her husband, a childless couple, had been promised a baby for adoption. It was expected to be born about February 15. All of the preliminary arrangements had been made, but the bassinet they would need had been loaned to a friend in Tulsa, many miles away.

Suddenly on January 13, a full month ahead of time, and even though a blizzard was raging, the woman decided to leave her work and go and get the bassinet. Her husband objected. The baby was not due yet, so what was the great hurry? She agreed to all he said, but she just had to go anyway.

The trip was hard and slow, but she got back with the bassinet late on the night of January 14. Early next morning they were awakened by the telephone. The baby had been born at 3:30 that morning. She was an eight-month baby, and she was in her bassinet that night.

If such experiences are instances of ESP, as some of them very well may be, they suggest something about the way ESP works. They are cases in which apparently an ESP message is received at some level below the conscious threshold. At that level, information cannot always easily pass into consciousness. Everyone sometimes experiences this when he tries to recall something that he did some time ago. Most of us, most of the time, can recall past experiences fairly well. But sometimes we forget. We cannot remember the name of someone we met last week. Perhaps we recall a little of it—it began with a K and was about two syllables long.

Or we may wake in the morning and remember that something good or bad happened yesterday, and we feel good or bad accordingly. For a moment we remember only the *feeling*, although we soon recall the reason for it.

These circumstances in connection with memory show that when information needs to be recalled to consciousness, it must cross the so-called threshold which one can think of as the level where unconsciousness and consciousness meet. But the information can be obstructed there. It appears that this threshold presents a kind of barrier that not everything in unconscious levels can cross. Probably it serves to keep memories *out* of consciousness so that one can have a clear mind for the present job and not be constantly overwhelmed by memories of everything that he has experienced.

Just so, it seems that when ESP messages are to be transferred to consciousness, the threshold presents a barrier. Often, just as in imperfect recall, only part of the message gets through. Frequently the part that does is either only the emotional component, as with the woman who had to thank God, or the worry of the girl whose clothes were going to burn. In each of these cases the person could do nothing about it. Her emotional response did not tell her the reasons why.

It was different with the other three, however. One could go to her parents' store, one could go home, the other could get the bassinet. All three of them took the proper action as if they had inner guidance, as indeed they probably did.

It is just as reasonable to think that the imperfect cases of this intuitive kind are caused by the difficulty of getting information over the threshold into consciousness, as it is to think it explains difficulties in memory recall. And here, too, it could be that much material from ESP as well as from memory is screened out, to prevent the complete bedlam that total memory *and* total ESP awareness would produce. At any rate, it seems that in both, the obstacle is the difficulty of crossing into consciousness, even though in one case the message comes from ESP, in the other from the memory of earlier actions.

Intuitive ESP experiences, whether complete in meaning or incomplete, are reported so often that this seems to be the most favored method of getting ESP information into consciousness when the person is awake. But it is not the only kind, for hallucinatory experiences, by definition, occur when the person is not sleeping. A study of them tells something about the psi process.

20. A Study of Hallucinatory ESP Experiences

A nurse with two young children to support had placed her eight-year-old girl in a Catholic school and, some twenty-miles distant, the older child, a boy, in a boarding school. She was called one day by a nun at the girl's school, who told her that the child was quite upset because she claimed her brother had come and stood beside the sandbox where she was playing alone. She said he had been trying to tease her by beckoning with his finger, and that he would not go away. Of course the nun knew it was all imaginary, but the little girl was quite disturbed nevertheless, and the nun, thinking it was strange, decided to tell the mother about it.

The mother, fearing she knew not what, called the boy's school and found that he was just recovering from a serious accident. He had waded into a low-tide heavy-current river and had fallen into a thirty-foot channel. He had gone down several times before he was rescued by a diver and given artificial respiration.

The little girl's experience could have been an ESP message "triggered" by her brother's crisis. Of course, she did not see him by ordinary vision because that occurs only when light waves bring the message. Here, instead of light waves, the ESP message could have resulted in pseudo-sight based on her memory of him.

In all such pseudo-sensory experiences a necessary aspect is that the person so seen or heard seems realistically to be there where he is seen or heard (1). Usually he appears just as the person remembers him. This indicates that the impression is based on memory. But this kind of experience is bound to be misleading because the person seen is not really there. The experience is hallucinatory. The little girl thought she saw her brother as if he were teasing her, as doubtless he had often done. She also saw him as if he were actually present because that was the only place she *could* visualize him.

In an auditory case a woman in California, the wife of a man who worked on a drilling rig as a derrick man, was lying in bed reading a very interesting book one night. Then she heard her husband call her name, although he was at work on a shift that lasted until midnight. Thinking that for some reason he had come home unexpectedly, she went to the back door where he usually came in. He was not there, so she went to the front, thinking he had parked in front instead of the driveway as usual. But no car, no husband. She went back to her book, puzzled, noting the time, 9 P.M., as she did so, and not thinking too much about it.

The next morning her husband said he had had quite a scare the night before. He had gone up the rig and carelessly had neglected to put on the safety belt which was standard equipment. His job was near the top of the rig, and he somehow lost his balance and fell, but fortunately was caught by one leg and hung there until he managed to pull himself back to safety. He said his first thought was of his wife. She wondered when it happened, and he said about 9 o'clock.

Presumably the wife had an ESP message about the accident, but of course, no air waves brought a call to her. Instead, a memory of his usual call created an auditory "image" which was indistinguishable from a real one. Even though he probably did not actually call—and in such experiences sometimes an actual call is uttered, sometimes not—it produced a pseudo-auditory experience. Again, as in the visual case, the effect was experienced as if it were where in reality it would have had to be if real.

Occasionally something different, though still an auditory hallucination, is reported. This is the kind of case in which a knock or other type of sound, not a human voice, is heard and seems to bring a message, even though no reason for it seems to exist.

For instance, one night in Virginia, a woman was sleeping soundly when she was awakened by a knock on the front door.

She sat up and listened; it came again. She turned on the light and saw it was 2 A.M. She looked out the front and back and saw no one. She thought it strange the dog did not bark as he usually did when anyone knocked. She sat in the darkened living room for a while, thinking if it had been a burglar she might hear something again. Then at 2:35 the telephone rang. Frightened, she answered. It was from the hospital, calling to tell her that her brother was there with a heart attack and was not expected to live until morning. He was then in an oxygen tent getting intensive care. (He eventually recovered.)

In cases like this, presumably the person hallucinates the sound of the knock, just as in the other case the woman hallucinated the human voice calling. But here there is another possibility; the sound could be the result of a PK effect. That is, the actual knock could have been the result of PK. Then air waves would have brought the sound. This is a possibility to be considered, now that PK is known to occur. It is only a possibility, of course, but one study of pertinent cases made a few years ago seems to support it (2).

In the study the point was to find out in cases involving a second person present at the scene, whether he too did or did not hear the sound. For this study the two kinds were contrasted; first the "call" cases, those involving the human voice; and second, those in which a knock, a bell, or other sound was heard. The study showed that hardly any of the call cases were heard by other persons present. On the other hand, nearly all of the mechanical sounds were heard by anyone within earshot. This looked as if the call cases were hallucinatory, while most of the others were probably something else, either instances of PK or just sounds made by undetermined natural causes that by coincidence came at significant times.

One other kind of experience can probably be considered hallucinatory, the kind represented by the experience of a high school girl who wrote:

My boy friend was hurt in a car accident. I did not hear of it until two days later. But at the time of the accident, I had an awful ache in my head at the exact spot where his head was cut. It went away about the time he was in the doctor's office.

In such cases when one person seems to feel another's pain it looks as if the sensation was hallucinatory rather than real. If so, it would mean again that by ESP, unconsciously, information had come about the accident and even the exact place of injury. Then by what one could call unconscious sympathy, the sensation was actually felt as if it were the person's own.

In a similar way, and not too infrequently, pains like those of childbirth, even complete with muscular contractions, are sometimes felt by a mother, sister, or even friend of a person having a baby. One woman who knew her daughter was expecting a baby, but not when it was coming, was suddenly stricken with "terrible pains," her stomach swelling and contracting every few moments, until the family wanted to call a doctor. But she told them to wait. Maybe her illness meant that a grandchild was coming.

It was, and ironically, the daughter had had little pain, even though nothing had been given her to ease it. Instead, her mother, who knew what a birth might feel like, seemed to have had the pains for her. And she had them at the proper time.

In a few still more curious cases, the other person may be of the opposite sex. A woman in Wisconsin, after five years of marriage with no pregnancy, had about given up hope that she and her husband would ever have a family. Then one morning the husband woke up nauseated at the sight or smell of breakfast. He rushed to the bathroom to vomit. The next morning the same thing happened. They wondered if he could have ulcers. Then they realized that the wife was pregnant. She had no morning sickness, but her husband's continued up to her fourth month. It persisted even when he went hunting miles away from his wife, and even though he got mercilessly teased by his companions. At the start, the sympathetic effect presumably could have been the result of ESP, though after they learned of the pregnancy, just a sympathetic reaction to an imagined situation must have produced the effect.

In the intuitive cases of Chapter 19, it looked as if an ESP message often got blocked, or partly so, when it reached the threshold of consciousness. But in these hallucinatory experiences it looks as if the blockage comes earlier in the process. When the ESP message first arrives at an unconscious level, instead of proceeding right up to the threshold, it seems to get stopped in its tracks before it ever gets that far. It is stopped because the person's memory blocks it. Instead of carrying the message on up to the threshold, the person, let's say the little girl playing in the sand pile, remembers her brother as he affected her in the past. And that memory becomes the whole thing. She does not become aware of his danger, only of what he had so often meant to her.

That explanation, however, does not tell why she should think she actually saw him when he was not there. Or take the case of the woman reading in bed. Even if she had an ESP message about her husband's danger and allowed her unconscious memory of the way he usually called when he came home to *block* the actual message, that still does not explain how she could hear a call when her husband was not there to utter it.

It seems as if people who have experiences like this, whether visual or auditory, have a tendency that permits them to get sensory impressions for *internal* reasons instead of only for external ones like air and light waves. In these ESP cases, the internal reason appears usually to be a memory. But since the number reporting hallucinatory ESP experiences is much smaller than those reporting ESP intuitions or dreams, it seems likely that the majority of people are unable to have hallucinatory experiences. Of course, as everyone knows, when ESP is not involved, most of the hallucinations that are reported occur under unnatural physical conditions like delirium, or when under the effect of certain drugs. From all this it seems safe to say that probably few of those who never have such an experience *could* have one. They could not see a ghost no matter what. A haunted house to them would be just another house.

It may be that the emotional quality of the situation *does something* to people who are susceptible to hallucinatory experiences that especially tends to block the real message and substitutes a memory instead. At any rate, in the great majority of hallucinatory experiences of whatever kind, the person "seen," "heard," or even "felt" was a very close relative or friend, and usually he was undergoing a crisis that was not only emotional for him, but could also create emotion in the one who had the hallucination. It is easy to see that this kind of experience is deceptive and that the person himself cannot realize that his unconscious has played a trick on him.

Certainly as a message bearer from deep unconscious mental levels into consciousness, the hallucinatory ESP kind is a most difficult and inefficient one, for it is very rarely that a person gets an intelligible message from such an experience. Usually, as in the examples, he gets only a suggestion. But deep down where the ESP message, shall we say, is "loaded" onto the vehicle that will bring it into consciousness, apparently the one that for some reason is the most handy is chosen, and not necessarily the one that will do the most efficient job. At least one can make a guess that way even though realizing that at this stage of our knowledge of ESP, it can be only a guess. At any rate, it is clear that an image of a well-known person, whether visual or auditory, can tell very little about him. As imagery it is too restricted. For real imagery, the person usually must be asleep. The dream-maker can do it better.

21. Dream Copies

One bright Sunday morning in a southern town, a young woman was smiling to herself while fixing breakfast. Her husband came in.

"You're looking mighty happy this morning!"

"Yes, I was thinking of a dream I had last night. I dreamed that an old beau of mine came back. I haven't seen him in years and years. In the dream I thought it was about five o'clock, and I was in the kitchen, getting supper. You had just come home, and as you came in the doorbell rang. I asked you to go to the door. You opened it and there he was."

That evening at five o'clock it was not a dream. She was in the kitchen preparing supper. Her husband had just come home, and as he came into the room the doorbell rang. She asked him to answer it. He came back a few minutes later and told her, "Your old beau is in the living room."

"You're just teasing me because of the dream."

"Go and see for yourself."

That final conversation was the only item that wasn't in the dream: that and the shock, not only at seeing her old beau, but at finding that her dream was true.

Yes, the dream-maker can do it better than it is done in hallucinatory experiences. In them the person is not asleep and usually can make only tight, little, restricted imagery based mostly on his memory of the person or thing involved. But when asleep, the range is greater. The details of how it is done are still among the secrets that psychologists do not have. But one can see at least that the ESP message in dreams is treated more as it is in the hallucinatory form than in the intuitive, for it does not break through into consciousness directly (1). Instead, it is diverted and the meaning transformed into imagery which then must be remembered upon awakening.

In realistic ESP dreams, like the one above, it is easy to see that when he tries, the dream-maker is an excellent copier. He can picture a real scene almost as in a photograph. But what photographer ever took a picture beforehand? The dream-maker does not seem to mind. He can take his pictures either in the present or in the future. And Xerox could scarcely do it better.

Another dream-copy—this one in the present—was of Happy, a smooth-haired terrier, almost ten years old. Nearly all of those ten years he had lived with his family in Chicago. He was almost one of them, a house dog who was pampered with root beer, ice cream, and even dill pickles. In spite of all this, however, he had his urges for freedom, and one night he was successful. He slipped out and away. His mistress was really worried when by midnight she could still see no sign of him. She was more and more worried and almost could not sleep. After all, she had raised him from a puppy, and he followed her around the house all day. She had a "missing son" complex, her husband teased.

But she did fall asleep, and she had a dream. She was in the kitchen. The clock said five. She raised the blind and looked out into the alley. There sat Happy holding up his right front paw. She awoke and walked into the kitchen; it was 5 A.M. She raised the blind and looked out into the alley. There by the garage in the exact spot of her dream, was Happy with his right front paw upraised, his customary sign of a guilty conscience.

The dream picture of Happy was obviously a "still." But the dream-maker can follow action too, as the experience of a woman now in California shows. At the time she had her dreams, however, she was in Texas, her husband in an army camp in Louisiana. He wrote that he was coming home on furlough, but was short twenty-five dollars on the fare and would she please send it by Western Union. Later she received another telegram asking her to send five dollars more, to a little town in Texas.

The night before her husband was to arrive, she had what seemed almost like a night-long nightmare. She could see her husband "sloughing" through snow, walking with his head against the wind. She saw him in the back of a truck with the snow falling, the wind whistling. When she woke the next morning, she didn't even expect him on the designated 8 A.M. train, but went to work as usual. At three that afternoon he appeared at the place where she worked, bleary eyed and unshaven.

"What happened," he asked. "Were you broke or something that you only sent twenty dollars when I needed twenty-five dollars?"

It turned out that Western Union had made a mistake and only gave him twenty dollars instead of twenty-five, and when he got to the little town in Texas to pick up the extra five dollars it was after hours and the place was closed. So he walked and hitch-hiked—was picked up by two different motorists, one in a truck, and eventually made the rest of the trip by streetcar. The blizzard was so bad that even the buses were marooned. It appeared that the ESP dream-maker had been right along with him in the storm.

Dream copies, however, are not always perfect. And some of the ways in which they may be defective can tell a little about what goes on in the realistic dreaming process. Sometimes a detail is missed. A soldier in a military camp had a curious dream one night, which he remembered mainly because it was so odd. He thought he was on a train sitting beside another man. A second man came up. He was wearing some kind of a dark uniform (a Xerox copy would have shown just what—the dream-maker slipped up on this one) and sat down opposite. The man beside the dreamer asked the one in uniform, whom he apparently knew, how things were going. The other answered, "Going pretty well. But there's one old geezer in the next car who doesn't seem to know where he's going." About a week later the soldier was going home by train, and another man was in the seat beside him. The conductor, in a dark uniform, came in and sat down opposite. The man beside the soldier said, "Well, George, how's things?"

"Going pretty well, but there's one old geezer in the next car who doesn't seem to know where he's going."

The slip-up on that unimportant dream was minor. The missing item may not have been *worth* reporting. The reasons why some copies are imperfect vary a great deal. It may be sometimes that the dream simply ends too soon. But sometimes, too, something may seem to have been blocked out for a reason. A woman in Texas dreamed over and over for months during World War II that her husband came home very changed and seemed uninterested in his family. In each dream he said he was very tired and wanted to be left alone to rest. Then when she finally went into his room, he was gone. It happened that way exactly, right down to the very words she dreamed, and of which, of course, he knew nothing. When he returned he did seem changed. He said he was tired and wanted to be left alone. Later, when she went into his room, he was gone. *He never did come back.* This significant feature in real life was not covered by the dream, although obviously it led right up to it.

Sometimes the dream sequence seems to be affected or changed in some aspect or detail, as in a schoolgirl's dream that the principal excused the eleven o'clock Spanish class because the ceiling of the classroom had fallen and trapped the professor. The next day school was dismissed at eleven because the professor had had a fatal heart attack.

One can suppose in such a case, perhaps, that the dreamer could not quite face the idea that the professor was dead, and so made up a less disturbing situation. Or it may be more disturbing. People and circumstances differ.

An Ohio woman, while ill and in the hospital, dreamed the doctor came in carrying a flat wooden box which he opened. Inside lay a pistol on a white lining. He picked up the pistol and she knew he was going to shoot her. It so frightened her that she awoke.

Soon after, her husband came, and she was telling him of the fright she had had, when the doctor came in with a flat wooden box which did contain a pistol on a white lining, which he picked up and showed her husband, telling how he had just bought it. Obviously the idea that he was going to shoot her was her own addition to the actual correct dream imagery.

Another occasional kind of imperfection in realistic dreams involves the identity of the one dreamed about. Sometimes the identity that is given is the wrong one, or it may not even be revealed. For instance, a woman in Ohio dreamed she was at a funeral in an attractively furnished and painted house, with all her relatives. But she could not tell who had died. Two days later her cousin was killed in a car accident. The funeral scene was as in her dream house in detail, but the casket was closed because the cousin had been injured so badly. The dream picture was true enough. It gave the objective facts. But it did not tell the important item of identity.

Pictures, of course, give only facts. The photographer knows the reason why he takes them. Dream copies, too, are made by a "photographer," and quite obviously he has a reason. But his reason may be a very trivial one (the old geezer in the next car who doesn't know where he's going) or it may be very significant (the husband who never came home again). Whichever it may be, trivial or important, the dream-maker has a job to do, and if he so desires, he can shape the details a bit this way or that and "touch up" the picture according to his fancy.

But the person then may fail to understand, or add to or subtract from the real meaning, just as if the photographer had been someone else. Such cases show fairly clearly that the mental processes involved go on at different levels and that these levels are separate in some sense, so that in the conscious part, the imagery alone, must tell the story. The photographer keeps his reason for the picture "underground."

This split-level feature means that the dream as it is remembered may or may not be an exact copy. Accordingly, the inexactness that results in most of the incomplete realistic dreams shows that they must not be taken too seriously. Even if the dreamer could tell beforehand that it was an ESP dream (which of course, he cannot do) he still could not be sure that any of it was true until he could check up.

But realisitc dreams are usually fairly complete. The dream-maker generally tells it like it is, and so makes this the most effective form of all for expressing ESP messages.

22. Dream Drama

Joy worked in a photographic studio, and one day a young man came in and they fell to talking. They had some coffee. He walked home with her. That night she had a particularly vivid dream.

In it she saw an old rundown Virginia-creeper-covered house on a hill, with a vine-covered gate in front. By the house a girl was standing and very angrily she told Joy to leave Gil alone. She said he was "her property."

Joy thought she replied in a sing-song, "All is fair in love and war. If you can keep him you can have him. I don't care." But she awoke covered with perspiration and quite convinced it was no ordinary dream. She decided it meant that Gil was married and that she'd better stay out of trouble and not see him any more.

The next time he phoned, she said, "No, you're married." He said she was crazy, but she hung up. He phoned again, with the same result. Finally she did see him and decided to tell him of the dream. He looked startled and she was not surprised that he said nothing for a bit.

Then the narrative skips to their honeymoon, when, three hundred miles from home, he said he wanted to show her something. He led her up a hill, through a winding trail, and there was the house of her dream. He told her then that for six years he had been engaged to the girl who lived there but the very night after he met Joy he wrote to the other girl to break the engagement.

He knocked on the door, and her parents opened it. There on the wall was a picture of the girl of Joy's dream. The girl's parents said she had gone away to work after the engagement was broken. Gil then told Joy that he had not wanted to tell her how truly she had dreamed; he was afraid of the effect on her if he told her then of his long engagement. And so he had waited until they were married to tell her.

Joy's dream was not a copy (1). But by a little imaginary scene it told the truth, though not quite all of it. It left only a slight uncertainty, so that her interpretation was nearly, but not quite, correct.

It was different with an older woman in Pittsburgh. One morning she told the family that she had had an odd dream the night before about a young man the family had known some years previously. But for several years none of them had seen or heard of him, as he had married and moved away.

In the dream he had come with his wife and two small children (which he actually had, but she did not know it), said he was only able to stay a minute, put his arms around her, and kissed her goodbye. She said she could not imagine why she should dream of him. She had not heard his name mentioned for a long time, and they had never been close, although he used to come to the house when the children his age were there. Later she learned that he had been instantly killed in an auto accident that night, a few hours before her dream.

It was another unrealistic dream, the imagery a dramatization, and one that did tell a truth, but indirectly. The dream-maker must have "known" of the death, however, in order to produce a drama to fit.

The dreamers in cases like the two above apparently are excellent dramatists, at least when the process can go on unconsciously in sleep. Probably few novelists could conjure up the necessary imagery almost instantly that some dreamers can. But in ESP dreams the ability may not be an unmixed blessing. It adds to the uncertainty of trying to understand a dream beforehand, as individuals often try to do, without the safeguard of corroboration.

Take, for example, the dream of a young California woman, who was expecting her first baby. Somehow she and her husband had tacitly come to assume that it would be a boy. They talked about "him" fairly often. Three weeks before the birth she had a dream. She thought the baby came and that it was a girl with long black hair. The rest of the dream seemed foolish, for she thought the baby *walked* out of the delivery room.

The doctor said sometime before that he thought the baby would be fairly small. But he was wrong. When it was born it was a girl with long black hair, it weighed nine pounds, three ounces, and the nurse exclaimed, "My gosh, this kid is big enough to walk right out of here."

Another pregnant woman in a comparable dream two months before her baby came, dreamed she had triplets, that the nurse gave her only one baby and told her it was a girl. The nurse then paid no attention to the other two, and neither did the dreamer. The dream of course made little sense because by then she knew that no triplets or even twins were in prospect. The plans were all made for a home delivery, but a complication arose and she had to be taken to a hospital, where two other babies were born within minutes of her own, a little girl.

Dreams like these suggest that dream-making is not always the job of experts. The tendency to jump to conclusions without examining the evidence carefully, can show up even in dreaming. These dreamers, it would appear, allowed some of the details to be confused, and when awake they were just as prone to draw the *wrong* conclusion, as if the imagery had been made by someone else.

Perhaps one of the most generally believed ideas about dreams is that many of them are symbolic: that they have a hidden meaning, and books on dream interpretation have a market accordingly. Since the time of Freud, psychiatrists, often with only a little evidence and plenty of imagination, have made a point of finding the hidden meaning in dreams their patients tell. Fortunately, perhaps, those dreams very rarely involve ESP. Consequently no checkup can show the correctness or incorrectness of the psychiatrist's interpretation, and so apparently all goes well. Neither the doctor nor the patient needs to raise a question. With symbolic dreams in parapsychology however, it is not safe to be permissive. Here the point is to try to find out the processes that go on and thereby better understand the way that psi fits into human life. Guesswork here would be like guessing the way home in the dark and in strange territory. One might get somewhere, but it very well might not be home.

However, certain kinds of dream dramatizations are often considered to have a psi implication, as, for instance, the case of a young woman who one night screamed in her sleep, waking herself and her husband. She told him she knew Death had just touched her. In the dream she thought she was sitting on the porch at home, with her mother and an aunt, when a figure glided through the screen and laid his hand on her shoulder, a fairly tall man in a straight black suit, but with the face of a mummy. As she screamed he glided out through the screen. Her husband consoled her. It was "just a nightmare," he said, but three weeks later her older sister, to whom she was very close, died in childbirth.

Was there a connection? The family thought so, and that the dream was a "sign" of it. Possibly so, but not necessarily. The husband may have been correct. It may have been only a nightmare. No single detail was realistic. Any death that might have occurred soon after could have seemed a fulfillment.

Among the possible psi dreams that are reported, truly symbolic ones like this dream of the figure of Death, are relatively scarce. Many more death dreams are realistic and leave little doubt about their meaning. Some are unrealistic, like the one above about the young man who said goodbye to his old neighbor. Only a few can be classed as truly symbolic. Add to that the fact that one can seldom be reasonably sure that the symbolic dream was not just a nightmare, and then one realizes that the convincingness of symbolism in psi dreams is exceedingly low.

But even in the unrealistic experiences that are certainly more truth-telling than those that are symbolic, what, if anything, goes on? Obviously the dream-maker in these, when an ESP message is received, blocks the message at the start, and then unconsciously lets his fancy roam. If it's the girl with whom her boy friend had been going, she, like Joy, acts out the part. If it is a neighbor boy's death, he comes and says goodbye, and just possibly if, to this person, a figure in black with the face of a mummy means the figure of Death, then that figure could be a "sign" of the family tragedy three weeks away.

And so in ESP dreams, both the unrealistic and the realistic forms occur. Statistics are lacking to show whether the two tendencies occur in similar proportion in non-ESP dreams. Certainly in ordinary dreaming, fantasy is more likely to seem interesting, and therefore to excite comment, than a more realistic style of imagery. But the realistic style in ESP dreams, is the much more striking. It also is more frequently reported.

The fact could mean that more people tend to dream realistically than otherwise, and that therefore more realistic ESP dreams could be expected. Or it could simply be that the realistic ones are more easily identified as true than those that involve dream drama. At any rate, supposedly each person selects the form that for him comes most naturally. And the unrealistic ones can show quite clearly that some persons, whether or not they recognize it when they are awake, are inherent dramatists.

23. Closeup on PK Experiences

The A. and B. families in Brooklyn were strangers, although their houses were crowded close beside each other. The A. family's house had a small side porch, and when they were away, they found it an excellent place to leave their two pet dogs. They never heard them barking and apparently never gave a thought to whether or not the neighbors did.

But Mrs. B.'s bedroom window faced that porch, and when the A.'s stayed out late at night Mrs. B. knew it, and as it was repeated her exasperation grew.

One day, before she notified the authorities of the nuisance, Mrs. B. was telling the cleaning woman all about it. Just as she was saying in no uncertain terms what she thought about the A.'s a large picture in the room, the enlargement of a photo of the quiet vacation country of her youth, shattered to the floor.

She said to the cleaning woman that that was her pay for saying such mean things about her neighbors.

Was it? Or was Mrs. B.'s idea "just superstition"? In Chapter 8 a glimpse was given of experiments that showed the human mind as seemingly able to affect the physical objects, dice, that were thrown or fell onto a surface. But perhaps many persons still feel that even if they must accept the experimental data, it is quite impossible to think that effects in real life, like this one above, are anything more than chance coincidences. It probably seems to many even more farfetched that something like a falling picture had anything to do with the human situation or that a stopped clock could mark the time of a death, than that the figure of Death (Chapter 22) could mean that someone in the family was going to die. For ages, falling pictures, stopped clocks, and other such occurrences, have been taken as "signs" by some and put down by others, particularly the better educated, as superstition pure and simple.

By now the idea of symbolism in dreams has been around so long that people in general tend to take it seriously. Not so, however, with the idea of PK in daily life. It is too new and runs too strongly counter to common sense. Yet it has much going for it on the experimental side, while symbolism has nothing (1). Besides, if PK happens in the laboratory, why not spontaneously?

In the laboratory PK occurs best when the general emotional situation is at a peak, when those involved are interested, enthusiastic, and excited, as much as they can be in a laboratory. It should therefore be expected that in real life it would occur when the situation is highly emotional. In real life psi effects as shown in the various forms of ESP begin, it appears, by unconscious awareness of an event, often one that would create strong feelings in the person if he did become aware of it consciously. When occurrences that could be instances of PK are compared, practically all of them seem to coincide with strongly emotional situations. The emotions involved from case to case may vary, from anger to fright to sorrow to grief. The nature of the emotion seems less important than its intensity.

Grief, for instance, would have been the emotion involved in an experience that happened one night just as a little girl and her mother were about to relax for the evening. The mother opened the closet door in her bedroom and exclaimed, "Oh, how strange."

"What, Mama?" asked the little girl.

"Why, you know I have the pictures of all you four children stuck between the two panels in the closet wall, and just as I opened the door, the one of Harold fell out of its place."

Harold had joined the navy shortly before. As the family soon learned, he had contracted dysentery and he died two days later. Whether the picture fell before or after his death was not reported, but at least it was before the family knew of his illness. Either way, it could have been a PK effect.

Along with the many cases like that occurring at the time of the death of someone emotionally close, a few involve persons that were still living, as in the case of a woman in Ohio. One Sunday night she was watching television when she heard a loud squeak from a rocker her mother had given her and saw that it was rocking madly back and forth. Wondering, she looked at the doors and windows, and none was open nor had a noticeable vibration of the rather solidly built house occurred. Meanwhile, many miles away, her mother, in the hospital with a broken hip, told a daughter who was with her that she had been "on a trip" to see the distant daughter, and that all was well with her. Her mother didn't mention it again, and lived for several days. Possibly the dying woman's strong thought of her daughter called out in the daughter the PK effect on the rocker that was reminiscent of her mother.

In other instances, effects, even that of a rocking chair, are said to occur after the person who seems to be involved is dead. Such a case was reported by a man in Texas. As he was shaving in the bathroom he was thinking strongly of his mother who had died several years before. Then he thought he heard his mother's rocking chair in the adjoining room creak as if someone had sat on it. Thinking someone had come in without his hearing, he stepped out of the bathroom. The chair was rocking gently to and fro, but no one else was around. Almost feeling his mother's presence, he watched it for several minutes until it gradually came to rest.

In this instance an interesting and possibly significant added fact was that as a boy playing dice, this person had felt that he could almost always get the face he threw for the first few times around the die and that gradually he would be unable to do so.

A feeling like this, of course, is vague evidence, yet not all boys throwing dice get such an impression, so that it could be possible that this one did exercise PK rather more frequently than most, and that that characteristic in turn might have made an episode like the rocking of the chair more likely for him than for some person who had never had a suggestion of PK ability. This supposition, like the one about symbolic dreams, cannot be either proved or disproved, but at least this one has some plausibility.

And it ties in with the cases like the one about of Mrs. B. and the barking dogs. If these are instances of PK in daily life, then the PK must be exercised by the person who observes the effect. The daughter, the son, both no doubt associated the rockers with their mothers. The only difference was that the man's mother was dead. While that could seem like a post-mortem effect produced by his mother, it could just as well, even if not so obviously, have been his own psi ability that did it, just as it must have been in the case of the woman whose mother was still living. She was like the woman in Brooklyn, who had no post-mortem entity to whom to credit the falling of the picture. If anyone "did" that, she herself must have been the one.

Cases like that of Mrs. B. in which no other person was involved, have not been reported very often until recently. It seems likely that such persons themselves could not believe that a connection existed between their feelings and the physical happening. They did not know about the PK ability. However, in all such instances when only one person is involved and something physical happens, the records show that the person was in an emotional state. He appears thus to be the one who compares to the subject in a PK test, who also is keyed up, although perhaps less strongly. On this account it looks as if the person who does it is the one who sees the effect: the mother looking at Harold's picture in the closet; the woman watching television as her desperately ill mother thinks of her. And for all these, the emotional state, whether conscious or unconscious, causes the PK effect that marks it, often on some object the subject associates with the one in crisis, when such an object is involved.

When a PK effect like any of these occurs, of course, it is quite different from the dreams and intuitions of spontaneous ESP. But the way it begins in the unconscious is probably the same. Again, when the information is received, apparently it is blocked, but instead of triggering any kind of imagery, as in a dream or hallucinatory experience, the PK force is released. Just how this is done is still mostly a mystery although a strong emotion is almost certainly a necessity.

The PK form of psi communication, however, is not reported as often as the others. This may mean that fewer persons can have spontaneous PK, but also it certainly seems that instances of it are less likely to be recognized when they do occur; it is too easy to think that they must have been the result of chance or some ordinary cause that was simply undetected.

In summing up the value that the case studies have, the main one is probably the fact that they come in forms that in themselves are not strange or new or even special, but are the commonly used ordinary vehicles of mental experience. They represent the methods by which information in unconscious levels is transferred to consciousness, whether that information is supplied by ESP or by the senses or by recall.

This observation may never be open to experiment, but it fits in with the known facts of psychology and parapsychology. It makes sense of ESP both as shown in the laboratory, where it usually takes the form of an intuition, and in everyday life where it may take any one of the five. It makes sense because these forms all originate in unconscious levels where somehow, by means of the psi ability, the mind obviously can come into direct contact with the real world.

SECTION FIVE

Life After Death

24. Psi Experiences Involving the Dying and the Dead

Anne, a young woman in Michigan, woke one night, sobbing because of a vivid dream. In it she seemed to get a message from her mother who had died six years earlier. In life, Anne had often fixed her mother's hair, and in the dream she was doing it again. But her mother was weeping and trying to tell her about Anne's unmarried sister, Phyllis. She said Phyllis was going to have a baby. She had fallen in love with a young man and learned too late that he was married. He had walked out on her when he learned about the pregnancy.

Later a letter came from Phyllis. Almost before she opened it Anne knew the sad story it would tell. Phyllis had a tragic love affair, and her baby had been born the night of Anne's dream.

Experiences in which a dead person seems to bring a message to a living one have occurred many times and in different forms over the years. Also, instances have been reported involving a person not already known to be dead, but who, as it proved, was dying at the time; for instance, as in this experience of a thirteen-year-old girl, Mary, in Canada. Her grandmother, a "strict and proper Scotswoman" had had a stroke and was very ill. One night as Mary and her sister went to bed, their mother told them that she and their father were going to drive over to grandma's to see how she was.

Sometime later still, wide awake, as she thought, Mary suddenly saw grandma standing in the doorway. She had on her suit and the mink fur that she always wore. She had her handbag in one hand and her suitcase in the other. She looked at Mary, smiled, and said in her familiar Scots accent, "Don't worry, pet. I'm just going on a wee trip." Then she was gone.

Mary was not frightened, but she was puzzled. She thought grandma was home sick in bed, so how could she be here too? Her parents returned some time later. Mary jumped out of bed and ran to them excitedly.

"Mommy, Grandma came to see me while you were away."

Her mother looked at her queerly. "You must have been dreaming. Grandma died tonight. She's gone, dear."

Mary went "all shivery," but she knew that grandma had really come to say goodbye to her. A comforting thought—whether actually a true one or not.

Reports of such occurrences have always raised the "survival" question (1). "If a man die, shall he live again?" Of course it is one of the greatest, for it affects everyone, not only for its bearing on the answer to his own personal destiny, but also for his relation to other people. This, in turn, affects the kind of society that develops. Will it be a peaceful one based on the idea of "Do unto others as you would have them do unto you?" or a Hitlerite Germany that tries to exterminate whole races that it considers inferior?

The survival question has a history as old as the human race. It has been given different answers in different places and ages. However, little of that history need be mentioned here, except to say that in the main the answers have come from the religions. Different religious leaders had different answers. In the religions most familiar to Westerners now, the answer is immortality, the doctrine that man has a soul or spirit that lives on when the body dies.

A century or so ago, many people were beginning to ask for proof of important doctrines such as that; they were no longer willing to accept blindly the answers handed down on authority. Even the idea of immortality began to be questioned by some. They wondered if it could be proved.

Yes, some said, because many people think they have had messages from the dead. If this is really true, then of course the dead still exist. Even though it might not be possible to prove that they live forever, as immortality would require, it should be possible to find out if these reports mean what they appear to mean, that the dead can communicate with the living. The reports can be treated as scientific data and evaluated accordingly.

As already mentioned, among the persons who a century or so ago took up this job of proof were the founders of the Psychical Research Society in London. In the 1880's they went to work on the question with great determination. Then soon after an American Society in New York City was founded for the same general purpose.

The methods used by these Psychical Research societies were the best and most careful ones known at the time. The results they achieved over the following fifty years cannot be written off, even today, except that it is necessary now to interpret them differently. This is because of general advances in knowledge and scientific method.

These advances have shown that the correct answer is more difficult to get than seemed likely at first. Like the answer to the telepathy question, the one about survival is more complicated than it first appeared. But like that one, the answer could be even greater than has been supposed, just as one could say about the early idea of the shape of the earth. Once people thought it flat, and certainly most of them were satisfied with it that way. But when the truth was known and it was found to be spherical, it made a much greater, more interesting universe. The answer to the survival question, whatever it may be, could well be similar.

It is easy to see why in the past an experience like Anne's, when her deceased mother seemed to bring her information, often convinced the living person that the answer to the survival question is Yes, and that the dead person actually did communicate. But now, with knowledge that the living person has ESP ability, that is too easy an answer to solve such an important question. After all, the dream was not essentially different from some of those given earlier, for instance, the one in Chapter 22, in which the girl named Joy dreamed of the person her new boy friend had jilted. The main difference was that Anne's mother was dead, the jilted girl was living. Obviously the dreamer must have gotten the correct information about the jilted girl by ESP. And then the dream-maker constructed the drama in which it seemed that the confrontation occurred and correct information given. If that dream-maker could so dramatize the ESP information, then presumably Anne's could do the same. She could tell her sister Phyllis' story to herself just as their mother would have told it had she been alive. Anne's own memory of her mother would have been the basis of that aspect of the dream just as much as it was in the item about fixing her mother's hair. Obviously, then, it is impossible to conclude that the deceased mother actually caused the dream.

Another kind of personal experience that often involves the dead or dying is the hallucinatory. For instance, take the case of a woman and her fifteen-year-old daughter. They had recently moved to California from their previous home in Washington, D.C., where they had left the woman's father very ill. One day not long after, as the woman went into the dining room, to her great surprise, there stood her father.

"Why, Dad, when did you come?" she exclaimed. Her daughter turned to look and she too saw the figure, she said, with hand upraised in a gesture of blessing. But then he faded away, and they both realized that he was not really there. Before long a telegram came: FATHER PASSED AWAY TODAY.

The experience was a visual hallucination, the same kind the little girl experienced in Chapter 20, when she thought her brother was teasing her just when he actually was about to drown. Or take the experience of fifteen-year-old Judith. One night after she had turned out the light and was composing herself for sleep, she turned on her side and closed her eyes . . . but what was that?

A whitish misty form, it was Susy, her best girl friend . . . looking very serious, not her usual happy-go-lucky self. Petrified, too stunned and terrified to move or call, Judith watched the figure disappear. Then she screamed, ran headlong to her parents' room, weeping and trembling. Gently they tried to convince her that she had just been dreaming.

The next morning the family learned of a terrible accident the night before. Susy was pronounced dead by the physician at the scene of the wreck. As close as could be figured, this was the time that Judith had seen her in the bedroom.

But wait, the story is not finished yet. The physician checked again before leaving and discovered the faintest heartbeat in the badly burned and broken body. Susy did not die, but lay in a coma for days. Later the nurse asked Judith if she was the one Susy had called for.

Susy lived, and the two were still close friends some twenty years later when Judith reported the experience to the Parapsychology Laboratory.

In the past it seemed obvious that an apparitional experience meant that in some nonmaterial sense the dying or dead person was "there." His appearance was usually taken to mean that he had come to say goodbye. But in that past time cases like Susy's in which the person did not die were not likely to be taken seriously because, before ESP was known, they did not "make sense." Now that it is known, the old explanation is no longer the only one. There is no reason why the situation is any different if the person seen or heard is dying or dead than if he is still living. The one who has the experience could simply be expressing his ESP information in the hallucinatory form.

This newer explanation makes such experiences seem much more ordinary than the old idea that the dead could actually come and show themselves to their living friends. It makes clear too that they seemed to "come" not because they actually did so, but because the person created their image according to his own design and in his own perspective.

But then, what if the person seen is a stranger? No memories cling to him and dictate the image that develops. This sometimes happens, though not as frequently as the image of a friend or relative. For instance, in England a family had just moved into an old house but one quite new to them. One of the daughters awoke one night with the feeling that someone was in the room with her. By the dim light she saw in her rocking chair, gazing at her, an elderly gentleman with a clipped moustache, dressed in old-fashioned plus-fours and a tweed jacket. He at first appeared quite real, but faded away in a few seconds.

The experience impressed her, even though she felt no fear. In the morning she told her mother and even drew a sketch of the man she saw. A few days later her mother was talking to the landlady and mentioned the experience. The woman was amazed. She said it was a perfect description of her husband, a retired Indian army colonel. He had had a heart attack after mowing the lawn a year before. He had died in that room.

That situation was a little different because no memories were involved. But there the person who had the experience, by ESP presumably, could "sense" the earlier history of the place in which she was. She expressed her impression by recreating the old gentleman—sensorially—as he actually used to look, but as if *gazing at her* just as she would have expected him to do if he had actually found her there.

And so the appearance of a dead person in a psi experience does not necessarily mean that he was there and made a communication. The living person could have created it all himself.

It is possible of course that such experiences can be of two kinds: one explained as an instance of ESP, the other as the effect of a surviving spirit. But if so, no way is now known to separate them. Therefore, they cannot be thought of as evidence for survival. Careful thinkers need evidence that can have only one interpretation. Anything less could only be evidence of wishful thinking.

25. Can the Dead Speak through Mediums?

Mrs. Leonora Piper was a famous Boston medium in the 1890s. In 1892 a young lawyer, George Pelham (G.P.) was killed in an accident. A few weeks afterward a friend of his, a Mr. Hart, went to Mrs. Piper for a sitting hoping to get a message from G.P. (2). Mr. Hart's arrangements with the medium were made by a third party. Mrs. Piper did not know the name of Mr. Hart or that he wanted a message from G.P.

Mrs. Piper was a trance medium. When she was in trance it was as if a deceased person, a "communicator," was speaking through her lips. In this instance it seemed to Mr. Hart to be G.P. who was speaking. Among other references then, G.P. began to talk about a Mr. and Mrs. Howard whom both G.P. and Mr. Hart had known. And then came a couple of sentences which at the moment seemed to Mr. Hart to have no meaning, but which turned out to be the most "evidential" of all (evidential because they proved to be true and something the medium could not have known normally).

The words, apparently from G.P. to Mrs. Howard, were, "Tell her. She'll know. I will solve the problem, Katherine." Although Mr. Hart did not know until later when he compared notes with Mrs. Howard, G.P. had once lived in the Howard home, and he had often talked with Katherine, their fifteen-year-old daughter, about such topics as Time, Space, God, and Eternity, and he told her he didn't think that the current explanations of them were satisfactory. He had told her that sometime he would solve these problems and let her know.

In 1927 a Mr. John F. Thomas of Detroit, Michigan, had gone to a London medium, Mrs. Vickers, to see if he could get a message from his wife, Ethel, who had died some time before (4). His sitting, too, had been carefully arranged "blind" so that the medium could know nothing of the identity of her sitter. Part of the sitting went something like this:

A name like Eric . . . a great big E, I see . . . quite an ordinary name . . . but I can't get it . . . Eth . . . I am not getting names very easily this morning. It is like Ethel or Emma . . . I don't know if it is Effie or Ethel . . . I don't know if it is her name or someone she is referring to. . . .

Later, while still in London, Mr. Thomas and his secretary went to another medium, Mrs. Garrett (of whom more later), who also attempted to identify Mr. Thomas' deceased wife, Ethel:

Do you know a little name beginning with E, too, that she's interested in, because I see E near her. Eff . . . Effel, that comes up rather close, too.

And then later:

Please, is there anyone she knows well, Hetty, Hatty? Hatty and Hetty is connected with Etta . . . Ethel!

Mrs. Thomas did have an Aunt Hatty.

A few illustrations like these can give only the slightest idea of the way the mediumistic material was given. It was seldom the direct kind of statement one expects when the person is fully conscious. The medium did not say to Mr. Thomas anything specific like, "This is your wife, Ethel." And the communicator G.P. did not say through Mrs. Piper, "I told Katherine Howard that I would solve the problems for her." Instead, more groping and round-about phrases were usually used. One can recognize the kind now as characteristic of the semidream like form that material slipping over the threshold of consciousness from unconscious mental levels may take.

The Mrs. Piper mentioned above was only one of the many that were carefully studied by the Society for Psychical Research. One of the first problems of the investigators was to be certain that the mediums they worked with were genuine. Among the so-called commercial mediums so many were fraudulent that it was a question whether there were any who were not. The Psychical Research investigators, however, worked mainly with selected individuals whom they regarded as honest and self-respecting individuals and who neither then nor later were ever found to engage in trickery.

Even working with presumably honest sensitives, the techniques these investigators used were such that they knew that any correct information the mediums gave them was not learned beforehand and then palmed off as if coming from discarnate sources. Not only were the experimental mediums kept ignorant of the identity of the sitters, as in the cases of Mr. Hart and Mr. Thomas, but in some of the most thoroughly controlled studies, the medium lived for a time in the home of the investigator, and all of her mail and other outside contacts were carefully controlled.

Under ever stricter conditions then, for fifty years or more a great deal of material was secured by different investigators that could not have been the result of fraud of any kind. The words of the mediums were taken down stenographically or their written messages transcribed, and the records became the basis of study by some of the best minds of the time. The verdict was unquestionably that these mediums had shown knowledge they could not have known by sensory means. The episode from Mrs. Piper's record given above is not even the proverbial drop in the bucket of all the material she gave the investigators and which they considered significant because she could not have known it by ordinary means.

The best of all the material collected by the Society for Psychical Research over the years up to and after the turn of the century came to be called the Cross Correspondences because different mediums seemed to contribute in an interlocking pattern that could not then be accounted for in any known way (1). The complicated mass of material fills many volumes of research reports and can well excite amazement even today. Its quality was such that many persons were convinced by it that nothing but survival could explain it, though others remained uncertain. They could not explain how the mediums got the information they gave, because ESP was not then known. At the time they were probably still mystified by the manner, the trance, the automatic speech and writing which was sometimes used because unconscious mental levels had not yet been recognized. Still, they were too careful to jump to a quick conclusion on a question as important as survival.

The case of John F. Thomas in the reference above was one of many that came later in the 1920s and in which much evidential material was secured. Mr. Thomas worked with many mediums both in the United States and in England. Sometimes he was not even present at a sitting but sent only a secretary to take down the medium's words. Even so, his wife, Ethel, "came through" so often and so correctly that it seemed almost miraculous. Sometimes the facts given at a sitting proved to be correct when neither Mr. Thomas nor anyone present knew them, and they could only later be shown to be correct by research in old archives and on moss-grown gravestones.

The case that was made for the reality of communication from Mrs. Thomas thus grew very strong. But Mr. Thomas, although deeply impressed, for a time remained skeptical. He wanted expert opinion, and decided that the psychologist Dr. William McDougall at Duke University was the one to give it. In order to ensure personal contact, he engaged JBR and myself, then two young graduate students, at Cambridge, Massachusetts, who had already been studying his records, to go to Duke that fall (1927) and bring the Thomas material to Dr. McDougall's attention.

We knew the records had been collected in such a way that the hits could not be explained away as the result of fraudulent mediums or normal "leaks" of any imaginable kind. Dr. McDougall was very much interested, but after careful study it remained unclear to him whether or not it all came from a surviving Mrs. Thomas or from some source within the mediums. However, as more evidential material accumulated, Mr. Thomas eventually became convinced, though the rest of us did not.

We could not be sure. What if telepathy was a real mental process? Perhaps the mediums got their information by telepathy and play-acted (unconsciously) the rest? It really was important then to find out if this was possible. So began the series of experiments detailed in Section Two.

About the time JBR had been fairly well convinced that the extrasensory way of getting information was a fact, the medium Mrs. Garrett, mentioned above, came to Dr. McDougall to be tested (3). She had recently come to the United States, where, as in England, she had an excellent mediumistic record. She was unusual not only in the amount of correct information her sitters claimed for her, but also in coming, of her own free will, to a psychologist to be tested. No other medium of her standing in all the years since has done similarly. But Mrs. Garrett was so puzzled by her ability that she herself wanted to find out about it. She especially wanted to know about the "control" who seemed to take over her body when she went into trance. It was as if this were an outside entity which "possessed" her and helped the deceased spirits to communicate. Mrs. Garrett wanted to know if these (she had several at different times) were actually out-of-the-body spirits, as they claimed, or only split-off parts of her own mind acting like separate personalities. She thought Dr. McDougall, with JBR working under him, would be the one to find the answer to her question.

In the research that was then done with Mrs. Garrett, all the rules for getting safe material, learned over the years by other investigators, were observed and with an important addition. Earlier, it had never been possible to have a medium's remarks judged "blind" because the sitter who knew the answers had to do it. Now a way around that defect of method was worked out so that no critic could say the results were biased by a sitter's wishful thinking.

The necessary technique was complicated, slow, and laborious compared to that for judging a run of ESP, for instance. But the method was decided on in time and became the basis for other instances when "verbal" material, like that of experimental dreams (see Chapter 12), had to be evaluated. The method used with Mrs. Garrett required that she give sittings for a number of different sitters. One after another these persons were taken into a room separate from hers, so that she never met any of them or was given any information about them. Neither did any of them hear her responses, or know who the other sitters were.

Then later each sitter was given typed but unidentified

(coded) copies of all Mrs. Garrett's responses to all of the sitters, not knowing which was his own. He was instructed to mark all of the points in all of them as true or false for himself.

The result, of course, if positive would be that he would have many more hits on the responses when he was the sitter than on the rest. It was arranged so that the hits could then be evaluated statistically. When Mrs. Garrett's reports were treated this way the results were statistically significant. In spite of the "blind" judging, she had shown that she had known too much about the sitters she never saw or heard of for her responses to be the result of chance.

All of this, although it did not answer Mrs. Garrett's question as to the nature of her "controls," showed again the same thing that all the hundreds of pages of reports of the Psychical Research societies showed, that it is possible for a medium to get information about people that she could not know by sense perception, and material, too, that often was known mainly by someone who was dead. But all of it, of course, had to be checked against some still existing record or memory, for only then could anyone tell if it was correct or incorrect.

And so Mrs. Garrett's records just like the old Psychical Research reports raised the question: where did the information come from? Did the spirits of the dead bring it as claimed? Or was it drawn from the records or memories that still existed? It was the question of telepathy again.

Telepathy at that time was still a blanket word. Today the question would be: was it ESP? The advance of the previous years at the laboratory, at least, had brought a method for putting this question to the test. It was available then, and Mrs. Garrett was tested for ESP. She passed all the tests very well. In fact, her scores showed her to be a very good ESP subject.

The tests gave an answer of sorts to the problem of her mediumship. They did not *prove* that she got her information by ESP but they did show that she could have done so. And if she did, of course, she could then, quite unconsciously and almost as if dreaming, have dramatized the information into the form of responses from the deceased persons, for she knew that sitters were usually looking for messages from their deceased relatives and friends.

After this outcome with this medium, the value of mediumistic material in survival research quite naturally fell into question. Consequently, little of it has been done in recent years and none that matches in complexity that of the early Psychical Research reports. It is as if the serious study given earlier to such mediums as Mrs. Leonard in England and Mrs. Piper in the United States in a way "created" them, for even though they have successors, it seems that in this area, at least, the days of giants are past.

Still today, then, no way has been found to show for sure that the dead speak through mediums. Just as personal experiences (see Chapter 24) could be produced by ESP plus the person's ability to create imagery and dramatize it unconsciously, the medium could do it the same way.

When the search for evidence of telepathy began, it seemed that if it was a reality it would make the survival hypothesis seem more possible because it would be a way by which spirits could communicate with living persons. Instead, it prevents that conclusion because it makes it obvious that the living person can do it himself by his psi ability. Again, as in the cases of Chapter 24, if the deceased communicate, the times when they do so are not distinguishable from those when the medium does it all herself by her ESP ability and her tendency to impersonate, and of course her ESP ability would be a necessary factor in either case.

26. Hauntings and Poltergeists

Katherine and her husband, grandparents now, lived for a long time in the old mansion in southern California in which she grew up. It was old when her father bought it many years ago, and its earlier history had been long lost in the mists of time.

One Christmas their daughter, Mary, and her children came to visit. One day while they were there, and Mary had gone on a shopping trip, the children began to explore grandma's house, and the two little girls, five and eight, went to the cellar. Not long after, they came racing back upstairs in fright. The five-year-old was crying and shaking so badly that grandmother (Katherine), trying to calm her, was afraid she was having convulsions. It developed that the child thought she saw, standing in a corner of the cellar, an Indian girl, with long black hair, a "raggedy" dress, and moccasins, who turned and stared hard at her. It so frightened the child that she began screaming, and ran upstairs. The older child saw nothing but by contagion was frightened too.

Katherine finally convinced the five-year-old that she had imagined the whole thing. Later, when she told her daughter, Mary, about it, Mary gasped, went white, and then reported to her mother something that had happened at the same place when she was small and in the cellar.

It was about 1943, during World War II, when Katherine's husband was overseas, and Katherine herself was in the hospital with appendicitis. Her mother-in-law, Mary's grandmother, was staying at the house with the child, who was then about five years old. One day she went with her grandmother to the cellar. And then she saw standing in the corner an Indian girl with long black hair, moccasins, and in an old brown dress. The Indian turned and stared at her.

Frightened, the little girl started to cry and clutched at her grandmother's skirts. But the grandmother saw nothing and was so annoyed at the child when she said she saw an Indian girl that she shook and slapped her for telling lies. She said if Mary ever told such a story again she would give her a whipping, and she especially warned her not to tell her mother and worry her when she came home from the hospital. The impression was so strong that Mary never did. In later years she decided it must have been imagination, and so because it might sound queer she never mentioned the occurrence until now when her child had apparently had the same experience.

Well, so what? The story could be called a case of haunting; and if two five-year-olds saw the figure, even though a generation apart, it would seem that it must reflect some kind of reality. Of course, it was not actually an Indian girl because neither of the other persons present on either occasion saw her. Both children experienced an hallucination.

The question is: why?

Had an Indian girl once had a significant reason for being in that cellar? Unfortunately, like so many such accounts, there is a gap in the evidence here. No one knew if sometime in the long ago a connection involving such a person had existed, and so no conjecture made now can have actual reliability. Still, since both experiences were so similar, the question Why? needs answering. Three different possible ones can be suggested.

First, if an Indian girl had once been associated with the cellar, then both experiences could have been clairvoyant ones (of a past event), like that of the girl in Chapter 24 who saw the apparition of the deceased owner of the house looking at her. Then presumably the two children hallucinated and did so because of an ESP awareness of an earlier situation at a *place*.

Second, if no Indian girl had ever been associated with that place, then Mary's experience in 1943 must indeed have been an imaginary one. The second little girl's experience, then, could have been based on it, possibly by ESP of the telepathic kind.

Third, if the Indian girl had actually existed and her spirit caused the two sensitive children to have hallucinatory impressions of her, it would have been a survival case.

The first and second possible explanations have parapsychological bases. With complete information about the Indian girl, one of them might be the answer. The third possibility has no experimental basis. Even if an Indian girl had once been there, and if by ESP these two children became aware of her, no way is known at present to decide that this, rather than the ESP explanation alone, is the true one. It is an impasse . . . the same one reached in Chapters 24 and 25.

Stories of hauntings are reported under so many different specific conditions that no single illustration can be typical of very many. But they usually are similar in that they seem weird, "scary," hair-raising. This, of course, is largely because, as reported, they are mysterious and seem to be contrary to all known explanations. It must be remembered that this result follows necessarily because the idea began without the knowledge of psi ability, and when even simple signs of it, like cases of ESP, were often considered supernatural. And also, both long ago and even today, they are experienced by people who still, not far beneath the surface so to speak, believed in or were *ready* to believe in the idea of spirits, invisible entities with intelligence of their own who can affect human beings.

With this old superstitious background, one must expect that reports tend to be colored accordingly. Also, the events will be misinterpreted, even exaggerated perhaps, and shaded along preconceived lines, just as the effect that a magician might produce would be misinterpreted by a spectator who had a theory, but a wrong one, of the way the trick was done.

All of this makes it fairly impossible to arrive at an explanation for cases as they are reported, and usually firmly believed, by those involved. Some may sound weird, without necessarily being so at all. For instance, a Washington woman, very sane and matter-of-fact if one could judge by her reports of a number of fairly convincing ESP dreams and intuitions, had apparently and quite understandably come to take her experiences very seriously.

One night after a deep sleep she woke . . . nearly. She said she was neither quite awake nor really asleep, but aware of her surroundings. Then as she lay on her side, she felt a lump or something on her back, and dropped her arm down to feel what it was. IT WAS A HAND! She thought a large, firm, male one.

But the sequel tells what it was. The sequel was—she did not get frightened, but went back to sleep! That fact fairly clearly shows that the whole thing was not a hallucination, not an ESP experience of any kind, but . . . a dream.

One of the most frequently reported effects, and usually the most meaningless as far as can be determined, is purely auditory, the sound of footsteps. A woman in California, the wife of a policeman, who was accustomed to being alone with the children at night while her husband was on duty, one night had such an experience.

It was nearly morning when she wakened to the sound of footsteps coming down the hall. They sounded firm and masculine. She thought they meant a burglar. He came into the room, she thought, and probably wanted her jewelry. She thought it safer to lie perfectly still. He stood by her bed—but then turned and walked back down the hall. She waited to hear the heavy front door close, but no sound came. Later she checked and found that all doors and windows in the house were locked from the inside that night.

It happened again a few weeks later. This time she thought the footsteps were her husband's as he came into the room. This time she opened her eyes, but by the dim street light, she could see that no one was there.

Later, when she went on a visit and her husband was home alone, he heard someone walking down the hall. He turned on the light, but no one was there. At last account, the two are still wondering who walked down their hall and why he came.

Another experience, this one from the state of Virginia, is much the same. It is also from a woman, who, except for the children, was home alone one night. She, however, lived in a large old house inherited from her husband's ancestors, but unlike the house involving the Indian girl, this one had a fairly well-known history, including a poltergeist tradition dating back to the 1830s.

The last survivor of the older generation, Aunt Ann, had died at ninety-seven in 1958, and most of her possessions and the ancient furniture were still stored in the house. But more about that later.

The night in question, this person woke to the sound of footsteps. She got up, went to the children's room to see if they were up. They were sound asleep. She feared a burglar. And so she locked herself in the room with the children, listening for further sounds and debating whether she should yell out the window for the neighbors.

When her husband returned and she told him about her sleepless night, he was not much impressed. But about midnight some ten days later, when he was home and both were sitting up in bed reading, the footsteps started up again. This time her husband went to check on the boys. He too found them both asleep. The footsteps went on far into the night—and that's the end of the story as far as it was reported.

Now what about experiences like these? Are they meaningless, a combination of suggestion, fear, expectation, imagination, an unrecognized sound with an ordinary cause, a bit of hallucination? After all, sounds leave no effect. They cannot be traced later. When more than one person hears them the fact does a little—but not enough—to remove it from the realm of simple hallucination or imagination. But even if not a hallucination, what other explanation would fit?

The trouble is that all of these reports are still only case material, not the kind on which conclusions can be based. They are not like controlled experiments in which one can be certain of all the facts. They do recur, however, both to the same persons, sometimes, and to others. On that account they should sometime be subject to the kind of experiment that would give a reliable answer.

When the answer, or probably answers, is known then no doubt the chilly feeling such accounts raise in all but the most fearless and insensitive people will be dispelled. It will be like the difference between being terrified by thunder because it is a sign of gods angered by the wickedness of people, as the ancients used to think, and understanding as moderns do, that the noise is but the after effect of lightning, and has no relation to the good or bad behavior of human beings.

The ancient inherited furniture in the case above, as already mentioned, was stored for a time in a special room upstairs, and the woman and her husband who slept in a room below it were wakened repeatedly by sounds of footsteps above and of objects being pushed around, etc. Yet no signs of such movement were later visible. Eventually the furniture was removed and stored elsewhere, and then no more sounds were heard.

Soon afterward, however, as the woman and her husband one night were sitting in the living room by the fireplace reading, suddenly an object fell, seemingly from the ceiling. It bounced off her book and fell into her lap. It was a large, old-fashioned bobby pin. They had never seen one like it and could find no possible explanation for its presence, much less its arrival through the air. A few weeks later when again they were reading in the living room, the heavy ottoman on which her husband was resting his feet began to heave about as though being pushed up from below. No explanation. Still later, the woman awoke one morning to find herself covered and tucked in by a blanket she had left in the hall. She thought her husband had done it, and she thanked him for it, but he said he had had nothing to do with it, nor had he even thought she needed an extra cover. Still later, in the garden, when talking to the man who was working there, she was struck on the head by a large tulip bulb. No explanation. The man who saw it was so upset he nearly gave up his job.

One final episode—final as far as the report goes—was again purely auditory. Sitting sewing one day, the woman heard a sound of something heavy that fell and shattered. But no cause of the sound could be found.

The account of these varied occurrences is typical only in that all of them seemed to lack any cause or explanation. Hauntings are usually classed as *places*, poltergeists, as *persons*, that are associated with psi effects. Still in the old dwelling that had its traditional poltergeist, the suggestion was inevitable that the various happenings were somehow connected with the place.

Poltergeist effects, just like hauntings, have a timeless reference to the spirit theories of the past (1, 2). The word itself, from the German, means a boisterous spirit. The history of effects of this kind covers all sorts of physical movements, often of stones, dishes, household ornaments that fly through the air. Sometimes it is said they fly around corners. Other kinds of occurrences from exploding bottles to unusual electric effects are sometimes involved. Reports a hundred and more years ago, in general, sound as if the occurrences were often more violent and destructive than those reported in recent years. But the old reports are just that—old reports, and no way exists now to tell which, if any, were genuine, and which not. Mainly they attest at least to the fact that people then as now thought they happened.

In recent years some poltergeist effects have been validated to a greater degree than earlier. In several instances when investigators were present, and something unexplained happened, no evidence of trickery was found. Usually in these cases, as in the reports of long ago, the manifestations seemed to center around a given individual, and that person was one who appeared to be more or less unsettled emotionally. More often than not it was an adolescent boy or girl. Usually, too, while the effects seemed to center around him, he seemed to be unaware that he was causing them.

How far does this go toward an explanation, granting it may be correct? The only approach science can make today for "uncaused" physical effects like these is that the PK effect is real. The demonstration of it in the laboratory still is in its infancy. It has succeeded only on objects already in motion, as in experiments with falling dice or in PK "machines," and with living organisms, as is suggested by recent experiments. As discussed in Chap 14, no experimental attempts to move an inanimate object at rest had been successful, but it now seems likely that eventually experimental PK on stationary objects in the laboratory will be successful and if so a better basis for insight into poltergeist effects will be available than we have now. At least research in PK is promising an explanation for them that seems more rational than that a "boisterous spirit" causes them.

The only theory that has been suggested in modern times, to replace this old, outmoded one, is that of PK by the living person. The only theory to explain PK advanced so far that seems to have a certain reasonableness to recommend it is that PK is the force connecting the mind and the brain (supposing, as some do, though many do not, that the two are separate entities), and that it operates every time we think. If so, it is as natural as breathing, even though it gives no outward sign like breathing. Instead, it is so hidden that no one ever suspected its existence, except as it "gave itself away" in PK experiments and experiences. When it occurs in either of these, it would mean that this energy of the mind is then operating in an *extra*, unusual, eccentric, bizarre way, for instead of affecting its own brain, it goes outside its body, one could say, and affects a die or a PK machine in a test; in daily life, it would go from the mind of the person and affect the object, whatever it may be: a clock, a picture, or even possibly a table in a seance room. However, this is all speculative now, and should not be considered on the same level with the fact that PK does occur. Later—much later —it well may be that research will show whether this or some other hypothesis provides a true explanation. Today, parapsychologists are like Columbus when he reached San Salvador. He could not know about the mainland yet. For parapsychologists, however, it is a little different, for they at least *know* that they know only about the island, and that signs indicate that there is a mainland—beyond.

SECTION SIX

The bearing of psi on the concept of man's nature.

27. The Meaning of Psi

Experiments involving psychic phenomena were undertaken in the first place because they suggested that there may be an aspect of human nature not accounted for by the physical body. The fact that the experiments showed that psi ability is a reality, that man's nature does include a nonphysical component, gives parapsychology its meaning today.

Parapsychological research has shown that the mechanistic, or wholly physical, model of man is incomplete and needs to be amended. It thus has a bearing on the age-old question: Who and what am I?

Different answers to this question have been advanced in different times and places. In the Western world, and in times not long past, the answer generally accepted was theological, based on the teachings of religious authorities. Broadly speaking, that teaching defined man as part physical and part spiritual, a body and a soul.

The theological answer to man's question was: "I am an entity of importance because of the soul, the spiritual component." Even though obviously the physical side, the body, was temporary and at death dissolved into its elements, the soul lived on. In religious terms, it was immortal.

This theological idea of the nature of man was fairly generally satisfying. It gave a reason for existence. Those who accepted it, as a large number did, did so on faith. Authority said it was true, and believers scarcely asked the question, for they already knew the answer: "I am the child of God. I have an immortal soul." That was enough. The religious system of reward and punishment, heaven and hell, supplied the motivation necessary to make the person act according to God's law as the authorities proclaimed it. It was similar to the earthly family, in which the child of an earthly father, by a system of rewards and punishment, was led to obey the law his earthly father laid down.

But the time came when to many this religious answer was no longer convincing. In the last century or so, steadily increasing numbers of persons have been rejecting it. It is not that they have disproven it, but that they can no longer believe it. With the advance of science, the climate of thought has changed. The scientific method has been applied in the physical fields that affect their lives, and so this area, the religious, comes under scrutiny too.

The advance of science in the physical fields means, of course, that experimental methods for finding answers have been used, and the value of the results decided by statistics. By this method some of the old ideas have been shown to be correct, some incorrect, and whichever they have turned out to be, their meaning no longer depends upon authority, nor does it call for unquestioning belief. Today, a person who doubted the earth to a sphere could find out the truth about it for himself. Scientific method calls for questioning minds and answers that each person can evaluate for himself.

It follows, naturally, that now the question about the full nature of man becomes a serious one. The physical sciences have dealt with the physical aspects of the universe. The sciences of man, too—physiology, medicine, psychology—all deal with the physical person, none with the soul or spirit. Those are concepts that give no substance for experiment. No longer taken on faith, they leave no material residue. Physical methods could not be applied to them, or so it seemed.

As a result, in this scientific era the brain, not the mind, is studied. The brain is made up of cells, involves electrical reactions, etc. It is notable for its immense complexity compared to all mechanisms yet constructed. But even its status as of exceptional complexity among mechanisms may be only a temporary one because the process of discovery and invention is not yet completed. Considering the progress already made along computing lines, first with the abacus, then calculating machines, computers, super computer systems, and all at an ever increasing rate of invention, an actual computer-made man may seem to be just a few more steps (years) ahead.

The answer, to many, seems clear enough: "I am a temporary physical arrangement of molecules. I am very clever. I can build tremendous machines. But what real significance, what reason do they, or I myself have? None ultimately." And thus the answer to life itself would be: "So what?"

This turns out to be a widely unsatisfying answer, and has led to great unrest and demoralization in the present generation. Why do individuals and society itself feel it to be unsatisfying?

Perhaps it is unsatisfying because of a hangover from the old religious answer that promised more because it gave meaning to existence far beyond any physical one, a reason and a goal for living. Or perhaps it is because of something overlooked in the "temporary arrangement of molecules" model and that something intuitively leads to the suspicion that it is deficient. Or it may be that another reason is hidden just beneath the surface. That is, that this one violates a cardinal scientific principle which is that a conclusion must not go beyond its data. Jumping to conclusions is a breach of scientific method just as much as is operating without a control, or not judging the data blind. Any or all of these reasons could make the mechanistic answer unsatisfying and raise anew the question: "What am I? Am I really no more than this? Do I really have no more significance than my computers?"

Whichever may be the answer, certainly dissatisfaction with the mechanistic idea of man's nature appears to be the reason behind much of the unrest and upheaval of the current scene. It lies behind the present-day urge to question further. It probably is behind the current upsurge of interest in the mystical, the occult, and all the fringe areas that offer quick and easy answers to the question of the end and meaning of existence. If so, it is because of the implication, in all of these, of a mysterious "something more."

Now comes psi ability. It is not a concept founded on the authority of a priest or prophet. It is not a religious dogma. It is not an idea to accept on faith. Instead, it is a logical attempt to apply the methods of physical research to the question of a possible nonphysical aspect of man, but by adapting those methods according to the situation, just as each of the other sciences adapted its methods and techniques to fit its individual type of data.

The results of parapsychological research now have produced a simple scientific conclusion, that the psi ability is a reality. This conclusion has the same kind of basis as that of any other field of science. It has been established just as they were, by experiment and the statistical evaluation of results. The methods and conclusions of parapsychological research can be reexamined, their strengths and weaknesses judged by anyone who cares to take the time to do so.

The field of parapsychology is still comparatively young, the investigation still in progress as new aspects of its subject matter come under study and old investigations are repeated, corrected, enlarged. Section Three, especially, showed that in practically all of the current lines of research the present findings can still be considered as preliminary, suggestive, promising, but incomplete.

Even so, enough has now been established to show that the physical answer about man is inadequate. It does not account for all of him. Psi ability does not fit into the physical materialistic-mechanistic scheme. It interacts with mechanical principles, but they do not limit it. It operates in space and time, but goes beyond them, for clairvoyance is not confined to the immediate surroundings, precognition invades the future, telepathy makes possible even the awareness of thoughts in other minds. And all three types of ESP express themselves according to the same psychological realities of personality that serve the rest of human life. ESP, like sense perception, helps the individual to keep track of the world outside him.

PK, as already noted, seems almost like an Extra. No one knew it was even needed in the scheme of things, and so when in a few unusual circumstances, like dark-room seances, it seemed that objects moved by themselves, it did not make sense and was not easy to believe.

Mind over matter? Who needed it? Nobody. It appeared to be just a trick (which, no doubt, it frequently was). But still, hidden in all the dust and confusion, the PK ability was there, too.

Unnoticed, unexpected, unwanted, evidently it nonetheless

has a function. Possibly, when operating in its normal sphere, that function is to effect the connection between mind and brain. If so, however, it betrays itself only when it operates *outside* the body, as in the laboratory, sometimes perhaps in the seance room, or spontaneously in personal life in situations of sudden, strong emotion. It well may be that PK is an ability inherent in life itself.

All of this means that psi ability is part of the person just as much as is the body with all its mechanical processes. But for this the inverse square law, the laws of gravity, of motion, heat, light, electricity, even of physical causation, do not apply. This is something else.

Psi, however, does not conflict with the physical aspects of the person, but is simply evidence of another principle, also operating in the human system. It connects the personality to the world around it *without a mechanism*, or at least, without any mechanism sufficiently like those of the physical world to make it in any way similar.

Again like Columbus at San Salvador, this finding of the psi ability is the discovery probably only of an island preliminary to the mainland beyond. But its different nature from that of the physical world is now established, and that fact gives the stimulus and direction for further explorations in the future.

Even now it shows that part of man's nature is free from mechanics. To what extent is not yet known, but the glimpses given by experiments and experiences suggest a range in time and space potentially as great as personal interest dictates.

And so, with the discovery of psi ability as well as with all the advances that have been made toward the understanding of the physical side of human life, the answer to the question is: "I am a temporary arrangement of molecules, yes. But also something more. I have properties that no known arrangement of molecules has. Those properties are more like those once assumed by the religionists than like the mechanistic concept. As yet they have not been found to go as far as the religious answer does, but as far as they do go, they are solidly based, and will not disappear when subjected to the intellectual test."

This answer, of course, is not complete or final, but it goes beyond any earlier one, for it has in it the hope of meaning and the reliability of science. It therefore is an acceptable and encouraging answer and one well worth disseminating as far and as widely as possible—particularly since already too many persons have been frustrated and discouraged by the fear that the mechanistic answer is the ultimate one. This one dispells that, and sheds a bright light ahead for the searching mind to follow.

SECTION SEVEN

Miscellaneous Topics, How to Do It.

28. The Occult in School

The current upsurge of popular obsession with the occult quite understandably has spilled over into the public schools. It is a bit like a new virus in a population with no immunity. With the help of the media this one has been spreading like a flame in the wind and with very little but the inherent common sense of the community to restrain it. Unfortunately, the availability of information about psi and the part it does and does not play in occult practices is still too limited to be effective.

The problem raised by the occult fringe arises in the first place because the psi ability did not wait to operate until it was officially recognized by parapsychological research. It was operating upon occasion ever since man became man, and even long before. People of all times and places had to deal with it the best they could. From primitive magic and religions, down through the ages, occult beliefs and practices built up, with nothing firm and factual to support them except the fact that an element of truth, however misinterpreted, was in them. Without the psi ability it seems unlikely that even primitive religions, not to say more modern ones, could have persisted.

And this it is, this occult heritage from the nonscientific past, that still today confuses many school children and sometimes their teachers as well. Nancy's letters reflect this and other things, and perhaps the answers can give a bit of clarification.

Dear Dr. Rhine:
I have been reading *New World of the Mind* by J. B. Rhine. I think it is very interesting. Before I read it I thought ESP was a bunch of nonsense, but now I think it is very real.

I guess I should tell you who I am. My name is Nancy Green, I am thirteen. I have long brown hair, brown eyes, and I am in the seventh grade.

Now that I have explained myself I want to ask some questions. I want to know more about ESP and how it works. Can ESP be used to hurt someone, physically or mentally? Can someone fight ESP with ESP? I hope you read this letter and can tell me.

I have been conducting clairvoyance tests at home and at school. I have been using the 4-Ace test [see Appendix]. I took the test myself and got 27 hits. I gave the test to a boy named Walter twice, and he got 33 and 34.

I have had one psychic experience. A couple of years ago when I was about ten I had a dream that my father was crying in his sleep. He is in the navy. He was overseas on his ship. I woke up all of a sudden and it was around two in the morning.

The next day I found out that my grandfather on my father's side had died. Then I learned that my father had dreamed his father had died and he *was* crying in his sleep and it was around two in the morning that same night.

I hope I am not bothering you. Please write soon.

Sincerely yours,
Nancy Green

No Nancy, ESP could not possibly be used to hurt anyone physically or mentally. It is true that sometimes people get the false idea that someone is influencing them by ESP. They think it is by telepathy, but this is very unlikely. Telepathy seldom, if ever, works that way, for no one can send his thought to another person and *make him take it.* Let us call the one who tried to do it A. and the one he tried to send to, B. Even if A. tried to do it, B. would probably not know it unless his own ESP was very good; and even if it was and if he thought A. was doing it, all B. would need to do would be to ignore it. It would be even easier than if A. were actually present and threatened to beat up B. unless he followed A.'s orders. For B. it would be just like resisting a temptation of any other kind. And so B. would not have to fight off A.'s thought. It would just be a blank and he would not need to know or care anything about it. Only his own ESP, and not A.'s, could affect him.

The only way a person could be hurt would be by his *belief* that he could be so affected. It is possible sometimes for a person to "think himself sick" for other reasons and in the same way he could think himself sick by believing that someone was affecting him by telepathy. But, if so, his sickness would be caused by a mistaken suggestion, not by telepathy.

You surely did well on the 4-Ace test, and almost proved that you and Walter both were using clairvoyance. You should only get about twelve by chance, you know, and your score was twice that and Walter's was nearly three times as much. In the laboratory, the backs of the cards would have to be screened from sight because some cards are printed so that it is possible to tell what they are from the backs in certain ways of lighting (and squinting), but I doubt if either you or Walter got your scores that way.

Your dream was especially interesting, first because you were so young, and second because it was true. It probably was a combination of clairvoyance and telepathy, or a GESP dream. Since it turned out that your father's dream was occurring then, too, the combination was quite unusual. I am glad you told about it.

Dear Mrs. Rhine:

I was so happy to get your letter. After I wrote you the last time the other 7th grade at our school was having a seance in their class. It didn't turn out as one though.

Two girls in the seance got a picture in their minds of a boy named John tied to the ground and a pendulum with a blade on the end going back and forth over him. One girl was saying "back and forth" in a whisper. One of the girls said to John that he was going to die. John got scared and you can't ever imagine John being scared.

Can you tell me if anything will happen to John or not? The girls that told me about this were scared.

I have been reading a book about paranoid reactions to telepathy. A doctor says something about people having the power of wishing people to death. He calls it malignant telepathy, and says he found this out from many cases. I would like you to give your opinion on it. Also, I wonder what you think of the TV series that is running now and whether most of it is true or not. It got me interested in parapsychology.

Sincerely,
Nancy Green

No, nothing will happen to John because of that seance. The idea that those girls had was just cooked up in their imaginations by suggestion, even though they didn't know it. Many older persons too might make the same mistake if they did not know about the unconscious reactions they could stir up that way. It would be mostly because they think that the ideas they get at such times have some magic truthfulness. If they were on the playground and tried to scare a boy like John by telling him he was going to die, he wouldn't be affected because he wouldn't believe them. But he would be afraid of things said in a seance, because he wouldn't know they were not somehow magical.

It's because of all this that seances are not to be recommended for anyone except, perhaps, adults doing research. I hope the teacher will not let anything of this kind be repeated. So much that is good and wholesome is to be learned about parapsychology that it would be a shame to waste time on this kind of activity. It cannot teach the students anything and it can stir up unhealthy ideas. This one certainly did just that, not only for John but for others too.

Instead of a seance, some interesting ESP tests could be given. The 4-Ace test would not be so suitable for a schoolroom as for one or two persons alone (unless a lot of card decks are available), but formal tests could be given in which the teacher has the deck, and students try to identify cards and record their guesses on record sheets. This way they might get scores that would suggest ESP or even tell something about it.

Now about the idea of "malignant telepathy." It fits in with the answer I gave you before. It is an idea that is based on a mistaken notion of the way telepathy works. The author of that book does not sound like a student of telepathy but more like one of of abnormal psychology. He could have been a psychiatrist for instance and knew that mentally ill people sometimes think they have been harmed by telepathy, but, as I said, any such effect is the result of suggestion, not ESP.

The television show that was running when you wrote was made to be entertaining, not to represent parapsychology faithfully, and so it was really a showman's version, and certainly not very reliable. The best thing I know about such shows is that they may arouse an interest in parapsychology in people like you. If it led a few persons to make actual serious tests, then it was that much to the good. Otherwise, it was just entertainment —like science fiction, I guess, but nothing to take seriously.

Dear Dr. Rhine:

I got your letter and showed John the part about him. It was so funny. He went around the room yelling "Nothing's going to happen to me." He's a nut.

The tests I was doing are going to be started up again. The teacher saw your letter and told me to remind her.

My grandmother believes in ESP too. She also believes in reincarnation. She believes the soul, after the body is dead, waits for another body to live in. She says that maybe a soul that belonged to a person that was a coward can wait till a person that might be brave.

I had better close. I have to set the table.

Nancy Green

I was glad to know that my letter about John relieved his mind. He may have been quite worried, secretly at least, by something that had no real meaning at all.

About reincarnation? It's almost like a religion for some people. It is something to believe in if one wants to, but quite different from a scientific finding because the answer to it has not been proven. In some countries it is widely believed, and sometimes young children say things that make the grownups believe they are remembering an earlier life.

A psychiatrist at the University of Virginia, Dr. Ian Stevenson, has studied many such cases in foreign lands, and written a book about them called *Twenty Cases Suggestive of Reincarnation*. (1) It is very interesting but he does not claim that the cases prove reincarnation. To prove it finally would take a kind of experiment that at present seems impossible to make.

Dear Mrs. Rhine:

Now I have some dreams to tell you about. One was by Kathy, a friend of mine, and the other by my mother.

My mother's sounds like a precognitive dream. It started by her watching a plane that was taking a nosedive until it hit the ground. It was straight up and down in the ground. It was also red and white.

A few days later a red and white plane crashed. It was a nosedive. She did not know anyone on the plane or anything about it. It was in California.

My girl friend's dream was about her grandmother and they love each other very much. The dream was that Kathy's grandmother had a pistol in her hand. She raised it and pulled the trigger. Kathy knocked the gun out of her hand. She picked it up and pointed it at her grandmother who called her name in a sobbing voice. She dropped the gun and ran to her grandmother. They hugged each other and her grandmother said, "I'll put all my past sorrows with all your future tomorrows. It'll be all right."

Why should she dream like that? I know it might be in her mind, but I don't know. She is scared.

I had a clipping about a woman who can tell the future. Nine times out of ten she is right, it said.

Now my home-room teacher and my social-studies teacher are getting married. My room and his room are giving a party for them. We're all putting in twenty-five cents each for a wedding present.

Nancy Green

Yes, your mother's dream could have been precognitive. Did she see a picture of the wrecked plane in the paper? If so, her dream could have been based on that. At least it would be possible. Nearly all of the ESP dreams are about a person's own affairs, but occasionally they may be about strangers or news items.

Kathy's dream, on the other hand, was not an ESP dream, but just a rather unpleasant ordinary dream fantasy. No one could tell just why she should have had it because dream fantasies can hinge on the slightest causes. But she need not be scared. Tell her just to forget it.

The report about the woman who has nine out of ten predictions come true will do for a newspaper report, but it probably would not check out if it was carefully investigated. At least no one yet has had a nine-to-one record for precognition when everything was considered. It is not easy to know beforehand which experiences are precognitive, for instance, and then the impressions that do not come true will be discounted. You can see that it is like arguing in a circle. If they come true, then they are precognitive, if not they are not. In order to avoid this, it is necessary to make a test in which the number of hits and misses can both be calculated. Without such a test, only the hits get counted. That is why precognition could not be proven by dreams. It took experiments to do it.

And now, some different inquiries from different inquirers:

Dear Dr. Rhine:

I am making a reasonably important research paper for an assignment in my English class. I am sixteen and very much interested in all fields of the occult.

My paper is on witchcraft. However, ESP is involved as it is sometimes the witch's tool. I might add that I might someday join a coven if possible.

I would appreciate very much if you would answer personally the following questions and send me your answer as soon as possible. This is urgent as I need your interview as a reference and the deadline on my paper is about two weeks. Please hurry.

Thank you.
Mary Sue A.

1. Do you believe witches have ESP?
2. Do you believe in God as the Bible teaches?
3. Is ESP found in the Bible? If so where?
4. Can a witch kill another human being through psychic powers?
5. Do you believe a witch can talk to the dead?
6. Have you ever had a vision of God or the Devil?

Mary Sue, about all I can tell you about witchcraft in a letter is that it is a topic too big for a high school English class assignment. I can answer your questions only by saying that the idea of witches is a mistaken one which goes back to the time when spirits were thought to be real. But now we know differently. Instead, now we know that people themselves have ESP and PK ability. But you must study parapsychology to know all about that, and to understand that your questions really do not apply.

A letter like Mary Sue's can show the general demoralization that old ideas of the occult project on impressionable young minds. At sixteen how could a student possibly handle them? No one would expect a high school student to write a paper on advanced mathematics, or a scholarly critique on, let us say, Chaucer. But on the occult, the assumption seems to be, that no background is necessary, and this, unfortunately, is a big mistake. The teachers, too, need information to avoid the old "blind leader" effect.

Gentlemen:

I am a high school senior. Two friends and I are writing a report on witchcraft and magic and we are interested in obtaining all possible views on the topic.

We have been told of several cases of demoniac possession by a Catholic exorcist and would like to know how many of the supernatural powers displayed during possession could be explained by parapsychology. These include the power of astral projection, the ability to move objects without physical force, to read minds and to speak in foreign tongues.

We would also like to know if you have been directly or indirectly involved in any cases of supposed possession, and how you analyzed the cases. We would appreciate any information you could send us on the above subjects or the relation of magic and parapsychology in general. As the field of parapsychology is a relatively new one, it is hard to obtain current information.

Sincerely,
Daisy W.

It is fairly new these days for students to ask questions about old topics like magic and witchcraft. Until recently all such occult ideas were so generally held to be just relics of old unenlightened superstition that serious questions about them were not asked. That such questions are being asked now is one symptom (though probably not realized by these high school students) of the search for a better answer about the question of man's nature than the modern mechanistic-physical one.

One evidence that the old idea, magic, is long gone out of style is that the word today generally has a quite different meaning from what it had in connection with witchcraft. Today the idea of magic suggests a magician on a stage and a "rabbit out of a hat" effect. But long ago magic was a method by which it was believed, or hoped, that supernatural forces could be controlled. The method was mainly by incantation, charmed words or phrases by which some ill-defined force of gods or nature would produce the wished-for good effect. Witchcraft, on the other hand, usually referred to bad or evil effects which, it was thought, could be used against people, even innocent ones.

Both magic and witchcraft are long-outdated concepts. Thanks to having been born centuries later, we "wise men" of today have the benefit of the scientific discoveries of the ages. We know about the revolution of the earth around the sun, about the circulation of the blood, bacteria, the steam engine, electricity, unconscious as well as conscious levels of the mind. We no longer need to use spells, signs, or incantations.

However, at high school ages and even older, this heritage from the past is often unknown, or it may be unappreciated or discounted because it is familiar. Under such circumstances, to active, inquiring, and adventurous minds, the idea can seem attractive: "I might someday join a coven if possible."

Certainly, as already suggested, ideas like those underlying past beliefs in magic and witchcraft had a deeper and more tenacious hold on the people of their time than would have been true if psi effects had not been mixed in. Sometimes it must have given priest or prophet a proper answer the source of which was just as much a mystery to the priest as to his followers. And that leads directly to the question that comes up next.

"How many of the supernatural powers displayed during possession could be explained by parapsychology?" By possession, Daisy W. means certain strange and unnatural effects that an occasional person has shown and which since primitive times have been taken to mean that a bad spirit, a devil, has invaded and taken control of his body.

Before discussing possession, let us consider first the special questions about effects that were said to occur in it. Astral projection, the ability to move objects without physical force, to read minds, to speak in foreign tongues. The answers to these are a little mixed, but mainly, yes, they could at times have involved psi.

Astral projection is a term of misunderstanding. It was coined before ESP was established. But now ESP is established, and also the fact that it has nothing to do with physical distance. Just as a person in the United States can think of the North Pole, for instance, without going anywhere, so a person can by ESP be aware of a distant scene without "projecting" or traveling in any sense. The term, however, implies that the person *sends* his thought over the intervening space, as if his mind in some way actually traveled there.

An example would be that of the merchant-marine son of a woman in Connecticut. He was on his way to Australia when his mother was awakened one night, or thought she was, by hearing footsteps, light and quick, on the kitchen floor below her second-floor bedroom. She heard them come up the stairs and enter her room and then in the dimness she saw her son standing by her bed. She spoke aloud.

"Jim, is it you?"

He stood there a few seconds and then disappeared. She did not hear him go. Next morning she sent an air-mail letter to him telling about the experience and how real it seemed. The letter was awaiting him when he reached Sydney. She received the following reply from him.

That night I was standing on deck concentrating on the North Star, and the thought of you, when I found myself walking into the kitchen at home, going upstairs to your room, standing by your bed and speaking to you,

"Mother."

I tried several times but you couldn't hear. I didn't hear you speak either. When I returned to consciousness I was alone on the deck again.

It is not hard to see how, earlier, such an experience could be interpreted to mean that in some sense the son actually "came" to his mother's room and by "astral projection" was at his mother's bedside.

However, it is now clear that ESP operates outside of, or without, space. A person like the son, very much aware of the great distance actually separating him from home and mother, might well dramatize the thought into a pseudo-real sense of being there. And yet, no traveling was involved. The mother's experience could have been telepathic, expressed as a hallucination. The son's experience, whether involving ESP is doubtful, was distinguished mainly by his vivid imaginary awareness of the *place.*

The situation in cases of so-called astral projection, then, is one in which a person so dramatizes a distant scene that he feels as if he were actually there. If he also gets from his experience information about the scene he would not otherwise have known, then it was also an ESP experience. But it was not the *impression that he was there* that made it one.

The ability to move objects, seemingly without physical force, is psychokinesis, or PK. That movement of objects can occur without physical contact has been established in the laboratory (see Chapter 8), but it is still unclear just what kind of force actually causes it. The ability to read minds (telepathy) has also been shown to be a reality, at least to a fragmentary degree (see Chapter 7).

To speak in a foreign tongue, a language the person does not know? Here the question raised is different from the others. Here the evidence is in question. Does the phenomenon actually occur?(2)

Certainly sometimes it appears that way. A person in a peculiar mental state, usually apparently a kind of religious frenzy, speaks *as if* in a foreign tongue. Is it just gibberish, or is it an actual language? No reliable evidence on the topic, evidence that would satisfy a linguist who knew the presumed language, has been obtained. Until it is, the question remains unanswered.

The general verdict on these topics, then, is that in so far as any genuine phenomena are concerned, they are explainable as parapsychological realities. Because they are, they are not supernormal phenomena, but normal ones, the somewhat infrequent expressions of the natural human ability psi.

The idea that a person can be possessed by an extraneous spirit, a devil, like these others goes back to prescientific days. As discussed earlier, for primitive man, unexplainable happenings of many kinds could only be taken as evidence of spirits, beings that were invisible. Not only such occurrences as eclipses, thunder, lightning, which were beyond human control, had to be considered the result of supernatural beings; but also certain personal affairs of men, when beyond their own control, had to be considered as caused by other entities, angels or devils, depending on the situation.

When a person became mentally ill, or if he showed information he had no recognized way of knowing, the idea that he was possessed by an outside spirit was the only one the ancients knew. But on topics like these now, the advance of knowledge has cleared out the underbrush. Phenomena that once had to be ascribed to demoniac possession now fall in line as evidence of abnormal mental processes (best-selling novels and television programs to the contrary, notwithstanding). The fields of psychology and psychiatry can account for any elements of truth they may include.

Of course, the ancient religious rites of exorcism were the logical methods of cure, and many times, according to the records, they worked. Religious rites and religious dogma do not change rapidly. In some instances the rites of exorcism are still followed in cases that can be classed as "possession," although the psychiatric diagnosis would be quite different. Also, the psychiatrist would have quite a different "cure" from that of the priest.

The irony is that the old priestly method sometimes cured, and the psychiatric one, also, does sometimes. But on the question whether in the parapsychology laboratory cases of possession have been treated, the answer is No. The nearest to it have been poltergeist effects. But as discussed in Chapter 26, the theory that appears to explain these odd phenomena is not that of demoniac possession. Instead, as far as actual "uncaused" movement of physical objects is concerned, the force involved would be the result of psi, specifically PK.

Another irony too, involving ancient topics like magic, witchcraft, and possession is that their resurrection today brings out a fact long unsuspected. They can now be seen as testimony to the psi ability. It was a reality that people in nonscientific ages struggled with. They did not understand it. They misinterpreted it. *But they knew it.* In that respect they were wiser than the later generations who deny it.

29. How to Get into the Field of Parapsychology

Dear Dr. Rhine:

I have always been interested in strange happenings. Then I read your article about parapsychology.

I didn't know such a course was offered in our colleges, but if it is would there be a future in it as a career?

I am twelve years old, and I thought that if there were any courses that I should take in the next five years to prepare myself you might give me a few suggestions. Thank you very much.

Sincerely,
Bill W.

Dear Sirs:

I am a sixteen-year-old high school boy who has been seriously researching and studying parapsychology for approximately seven years. I have read literally hundreds of books, magazines and articles along with consuming other sources on this subject, and I consider myself something of an "expert" agewise, in this area.

Aside from my actual study, I confess that I, along with many other personal friends of mine, have experienced some type of psychic phenomena. I have been blessed with a high I.Q. and have been maintaining a high average in my academic studies.

Now my problem—I'd like to know what future I have in parapsychology. To be truthful what I need are facts and figures as to the demand, the requirements, the opportunities, the advancement possibilities, the pay, etc. Could I major in parapsychology in college? Which college provides the best education in this field?

In the past I have heard nothing but complimentary statements concerning your institute and now I appeal to you for some needed and vital information.

A prompt reply would greatly be appreciated. Thank you for your consideration in this matter.

Faithfully,
Harold N.

Dear Dr. Rhine:

I read your article and it encouraged me to write. My teacher told me to write to Duke University, but I didn't know to whom to submit this letter.

My reason for this letter is that I want to be a parapsychologist. I am only 13 years old now, but I am sure this is what I want. Could you send me some information on parapsychology, and how or what degree I should get in this field?

My teacher thought I should major in psychology, but I wish I knew if there is another degree for this career. Should I start now to be fully enlightened about parapsychology?

I would appreciate very much any information I can get. If you are unable to give me this information could you advise me of someone else to whom I may write? Thank you very much for your kindness.

Sincerely,
Sheri M.

Dear Sir (or whomever it may concern):

I am only a sophomore in high school but I am very interested in psychic phenomena. I have read all the books available, ESP, regular and self-hypnosis and others. (The others were not even good enough to mention.) The library in school does not have much on the subject, and the Public Library is not much better off.

I am much more interested in parapsychology than I am in anything else. That is I would like to make my future career of it. All my friends, and even my parents don't believe in parapsychology, but I am interested in the real happenings and real goings on.

I don't read ghost stories or about witches or any other mysteries and other fiction stories. I like to seek knowledge, I seek the truth.

The TV show has got me even more interested. All along I was reading about these things and imagining in my head. With the TV program I can actually see it. I know that they probably change it to make it seem better than it probably is, but the part the psychic investigator plays in the story is what I would like to be exactly, if I can make it.

The reason why I explained all the above is to prove to you that I am not just a crazy teenager, but that I am really interested in the field, I would appreciate it very much if you would send me some information.

I would like to know some colleges that go into parapsychology and what the requirements are for these schools, and what courses I would take. The thing is, I don't want to just take courses. I want to get into the field and actually do some investigations myself and actually witness these improbable happenings.

Please send the information I need to me.

Sincerely,
Waverly D.

Just because a boy like Bill W. is only twelve years old is no reason not to take seriously his question about a career in parapsychology, and especially not when a great many others older than he ask the same question. It needs to be discussed, particularly because the answer is not quite what one might guess.

Even if most of these young people do not lose their interest in the process of growing up, the realities in this particular field are such that most of them will be diverted to something else by the graduate school stage, if not long before. The realities make parapsychology a field of challenges not many will care to meet. They make it still today a profession for only a very few.

An air of mystery and novelty about the field still stirs up a lot of initial interest. It has been increased by radio and television programs. Of them of course, it must be remembered that they were made for entertainment, not for science. The producers of such programs, whether in parapsychology or any other scientific field, go on the supposition that sensation must be heaped on sensation to interest the sophisticated audiences of today.

Any entertainment program on parapsychology, then, is bound to be sensationalized, truth and fiction hopelessly mixed, as even a high school girl like Waverly D. knows: it must be made to "seem better than it probably is."

Not better, actually, but distorted. Ghosts, haunted houses, bizarre and exaggerated personal experiences are not really

HOW TO GET INTO THE FIELD OF PARAPSYCHOLOGY 213

"better" than actual ESP experiences however modest, nor more interesting than one good careful experiment that contributed another crumb of the "truth" that an idealistic child like Waverly seeks.

It would take more time and study and a different kind of skill than producers can afford, to so present a topic like this one that it would be both true and entertaining. Without that, of course, most of the interest aroused in young viewers will fade away along with the television production. But with a few, perhaps it will persist; and for them the question where to go to college and what courses to take needs an answer. It is something of a puzzler, however. There is no simple answer, though times are changing and probably the situation will soon be different.

Today, no systematic training is available anywhere. Parapsychology is a field which is still, as it always has been ,struggling on without much if any recognition from the academic world. It has not died out, because its problems are great ones, its phenomena real, even if not widely recognized. Hidden instead, and denied, the people who experience them usually say little for fear of disbelief and ridicule. The field, consequently, has not flourished. The real reason goes back to the fact already discussed: the occurrence of ESP and PK does not agree with the general idea of the world and man that today is prevalent.

All of this means that no college departments of parapsychology exist. It is not recognized as an area of study. Only a few courses in it have ever been given; but the trend is changing a little now, and more are listed each year. They are scattered here and there, mostly among the smaller colleges.

In the majority of such courses the instructor is an interested amateur, often a graduate student. The result is that the course reflects his own knowledge which he has picked up according to his own interest and attitude. It will naturally reflect his own limitations as well as his advantages. On that account, few courses can yet be counted on to give more than an introduction to the field, and certainly not proper training. Still today, as in the past, each person must acquire his own knowledge of the field mainly by his own reading and individual study.

The first requirement for such individual study is a bookshelf that includes accounts of the main experimental findings. The majority of research reports have been published in the *Journal of Parapsychology* (founded in 1937). Some have also appeared in the *Journal of the American Society for Psychical Research* and the *Journal of the Society for Psychical Research* (London). These findings have been gathered into a few general books and articles (see list of references at the back of this book), and quite recently a flock of guides to information about the field have appeared on the scene (1, 2, 3, 4, 5).

Historical items can be added to the bookshelf, especially the older publications of the Society for Psychical Research. Also, works of older personalities in the field, like F.W.H. Myers, Oliver Lodge, Charles Richet. The temptation of newcomers is often to indulge in current or older literature of the fringe type. But this can be a decoy and a waste of time. There is no use in studying about mediumship, materialization, levitation, ghosts, haunted houses, etc., before the necessary understanding of present-day discoveries has been acquired. It is no use trying to understand advanced math before one knows the multiplication tables. The comparison, however, is not a very good one, since no one would aspire to that, while every schoolboy would like to investigate a haunted house, even if he does not know the ABC's of ESP.

Of course, actually getting into the field is more than just reading about it, just as Waverly recognizes. The real thing is different from the television picture, but that does not matter, actually. The view of a mountain in the distance is always different close up, but it can be just as interesting and challenging, if perhaps more difficult and not quite as grand as it looks from far away.

The people in the field today started without special training, just as most of those who are at the student stage now will have to do. It is a research field mainly, and so any training for scientific research that can be picked up will be a help. Even though such training is not yet available in parapsychology itself, almost any good scientific background can contribute to it. To be recommended are majors in psychology, biology, chemistry, or physics. And because methods of measurement are important, training in mathematics, including statistics, is advisable.

Because parapsychology today is mainly a research field,

young beginners should try their hand at a bit of experimenting on their own. If the beginner has not done it at home in high school or earlier, often it can be managed in connection with a class assignment in some other field. It need not be an ambitious attempt but, however small, it will first of all tell the person himself if he really likes this sort of thing. And then, when he gets to the stage of looking for a job, the fact that he has carried out an actual experiment will be a good recommendation.

In parapsychology ready-made jobs do not hang around like ripe apples on a tree. It is still a pioneer field and jobs are not plentiful. Jobs that do exist go to those who are best prepared, and a bit of well-done research will count strongly as preparation. College degrees help, too, but they can come later. A young person who all through college intended to go into parapsychology but never tried to do an experiment would be likely to lose out, jobwise, in competition with an eager high school graduate who somewhere along the line had made a brave experimental attempt.

A great many young people who think they would like to go into parapsychology get discouraged when they realize that jobs are scarce and salaries likely to be low. In a way, this is a good thing for the field. It means that only the staunchest hearts, those who have a real reason to consider the field, will actually stay with it all the way. But for those few, the road is not closed. Openings, a few, are constantly available for those who give promise of being able to fill them. Furthermore, opportunities can be created by those with the will and push to do so.

The picture painted is certainly discouraging enough to weed out all who need certainty, security, and the promise of fringe benefits. It is a field in which only self-reliant and even inspired adventurers need apply. For them the outlook can be exhilarating. They will not be following worn and beaten tracks, but eventually, they may be able to discover their own new worlds. It will be difficult, often discouraging; honors and emoluments will be scarce, but self-satisfaction will be of the greatest. With Waverly, they will be seeking the truth.

And they will not starve!

30. How to Make a Successful Psi Test

Dear Dr. Rhine:

I am a sixteen-year-old High School student. My Biology class has to do a paper and an experiment in order to get an A. I want to do mine on ESP because it is so weird and fascinating. If our papers are good enough we have to present them to the Senior Academy of Sciences.

My trouble is that I don't have any ideas on how to show ESP exists and that it varies in people. I don't seem to find an experiment to help me. I have a game which uses cards and a board to test ESP but I am not sure how to use it.

If you could would you please help me? I need an idea for an experiment that would really work. There is no one in this town who is able to help me. I'm really sorry to bother you, but I can't find any books or stuff that gives a basis for any experiments. Any assistance you might lend me would be *greatly*(!) appreciated and needed. Thank you very much.

Sincerely yours,
Sharon S.

Dear Mrs. Rhine:

I'm doing research paper on parapsychology and I wonder if you could send me some information on experiments and research or anything you find interesting that I could read (like letters or books) I would really appreciate it.

I became interested in ESP last year when my friend Penny and I used to sit in study hall. We would think of a color, really concentrate and the other person could tell the color. It didn't work all the time, but usually we could get 3 or 4 out of 5.

We tried it with other kids, but it worked best with just us, maybe because we were such good friends. It seemed as though we could see the color first thing with our eyes shut.

In October I broke my leg (I fell downstairs). For two nights before I had dreamed I had to walk with crutches. Could this be ESP or was it probably chance?

My brother goes to college and he might take some courses on mind control, dealing with alpha waves and things like that. He said that at the end of the course you are supposed to be a psychic. Could you tell me what this is about?

I guess this college is one of the first places to give courses like that. I wish my school would but they don't believe in anything but English, French, math, science, and geography, almost. No history (only in grade 7) no theater courses or anything. Next year I will be in high school. Maybe that will be better (hopefully).

I'm sorry if I bothered you by writing such a long letter when all I meant to do was ask for information. But when I get writing I find it hard to stop. I want to be a writer or a journalist, I guess, in a few years. But here I go again, so I better say thank you and goodbye now. Thank you very much for listening.

> Sincerely,
> Sandy B.

Dear Sir: I am a fourteen-and-a-half-year-old student—9th grade. In my science class I was asked to make an interesting and unusual report on the subject of my choice. My choice was the new and interesting field of "PSI" which I knew very little about.

My science teacher liked my report and asked me to write for some of your simplest experiments so we could try them in class. I hesitated because your experiments are probably too complex to use in the classroom, and only students with a trace of ESP can participate. Nevertheless, I would be grateful for information.

> Sincerely yours,
> Mel G.

"My trouble is that I don't have any ideas on how to show ESP exists," Sharon S. writes. Hundreds of other young students as well as older persons whose curiosity about their own psi ability has been aroused have the same trouble. It is real enough. It is not easy to show that "ESP exists." If it were, the psi ability would have been a commonplace long ago and would not raise questions today.

It is not easy to prove that psi exists but, oddly, it is not difficult to try. Contrary to the fears another of the students quoted expressed, both individual and classroom experiments are easy and fun to make and need not be at all complex. Besides, since everyone probably has the ability, however hidden it may be, all the students can participate. The trick, of course, is to get them to show it. But after all, that's what tests are meant to do.

In or out of the classroom, the methods are very simple. They require no machinery or expensive apparatus, only paper and pencil and, for the easiest method, a pack of cards. Almost any kind of card deck will do, but a special ESP deck is a little more convenient.

Directions as to specific techniques are given in the Appendix, but they will probably be more successful if a few of the realities and obstacles are considered first. For instance, the person taking the test, the subject, is the most important part of it, although the experimenter himself is a close second.

The point to remember is that ESP is a spontaneous ability but test situations are artificial. For a subject, taking a test is a little like sitting for a photograph and trying to look natural. Only it is worse, because the photographer can still get a picture even if the sitter's features are frozen. But the ESP test will probably only show a chance result unless the experimenter can lift the freeze.

However, the experimenter today has the advantage over those who tried before ESP had been established. He knows that tests have succeeded even if the necessary conditions do make it less than a spontaneous situation. He knows it is possible to get scores that average significantly better than chance. And so today it is easy to try and to know it is possible to learn something, even if it is only to convince himself or skeptical friends that psi exists.

The way to unfreeze the subject in an ESP test is a bit like learning an art—if an art can be learned. It is something that cannot really be described but must depend mainly on the intuition and inspiration of the experimenter. Subjects are affected very much by the atmosphere he radiates. It must be the kind that stimulates the subject to want to perform well while it puts him at ease and makes him comfortable. (1)

One of the most important ingredients of the atmosphere the experimenter creates comes from his own interest and enthusiasm for his project. It seems to be contagious if it is genuine. If it is in any way simulated it is unlikely to have the same effect. But if the subject becomes really interested and eager to see how well he can do once the technique is explained to him, usually his scores will be a little different from those expected by chance alone. This may be the beginning of evidence of ESP. If it continues, even at a low level, so that a trend is established, the amount of the *deviation* from chance will be the measure of success.

Because the level of scoring is likely to be low, it is generally necessary to repeat the tests a number of times. This is where boredom comes in, and it is a killer. Even if the subject grows strongly interested and is eager to see how well he will do next time, it is best to make the session fairly short. The initial freshness soon wears off and a break is advisable. Let him try again another day.

If the calls the subjects made were nearly all correct, common sense would tell that ESP was involved. But even with the best atmosphere for testing, they are likely to be only a little better than chance alone would give, and so statistical evaluation is necessary. Fortunately this is easy, because the formulas and tables for it have all been worked out by statisticians and are about as easy to follow as a new cookie recipe, and not nearly as difficult as the directions for knitting a sock. Those necessary for simple ESP and PK tests are given in the Appendix.

A mistake easy to make is to attempt to do too much or to make a project too complicated. Even for advanced workers it is advisable to have the objective of the test clear and simple. In order to be sure the plan is not too involved, it is a good idea to see if it can be stated as one clear question. For instance, "Are ESP scores better in the morning when the subject is wide awake, or late at night when he is tired and sleepy?" Or, "Do Bill and Jane do better when tested at the same time or when each is tested separately?" Or, "Can I get evidence of ESP from my three-year-old sister?" Or, "From my grandmother?"

Whether to work with one person alone or with a group depends on the situation. But in any event an experimenter will do well to test himself first, partly to be certain he has the technique in mind and partly to know how it feels to be a subject. A few tests with one other subject will also be good practice. Naturally the techniques are a little different, depending on the number of subjects, but the basic idea is the same. It is simply to give the subject an opportunity to identify a hidden target and to do it in such a way that the result can be evaluated statistically.

ESP testing is a challenge, but psi is still a topic on which discoveries can be made by experimenters with the ingenuity and creative spirit that are necessary to carry out tests under conditions that have not been tried before.

A few of the comparisons that have been tried often but from which new ideas can still be generated, for experimenters who want to "show that psi exists," can be listed. Subjects are likely to score positively or above chance with experimenters whom they know and like, negatively or below with strangers or persons they dislike; positively if they "believe in ESP" (sheep), negatively if they disbelieve (goats); positively with subjects who are the gay, outgoing type, negatively if they are shy and withdrawn; positively if they tend to be spontaneous in their responses, negatively if they are logical or analytical; positively if they are in pleasant and happy moods, negatively if they are worried or depressed.

The list could be lengthened, but these suggestions give a general idea of the direction of response that contrasting conditions can generate. In spite of a great deal of individual fluctuation, sufficient data on contrasting situations will usually show that at least a low level of ESP was being manifested in them.

This discussion so far has involved testing for ESP more particularly than for PK. Most of it, however, will apply to PK tests as well. The attitude of the subject and of the experimenter is the most important factor in either one. The greatest difference between testing for ESP and for PK is the kind of technique to be used.

On techniques, an interesting contradiction comes up. Certainly more persons have had spontaneous experiences that suggested ESP to them than PK. And so it might seem they would be more likely to think they could show ESP in tests than PK. In general, however, that does not seem to be the case. Most persons are doubtful, at first, of their ability to guess hidden targets correctly, but much more quick to think they might be able to get a desired face when throwing dice. Perhaps the difference is that the urge to take a chance, to gamble on an uncertain outcome, favors the PK test, because the subjects have no particular faith in their ability to guess an unknown target correctly.

At any rate, the dice test is easy and cheap. A handful of "store dice" and a cup (as described in Chapter 8) are the only necessities. And since research on PK is still at an early stage, many problems concerning it are still waiting for answers.

For instance, the effect of numbers of dice used at a time, size, weight, etc., have yet to be tested sufficiently to show where the dividing line comes between their physical properties and the subject's preference.

Of course, in PK tests of different conditions the need for special apparatus soon comes up. Even testing for *place* rather than *face* will call for it. But a great deal can be done along this line by any ingenious high school student, since the equipment need not be sophisticated. In all such tests the need is only to be able to produce the desired end without a bias that would invalidate the result. Usually, however, this can be achieved by changing dice or targets in such a way that possible biases cancel, so that the remaining deviation shows the level of success.

Whether in ESP or PK, then, a successful psi test is not only that, but also a test of the experimenter, of his ingenuity, skill, and artistry. He must handle the social and psychological relations with his subject, devise any needed apparatus in PK, and know his technique by heart ahead of time. When giving the test he must not allow his attention to be diverted to the method, but have it well in mind. He should have on hand whatever he needs in record sheets, etc. If well prepared beforehand on points like these, and if thoroughly determined, he can succeed in testing for himself whether psi really occurs.

Appendix

Methods and techniques of testing for Psi, and tables for evaluating results.

ESP Tests

Long experience has shown that the most convenient and generally satisfactory way of testing for ESP is that in which a subject tries to identify the symbols on hidden cards. The ESP deck was designed specifically for this purpose.* With five suits of five cards each, the number of hits to be expected by chance with this twenty-five-card deck is one in five.

Although the regular playing-card deck could be used, the total number of cards is rather large, and the chance of making a hit only one in fifty-two. Subjects seem to be more encouraged if they see the target card frequently even though it is only a chance effect; also, the shorter run of twenty-five cards is more interesting than the longer fifty-two-card run. Although results with either deck can be evaluated by the appropriate formulas, those for ESP decks are given here.

The first precaution is to have the cards front and back entirely hidden from the subject. Next, the target deck should be so thoroughly shuffled that the order of the cards cannot be inferred. In more serious testing, the order is usually taken from a random number table.

For variety two general types of tests have been used: card calling and card matching (1). In either type the subject is first made comfortable and the kind of test explained to him. He should be told that it does not matter whether or not he thinks he has any ESP ability and he should not try to keep track of the cards but name or place each one spontaneously.

A. CARD CALLING (GUESSING) TESTS

Have standard record sheets (See example, p. 226) at hand and instruct subject to write his guesses in the call column.

*ESP cards and record sheets can be obtained from the Foundation for Research on the Nature of Man, College Station, Durham, North Carolina. 27708

1. Clairvoyance Card Guessing Tests.

In these no one knows the targets as they are being guessed. Two slightly different techniques may be used.

a. DT (Down Through) Test. The experimenter thoroughly shuffles decks of ESP cards beforehand and returns them to their boxes. The subject and the experimenter are seated at opposite sides of a table, the box between them on the table. The subject is asked to record his guesses as to the order of the cards in the specified deck, in the call column of the record sheet.

At the end of the run of twenty-five guesses the experimenter takes the record sheet and the box of cards and records the order of the cards in the card column. He then checks for hits as the subject watches, thus double-checking the results. The total score is written at the bottom.

b. BT (Before Touching) Test. This is similar to DT except that the experimenter picks up each card in turn and, without looking at it, holds it face down while the subject makes and records his guess. The experimenter then lays the called card face down to one side. The second card is placed in the same way, on top of the first. The checkup is as in the DT test except that the called deck must be turned face up for checking because the first one called is below.

In the BT test a small screen is needed between subject and experimenter so that the subject cannot catch a glimpse of the inverted card as the experimenter holds it. The screen should be about twenty-four by thirty inches (a pile of books could be used).

ESP RECORD SHEET

No._____

Subject_____ Experiment_____
Observer_____ Date_____
Type of Test_____ Time_____
General conditions_____
Use other side for remarks. Total score_____ Avge. score_____

With ESP cards use ∧ for star, o for circle, L for square, + for cross, = for waves.

1		2		3		4		5		6		7		8		9		10	
Call	Card	Call	Card	Call	Card	Call	Card	Call	Card	Call	Card	Call	Card	Call	Card	Call	Card	Call	Card

2. GESP (General ESP) Card Calling Test

This test does not distinguish between telepathy and clairvoyance. Telepathy tests are difficult to manage and are not recommended for ordinary use. Some subjects feel that they can "read a mind" easier than a card, and if so, this GESP technique may seem more encouraging to them than a pure clairvoyance test.

In this technique the experimenter picks up a card as in the BT test, but he looks at it as the subject "guesses" it. In order that no cues be given, the two persons should be in separate rooms with a signaling device so that the subject can indicate when he is ready for the next card. Second best is to use a large screen between the two or at least to have the subject seated with his back to the experimenter.

Synchronized watches may be used, or the subject may call "Ready," but the experimenter should not call as his tone of voice might hint to the subject whether or not his preceding call was correct. The checkup is carried out as before.

3. Group Tests of Clairvoyance or GESP

The foregoing instructions are for use when subjects are tested individually. When a group is being tested, the problem of checking is a bit different and also separate target sheets must be prepared beforehand so that each subject has his own. This avoids a complication known as the "stacking effect," which arises if a number of subjects guess at the same target list.

Individual lists can be prepared beforehand by shuffling a deck thoroughly and copying the resulting order in the card column. Or get the order from a random number table, and convert the digits into symbols systematically.

In this way the experimenter fills in the card columns for as many record sheets as there will be subjects, numbering each and making a carbon copy which he keeps in his possession. Each of the originals he then seals in a large opaque manila envelope and staples two record sheets with a carbon between them on the front of the envelope. These sheets are directly over the one inside with the targets. The envelopes are distributed to the subjects who are told to fill the call columns of the outer sheet with the symbols they think match those of the enclosed list. When finished, the subjects are told to tear off their outside sheets and pass them to the experimenter, but to keep the carbon record of their calls. The subjects then can open the envelopes and check their own lists. Later, with his carbons of the targets and the originals of the subject's calls, the experimenter can recheck the students' evaluations and be certain all are correct.

4. Precognition Card Calling Test

This is the easiest test of all to conduct. The subject is told to fill out the call column of his record sheet as he thinks the cards of the target deck will be when they have been shuffled after he finishes.

As discussed in Chapter 6 the method of getting the target order is now standardized, but complicated. For beginning tests thorough hand shuffling will suffice. After that the resulting order of the deck is filled in the card column and the checkup made as before.

With this technique the checkup may be delayed if, for instance, time intervals are being tested. If so, and if the subject is no longer present to witness the checking, the experimenter should get some other person to double-check his accuracy.

This test is now standard procedure when the subject and experimenter cannot be together at the time the subject takes the test, and when groups of subjects are used. It involves no more extra work for the experimenter than does the clairvoyance group test described above, and each successful experiment gives added evidence for precognition as well as for the special objective of the experiment.

B. CARD MATCHING TESTS

Five cards, one of each symbol, are laid out in a row before the subject. These are the "key" cards. The subject is given a well-shuffled deck of ESP cards (the target deck) and, keeping the cards inverted, is asked to lay each card beside the key card he thinks it matches. This technique is sometimes thought to be more gamelike than the calling technique, since the subject handles the cards and does not have to try to identify them, but just have them match the key cards. He need not try to place just five in each position but place them spontaneously.

A special record sheet is necessary in order to keep a complete record for later checking. It should have space at the top for names, dates, etc., if it is to be a serious test as in a planned experiment rather than just a semi-playful one such as a person might make spontaneously to satisfy his own curiosity. It should be made by ruling off squares like a calendar, five columns of about eight or ten spaces each to make room for uneven distributions. The tests may be either clairvoyant or precognitive in type.

ESP TESTS

1. Clairvoyance Matching Test

Two different types may be used.

a. OM (Open Matching) Test. In this the key cards are face up. In a careful test the experimenter before hand prepares a target deck by enclosing each card in a small black envelope, flaps turned in. The deck is then shuffled and cut so no one knows the order of the cards.

After the subject places the cards, the experimenter draws each card far enough out of its envelope to be able to see and record its symbol. The hits are then recorded and, at the top of the sheet, the record of the order of the keys.

b. BM (Blind Matching) Test. In this the key cards instead of the target deck are enclosed in black envelopes and shuffled so that no one knows which is which. In the checkup only the keys need to be removed from their envelopes.

2. Precognitive Matching Test

This test is the same as the clairvoyance matching test except that instead of key cards, five shallow boxes are laid out in a row before the subject for the key cards later after their order has been determined. The subject is given a preshuffled deck of cards which he keeps inverted as he distributes the cards singly opposite the box he thinks will later contain a symbol to match it. When the cards have been placed the experimenter turns each pile up and records them on a record sheet. Then the order of the key cards is determined (except in serious testing) by careful shuffling and they are placed in the boxes. They are recorded in order on the record sheet and hits counted.

3. Four-Ace Test

This is a clairvoyance matching test using the playing-card deck. It is especially appropriate for beginning self-testing because the cards are readily available and no other equipment is necessary.

In this test the four aces are removed and laid out in a row on the table to serve as key cards. The remaining forty-eight cards are then shuffled and kept inverted as they are laid out opposite the ace the subject thinks each one matches for suit.

While distributing the subject should focus on the aces and not on the card. In self-testing, of course, there would be no tendency to try to read the card from the back, but in strict testing a subject might occasionally get a cue if he concentrated on the back.

When all forty-eight cards have been distributed turn the piles over and check for hits keeping a record of scores for each run. By chance, twelve hits per run on the average should be expected. Ten runs through the pack thus should yield about 120 hits by chance alone. If the average secured in the test was fifteen instead of twelve, the total would be $10 \times 15 = 150$. This would be thirty more than chance, and in ten runs a score this high would be a strong indication of ESP.

EVALUATING THE RESULTS OF ESP TESTS WITH ESP CARDS (2)

Since the number of hits expected by chance is five per run, the level of success is measured by the number of hits above that secured per run. Suppose a test series includes twenty runs. The number expected by chance in such a series on the average would be $20 \times 5 = 100$.

The number expected by chance is then subtracted from the total number of hits made. If in the twenty runs, 125 hits were made, actual *deviation* from chance would be $125 - 100 = 25$. Or if only seventy-five hits were made, the deviation would be $100 - 75 = -25$. This deviation from chance is the amount that must be evaluated. Its significance is expressed as a critical ratio (CR) and this has a probability figure or extra chance value.

Statisticians have worked out the standard deviation (SD) for chance scores like those of ESP runs. It depends on the number of runs. The *square root* of this number then is obtained and multiplied by two. For example, in twenty runs the square root of 20 is 4.47. And $4.47 \times 2 = 8.94$. The values are given in Table I for selected numbers of runs from four to one hundred.

The critical ratio is found by dividing the actual deviation by the SD. If twenty runs yielded a deviation of 25, the standard deviation, 8.94 divided into 25, gives a CR of 2.8. The probability that a CR as high as that would occur by chance alone is .005. (In Table II, probabilities for selected numbers of runs are given.) Since in parapsychology a probability of .01, or one time in a hundred, is considered significantly different from chance, a score of 25 in twenty runs would be considered to mean that ESP was involved. If the score was − 25, it would mean that psi-missing had occurred.

Tables for Evaluation of ESP Tests

Table I
Standard Deviation
of Runs up to 20

Number of Runs	Standard Deviation
4	4.00
5	4.47
8	5.66
10	6.32
15	7.75
16	8.00
20	8.94
25	10.00
50	14.14
100	20.00

Table II
Probability Values
of Critical Ratios up to 3

Critical Ratio	Probability
2.5	.012
2.6	.0093
2.7	.0069
2.8	.0051
2.9	.0037
3.00	.0027
4.00	.000063

PK Tests

As discussed in Chapter 8, the most common PK tests have been conducted with dice. Usually the dice were thrown for face, and for impromptu testing this is the best technique since it requires no equipment except dice and a throwing cup. Recently more sophisticated methods involving automated machinery have been used for most of the PK research, but simple and possibly significant contributions can still be made without such equipment.

The dice must be thrown on a flat surface, preferably a padded one so they will bounce rather than slide. For serious work a "dice box" can easily be made from a heavy carton about two by four feet and six to eight inches deep. It can be lined all around and up the sides by a piece of heavy material stitched to the corners tightly enough that it does not have wrinkles. It can then be used on a low table.

Record sheets for PK tests can be ruled into squares with space for twelve to thirty-six entries down the column; at least six columns should be provided for ordinary tests. Space at the top should be provided for names of subject and experimenter, date, number of dice, target face, and any special conditions.

The number of dice may vary. Many subjects have shown a preference for several, usually about six, which is a good number since, with an expectation of one target face on each throw by chance, the subject again (as in the twenty-five-card ESP deck) is encouraged by seeing his target come up frequently, even if only by chance.

As a basis for evaluation of results, a "run" of twenty-four die-falls has been used, whether secured by one die thrown twenty-four times, or two thrown twelve times, or six thrown four times, or all twenty-four thrown at once. If the number of runs used as a "set" is a multiple of six the results can be evaluated.

Because dice cannot be assumed to be perfect, imperfections can be canceled by using each of the six faces as target an equal number of times. It is best, however, to make a dozen or more throws for a given face, as too frequent changes of target may be confusing to the subject.

Ordinary throwing from the hand does not prevent "tricky throwing." A cup in which the dice can be shaken and from which they can be thrown is therefore necessary. More sophisticated methods can be used, but for simple tests cup throwing is all right.

The target order should be chosen by a regular and consistent plan rather than at random or by the whim of the subject. A good one is to begin with the one face and follow in order around the die.

The subject should be instructed to shake the dice in the cup and throw them vigorously, keeping in mind as he does so the target face which he wishes to have come up. The experimenter tells the subject the target face and records it on the record sheet. The subject may choose his own rate of throwing and should be allowed to concentrate without distraction.

The experimenter keeps the record and should call aloud the number of faces as he records them so the subject can double-check for accuracy. These instructions are for single faces; although other kinds of targets, doubles, and place are possible variations, single-face throwing should suffice for beginners, particularly as other kinds of targets call for other equipment and other methods of evaluation.

Table of Standard Deviations for Evaluating PK Tests for Faces

Table III
Standard Deviations
for Faces Tests

Number of Runs, 24 Trials Each	Standard Deviation
6	4.47
12	6.32
18	7.75
24	8.94
36	10.95
48	12.65
72	15.49
96	17.89

EVALUATING THE RESULTS OF PK TESTS

This is no different in principle from the evaluation of ESP results. The standard deviation is found similarly; the square root of the number of runs is multiplied by two. The actual deviation divided by the standard deviation gives the critical ratio which in turn has a probability value, just as in the evaluation of ESP scores. The range of possible targets, however, is six rather than five, and the number of trials per run is twenty-four rather than twenty-five. The table for SD (Table III) is therefore different.

Areas of Problems: *From Old to New*

1. *Confirming Work Already Done.* While this could include such elementary questions as whether or not ESP occurs, or whether its types (telepathy, clairvoyance, precognition) occur, such questions should be recognized as on the ABC level, and can no longer add anything to existing knowledge. Instead, more advanced questions should be asked, and if results are achieved on them, these more elementary questions will be answered incidentally. More up-to-date questions might be on a level like these:
   a. Can precognition be demonstrated when targets are determined by computer? (This assumes a computer is available.)
   b. Can PK be shown to affect target objects regardless of differences in their mass, density, or other physical property? (Choose specific ones to test.)
   c. Does space, or time, or other kind of barrier have an effect if psychological conditions are equal? (Again, be specific. Do not try to prove too much in one experiment.)
2. *Testing Common Claims or Beliefs.* These are too numerous and varied for more than a few suggestions and will make feasible projects depending mainly on the availability of specific kinds of subjects or conditions:
   a. Do handicapped (e.g. blind) persons show more ESP than others?
   b. Do identical twins or engaged couples, etc., show more?
   c. Do those who have had psychic experiences do better in tests than those who have had none that they recognize?
3. *Exploring New Suggestions.* These are areas in which research already done awaits more confirmation or broader scope. Suggestions might be:
   a. Does a subject do better if he knows specific details about the target, such as where it is, how it will be determined (in precognition), etc., than if he is simply instructed to "guess the right one"?
   b. Does "beginner's luck" apply to psi tests? Or does the length of the

task or the session necessarily lead to lower results?
- c. Do persons who think they are lucky or unlucky get ESP scores accordingly?
- d. Are leaders (e.g., student leaders) more gifted than others?
- e. What is the effect of time of day on ESP scores? Do persons differ on this, just as some individuals study best at night, some in the morning?
- f. Can subjects tell beforehand how well they will do in a run, or on a given day, etc. (with mood and interest changes which can be specified beforehand)?
- g. Do some subjects do better when competing? When in solitude? When being watched? (Personality differences would have to be measured independently of ESP results.)
- h. Contrasting different kinds of targets, do results vary, according to whether the subject knows or does not know the kind being used? (E.g., compare symbols as on ESP cards with pictures or meaningful names, etc.)

4. *Extending Known Findings.* Problems here would lead into areas not yet explored or at least on which no results have yet been achieved from which guidelines could be laid down. Problems on this level would best be selected after the completion of successful projects in more well-trodden areas.
- a. In ESP, tests which attempt to correlate physiological responses and ESP (still in the early exploratory stage).
- b. In PK, tests of the effect on targets ranging beyond cubes, spheres, and discs. Also on static objects, or on living objects (strict controls here are necessary, and difficult).

Here are a few final words of advice to would-be beginning researchers in parapsychology. If you are looking for something easy, look elsewhere. If you are looking for something sure, do not take psi research. If you will be crushed by failure, do not try this. But if you are looking for something new, challenging, important, then go ahead. It might give you a bit of the excitement and sense of adventure Columbus probably had. You do not know if you will succeed. But he did not know if he would even come back alive. You will live—to try again, and you may very well succeed the first time.

Good luck!

References

Chapter 4

1. Gurney, E., Myers, F. W. H., and Podmore, F. *Phantasms of the Living.* London: Trubner, 1886. Reprinted, New Hyde Park: University Books, 1962.
2. Jephson, Ina. "Evidence for Clairvoyance in Card-Guessing." *Proceedings of the Society for Psychical Research* (1929), 38:223–268.
3. Richet, Charles. *Our Sixth Sense.* London: Rider & Co., 1920. Pp. 67–92.

Chapter 5

1. Rhine, J. B. *Extra-sensory Perception.* Boston: Bruce Humphries, 1934. Reprinted 1964. Pp. 47–49.
2. *Ibid.,* pp. 31–34.

Chapter 6

1. Rhine, Louisa E. *ESP in Life and Lab.* New York: Macmillan, 1967. Collier Books, 1971. Chapter 6. (Gives references to other experiments also cited.)

Chapter 7

1. McMahan, Elizabeth A. "An Experiment in Pure Telepathy." *Journal of Parapsychology* (1946), 10:224–242.

Chapter 8

1. Eisenbud, Jule. *The World of Ted Serios.* New York: William Morrow & Co., 1967.
2. Rhine, Louisa E. *Mind over Matter.* New York: Macmillan, 1970. Collier Books, 1972.

Chapter 9

1. Schmeidler, Gertrude R., and McConnell, R. A. *ESP and Personality Patterns.* New Haven: Yale University Press, 1958.

2. Thouless, Robert H. "The Present Position of Experimental Research into Telepathy and Related Phenomena." *Journal of Parapsychology* (1943), 7:158–171; see p. 160.

Chapter 10

1. Humphrey, B. H. "Introversion Ratings in Relation to Scores in ESP Tests." *Journal of Parapsychology* (1951), 15: 252–262.
2. Kanthamani, B. K., and Rao, Ramakrishna. "Personality Characteristics of ESP Subjects: III. Extraversion and ESP." *Journal of Parapsychology* (1972), 36:198–212.
3. _____. "Personality Characteristics of ESP Subjects: IV. Neuroticism and ESP." *Journal of Parapsychology* (1973), 37:37–50.
4. Kelly, E. F., and Kanthamani, B. K. "A Subject's Efforts Toward Voluntary Control." *Journal of Parapsychology* (1972), 36:185–197.
5. Morris, R. L., and others. "EEG Patterns and ESP Results in Forced-Choice Experiments with Lalsingh Harribance." *Journal of the American Society for Psychical Research* (1972), 66:253–268.
6. Rhine, Louisa E. *ESP in Life and Lab.* New York: Macmillan, 1967. Collier Books, 1971.

Chapter 11

1. Anderson, Margaret L., and White, Rhea A. "A Survey of Work on ESP and Teacher-Pupil Attitudes." *Journal of Parapsychology* (1958), 22:246–268. (contains references to earlier work.)
2. Bond, Esther May. "General Extra-sensory Perception with a Group of Fourth and Fifth Grade Retarded Children." *Journal of Parapsychology* (1937), 1:114–122.
3. Brier, Robert M. "A Mass School Test of Precognition." *Journal of Parapsychology* (1969), 33:125–135.
4. Freeman, John F. "Boy-Girl Differences in a Group Precognition Test." *Journal of Parapsychology* (1963), 27:175–181.
5. _____. "Sex Differences in ESP Response as Shown by the Freeman Picture-Figure Test." *Journal of Parapsychology* (1970), 34: 37–46.
6. Krietler, Hans, and Krietler, Shulamith. "Does Extra-sensory Perception Affect Psychological Experiments?" *Journal of Parapsychology* (1972), 36:1–45.
7. _____. "Subliminal Perception and Extra-sensory Perception." *Journal of Parapsychology* (1973), 37:168–188.
8. Louwerens, N. G. "ESP Experiments with Nursery School Children in the Netherlands." *Journal of Parapsychology* (1960), 24:75–93.
9. Rao, K. Ramakrishna. *Experimental Parapsychology.* Springfield, IL: Charles C. Thomas, 1957.

10. Stanford, Rex G. "An Experimentally Testable Model for Spontaneous Psi Events: I. Extrasensory Events." *Journal of the American Society for Psychical Research* (1974), 68:34–57.
11. Van Busschbach, J. G. "An Investigation of Extrasensory Perception in School Children." *Journal of Parapsychology* (1953), 17:210–214.
12. _____. "An Investigation of ESP in the First and Second Grades of Dutch Schools." *Journal of Parapsychology* (1959), 23:227–237.
13. Vasse, Christiane, and Vasse, Paul. "ESP Tests with French First Grade School Children." *Journal of Parapsychology* (1958), 22: 187–203.

Chapter 12

1. Ullman, Montague, and Krippner, Stanley. *Dream Studies and Telepathy*. Parapsychological Monographs, No. 12. Parapsychology Foundation, New York (1970).
2. _____ with Alan Vaughan. Dream Telepathy, Macmillan, New York, 1973.

Chapter 13

1. Honorton, C. "Relationships between EEG Alpha Activity and ESP Card Guessing Performance." *Journal of the American Society for Psychical Research* (1969), 63:365–374.
2. Honorton, C., and Krippner, Stanley. "Hypnosis and ESP Performance: A Review of the Experimental Literature." *Journal of the American Society for Psychical Research* (1969), 63:214–252.
3. Honorton, C. "State of Awareness Factors in Psi Activation." *Journal of the American Society for Psychical Research* (1974), 68:246–256.
4. Kamiya, J. "Operant Control of the EEG Alpha Rhythm and Some of its Reported Effects on Consciousness," in *Altered States of Consciousness*, ed. C.T. Tart. New York: Wiley, 1969. Pp. 507–518.
5. Lewis, L., and Schmeidler, G. R. "Alpha Relations with Non-Intentional and Purposeful ESP after Feedback." (Gives references to earlier articles on alpha activity and ESP by other authors.) *Journal of the American Society for Psychical Research* (1971), 65:455–467.
6. McMahan, Elizabeth. "A Review of the Evidence of Dowsing." *Journal of Parapsychology* (1947), 11:175–190.
7. Palmer, John, and Vassar, Carol. "ESP and Out-of-the-Body Experiences: an Exploratory Study." *Journal of the American Society for Psychical Research* (1974), 68:257–280.
8. Tart, C.T. "A Psychological Study of Out-of-the-Body Experiences

in a Selected Subject." *Journal of the American Society for Psychical Research* (1968), 62:3–27.

Chapter 14

1. Pratt, J. G., and Keil, H. H. J. "Firsthand Observations of Nina S. Kulagina Suggestive of PK upon Static Objects." *Journal of the American Society for Psychical Research* (1973), 67:381–390.
2. Puthoff, Harold, and Targ, Russell. *Research in Parapsychology* Metuchen, N.J.: Scarecrow Press, 1973. Pp. 125–131.
3. Schmeidler, Gertrude R. "PK Effects Upon Continuously Recorded Temperature." *Journal of the American Society for Psychical Research* (1973), 67:325–340.

Chapter 15

1. Barry, Jean. "General and Comparative Study of the Psychosomatic Effect on a Fungus Culture." *Journal of Parapsychology* (1968), 32:237–243.
2. Metta, Louis. "Psychokinesis on Lepidopterous Larvae." *Journal of Parapsychology* (1972), 36:213–221.
3. Randall, J. S. "Experiments to Detect a Psi Effect with Small Animals." *Journal of the Society for Psychical Research* (1971), 46:31–37.
4. Richmond, N. "Two Series of PK Tests on Paramecia." *Journal of the Society for Psychical Research* (1952), 36:577–588.
5. Vasse, Paul, and Vasse, Christiane. "A Comparison of Two Subjects in PK." *Journal of Parapsychology* (1951), 15:263–270.

Chapter 16

1. Grad, B. "Some Biological Effects of the 'Laying on of Hands': A Review of Experiments with Plants and Animals." *Journal of the American Society for Psychical Research* (1965), 59:95–127.
2. Smith, J. "Paranormal Effects on Enzyme Activity." Abstract, in *Journal of Parapsychology* (1968), 32:281.
3. Watkins, G., and Watkins, A. "Possible PK Influence on the Resuscitation of Anesthetized Mice." *Journal of Parapsychology* (1971), 35:257–272.

Chapter 17

1. Duval, P., and Montredon, E. "ESP Experiments with Mice." *Journal of Parapsychology* (1968), 32:153–166.

2. Osis, K. "A Test of the Occurrence of a Psi Effect between Man and Cat." *Journal of Parapsychology* (1952), 16:233–256.
3. Schmidt, H. "PK Experiments with Animals as Subjects." *Journal of Parapsychology* (1970), 34:255–262.
4. Schouten, Sybo A. "Psi in Mice: Positive Reinforcement." *Journal of Parapsychology* (1972), 36:261–282.
5. Rhine, J. B. and Feather, Sara R. "A Study of the Cases of Psi Trailing in Animals." *Journal of Parapsychology* (1962), 26:1–23.

Chapter 18

1. Rhine, Louisa E. "Subjective Forms of Spontaneous Psi Experiences." *Journal of Parapsychology* (1953), 17:77–114.

Chapter 19

1. Rhine, Louisa E. "Psychological Processes in ESP Experiences. Part I: 'Waking Experiences.' " *Journal of Parapsychology* (1962), 26: 88–110; see pp. 88–101.

Chapter 20

1. Rhine, Louisa E. "Psychological Processes in ESP Experiences. Part I." *op. cit.* pp. 102–110.
2. _____. "Auditory Psi Experience: Hallucinatory or Physical?" *Journal of Parapsychology* (1963), 27:182–198.

Chapter 21

1. Rhine, Louisa E. "Psychological Processes in ESP Experiences. Part II: 'Dreams.' " *Journal of Parapsychology* (1962), 26:172–199; see pp. 174–183.

Chapter 22

1. Rhine, Louisa E. "Psychological Processes in ESP Experiences. Part II," *op. cit.* pp. 183–199.

Chapter 23

1. Rhine, Louisa E. "Spontaneous Physical Effects and the Psi Process." *Journal of Parapsychology* (1963), 27:84–122.

Chapter 24

1. Rhine, Louisa E. "The Evaluation of Nonrecurrant Psi Experiences Bearing on Post-Mortem Survival." *Journal of Parapsychology* (1960), 24:8–25.

Chapter 25

1. Heywood, Rosalind. *The Sixth Sense.* London: Chatto and Windus, 1959. Chapters VIII and IX.
2. Hodgson, Richard. "A Further Record of Observations of Certain Phenomena of Trance." Part I. *Journal of the Society for Psychical Research* (1898), 13:297-298.
3. Rhine, J. B. *New Frontiers of the Mind* New York: Farrar and Rinehart, 1937. Pp. 221-228.
4. Thomas, John F. *Case Studies Bearing upon Survival.* Boston: Boston Society for Psychic Research, 1929.

Chapter 26

1. Owen, A. R. G. *Can We Explain the Poltergeist?* New York: Helix Press, Garret Publications, 1964.
2. Roll, W. G. *Poltergeists.* New York: Nelson Doubleday, 1972.

Chapter 28

1. Stevenson, Ian. *Twenty Cases Suggestive of Reincarnation.* New York: William Byrd Press, 1966.
2. _____, Xenoglossy; A Review and Report of a Case Proceedings of the American Society for Psychical Research, 31, 1974, 1-268.

Chapter 29

1. Ashby, H. *The Guide Book for the Study of Psychical Research.* New York: Samuel Weisner, 1972.
2. Psi News. (projected 6 issues per year, $8.50) Information Services for Psi Education (ISPE) P.O. Box 2221, New York, N.Y. 10001.
3. McConnell, R.A. *ESP Curriculum Guide.* New York: Simon & Schuster, 1971.
4. White, Rhea A. and Laura A. Dale. *Parapsychology: Sources of Information.* N. J.: Scarecrow Press, 1973.
5. Wolman, Benjamin B., Ed. *Handbook of Parapsychology.* New York: Van Nostrand Co., 1975.

Chapter 30

1. Rhine, J. B., and Pratt, J. G. *Parapsychology.* Springfield, IL: Charles C. Thomas, 1957. Chapter 7, pp. 131-197.

Appendix

1. Rhine, J. B., and Pratt, J. G. *Parapsychology, op. cit.* Chapter 8.
2. *Ibid.* Chapter 9.

Index

Alpha, 67, 99
Altered mental states, 90–98
  alpha and, 99
Anderson, Margaret, 74, 75,–77, 79
Anesthesia, in mouse experiments, 116
Anpsi
  definition, 122
  experiments, 123
  precognition tests, 123–127
Anxiety, in ESP tests, 64–65
Apparitions, 7, 26, 172
Astral projection
  definition, 206
  example, 207
  explanation, 208
Astrology, 12, 16, 19, 20
Attitudes
  and grades, 76
  of subjects, 67
Automatism
  as in automatic writing, 16, 84, 93, 95, 96, 177
  as in dowsing, 96
  as in pendulum, 96
  as in table tipping, 96
  as muscular action, 93, 96, 97
  as with Ouija board, 94
  origin of, 93–94

Barry, Dr. Jean, 109–110
Binary random number generator, 124
Blockage (forgetting), 144, 149, 150, 165
Bond, Esther, 73
Brain and mind
  controversy, 47
  relation of, 46
Brier, Robert M., 80

Clairvoyance, 28–32
  and distance, 38–39
  and expansive vs. compressive personalities, 63
  demonstrated, 36
  double-checking safeguard, 44
  in dowsing, 96
  in school tests, 75, 77
  in spontaneous cases, 47
  similarity to precognition, 41
  unaccepted by scientists, 44
  usual technique, 35
  vs. GESP, 227
Cox, Edward, 104–105
Curran, Mrs. John, 94

Dale, Laura, 85
Delmore, Bill, 66, 67
Dissociation, mental, 93, 94, 95
Dowsing. *See* Automatism
Dreams
  as copies, realistic, 153, 156
  as fantasy, unrealistic, 87, 136
  imagery of, 158
  induced, 86, 87
  measured by REM, 85
  symbolic, 159–160
  symbolism in, 163
  telepathic, 85
Duval and Montredon, 124–125

Eisenbud, Dr. Jule, 155
Electroencephalograph (EEG), 85, 86, 98
Evidential, 174
  meaning of, 174
Exorcism, 209
Extrasensory perception (ESP)
  ability, 48, 56, 120, 180, 224
  and personality influences, 63, 64

INDEX

Extrasensory *(cont'd)*
  cards, 5, 34, 39
  characteristics of, 56
  conditions for testing, 56, 59
  definition of, 47, 48
  distance test suggesting precognition, 41
  evaluation methods of, 40
  in the schoolroom, 73
  tests for. *See* Personality tests

Fisher, Dr. R.A., 30
Formula, statistical
  criticism of, 44
  for evaluating results in ESP and PK experiments, 34–35, 46, 50
  for getting targets for precognition, 40
  for negative scoring, 59
Fortune telling, 7, 59
Freeman, Dr. John
  test with retarded class, 79
  Sex and ESP responses in booklet tests, 79–80

Garrett, Mrs. Eileen
  method of testing, 178, 179
  question of "controls," 179
Geller, Mr. Uri, as a special PK subject, 103–105
General ESP (GESP)
  attitude of subjects, 227
  definition of, 47
  technique, 63
  technique in dream experiment, 86
  technique in Kreitlers' experiment, 82
Ghosts, 26, 150, 212, 214
Goats. *See* Sheep
Grad, Mr. Bernard, 114–115
Gurney, Mr. E., 28

Hallucinatory experience
  blockage in, 149–150
  deceptive effect of, 151
  illustrative case, 134
  in an auditory case, 147, 185
  in haunting cases, 182
  in shared pain, 149
  relationships in, 150
  relative numbers of, 150
  without ESP, 138, 139

Harribance, Mr. Lalsingh, 66, 67
Hauntings, haunted
  definition of, 186
  explanation of children's experiences, 181–183
  houses, 7, 26, 27, 150, 214
  in entertainment programs, 212
Healing, "healers," 113
  as at Lourdes, 114
  Mr. E., 114–115
Honorton, Mr. Charles, 99
Humphrey, Miss Betty, 45
  personality tests
    expansive-compressive, 63
    extravert-intravert, 64
Hypnosis
  as an altered mental state, 97–98
  associated with telepathy, 33

Intuition, intuitive ESP experience
  barrier or blockage at threshold, 145
  compulsion, 144
  frequency of, 145
  illustrative case, 134–135
  incomplete messages in, 97–142
  mechanics of, 145
  without ESP, 138

Jephson, Miss Ina, 30–36
Journals, (Parapsychology)
  of American Society for Psychical Research (J:ASPR), 214
  of Parapsychology (J.P.), 214
  of the Society for Psychical Research (J:SPR) London, 214

Kanthamani, B.K.
  extraversion-introversion difference, 64, 67
  neuroticism, 64–65
Keil, Dr. H.H.J., 103
Kelly, Dr. Ed., 67
Kreitler, Drs. Hans and Shulamith, 81–83
Kulagina, Nina, 103

Linzmayer, Mr. Adam, 62
Litvag, Irving, 94
Lodge, Sir Oliver, 214
Louwrens, Miss N.G., 78
Lundholm, Dr. Helge, 33

INDEX

Magic, 205, 209
McDougall, Dr. William, 32, 33, 36, 44, 48, 177
McMahan, Dr. Elizabeth (Betty Mc), 45, 46
Meditation, 100
Mediums, 21
 as a source of information, 177
 fraudulent and honest, 176
 move physical objects, 52
 use automatic writing, 95
 used in research
  Mrs. Eileen Garrett, 178
  Mrs. Leonard, 180
  Mrs. Leonora Piper, 174
Memory
 and blockage, or difficulties of recall, 144
 as the basis of hallucinatory imagery, 150
Metta, Mr. Louis, 109
Myers, F.W.H., 214

Neuroticism, 64-65

Occult, and ageless beliefs, 12, 192, 198
Osis, Dr. Karlis, 122-123
Ouija (board), 16, 18, 19, 20, 93, 95
 as an automatism, 94
Out-of-the-body experiences
 examples of, 90-92, 93

Parapsychological organizations
 American Society for Psychical Research (ASPR) · New York, 170
 Parapsychology Laboratory of Duke University, Durham, N.C., 4, 44
 Institute for Parapsychology, 4
 Psychical Research Foundation, Durham, N.C., 66
 Society for Psychical Research, London, 27, 29, 33, 170, 175, 176
Parapsychology
 and entertainment programs, 212
 as a scientific field, 8, 9, 12, 15, 16, 17
 courses in, 15, 213
 defined, 4

 prejudice against, 8
 recognition of, slight, 213
 topics included and excluded, 12
 training for 213-214
 use of statistical formulas in, 35
Pearce, Mr. Hubert, 62
Personality
 and direction of scoring, 65
 of subjects, 62
 tests
  Bernreuter, 64
  expansive-compressive, 63
  Primary Mental Abilities
   spatial relations, 80
   verbal reasoning ability, 80
  tests not adequate on ESP, 68
Physical effect. See Psychokinesis, PK
Piper, Mrs. Leonora, 174-175
Podmore, Mr. Frank. 28
Poltergeist, 7, 27, 184
 definition of, 186
 recent investigations, 187
 reported effects, 53
 studied by parapsychologists, 209
Possession
 description of, 206
 how explained, 208
 testimony to psi, 209
Pratt, Dr. J.G., 103
Precognition
 as an ability, 38
 as new territory, 36-37
 first experiment and indications of, 38-39
 in PK target selections, 54
 in the school room, 75
 method of getting targets, 40
 no high scorers, 203
 similarity to clairvoyance, 41
 techniques in tests
  in animal experiments, 125
  in Brier's experiment, 80
  in Freeman's experiment, 79
Psi
 ability, 1, 2, 14-15, 59, 61, 62, 180, 183, 208
 as a concept, 192
 as a basis for certain occult beliefs, 208
 definition of, 59, 193, 194
 effects, 206

Psi *(cont'd)*
  in spontaneous experiences, 137, 173
  missing
    as shown in scores, 230
    definition of, 59
    in personality tests, 63, 64
    in relation to alpha, 99
    subjects who are missers, 76, 81
  once seemed supernatural, 183
  origin of the process, 166, 198
  or psychic experiences, 2, 134–136
Psychic
  ability, 2, 4, 11
  shuffle, 39, 40
Psychokinesis (PK), 50, 52, 53
  ability
    an unconscious process, 59
    and temperature changes, 101–102
    characteristics, 56–59
    frequency of spontaneous effects, 165
    illustrative case, 136
    on living organisms, 55, 114
    on static objects, 54, 101
    origin in spontaneous experiences, 165
    technique for moving targets, face, 50–51
    technique for moving targets, place, 54
    unrecognized, 193, 194, 198
Puthoff, Dr. Harold, 104–105

Randall, Mr. John, 108–109
Random behavior trials
  description of, 125
  show precognition, 127
Rao, Dr. Ramakrishna, 64
Rapid Eye Movement (REM) technique as an indication of dreaming, 85, 86, 87
Realistic experience, illustrative case, 134
Receiver
  definition of, 28
  technique in early tests, 29
Reincarnation, 202
Retarded subjects
  in Bond school tests, 73
  in Freeman (teacher) test, 79
Richet, Dr. Charles, 29, 30, 36, 214
Richmond, Mr. Nigel, 107–108

Schmeidler, Dr. Gertrude, 64
  and Lewis in EEG experiment, 99
  in experiment on temperature and PK, 102
  sheep & goat experiment, 57
Schmidt, Dr. Helmut, PK experiments,
  and his mechanism for testing PK, 128
  with cat, 128–129
  with cockroaches, 130–131
Schouten, Sybo A.
  precognition experiment in mice, 125
  telepathy experiment in mice, 126–127
Scientific method, 21, 35, 192
Sender
  as agent, 86
  definition of, 28
  technique in ESP tests, 29, 82, 83
Serios, Mr. Ted, 55
Sex and ESP
  in Brier's *Read* test, 80–81
  in Freeman's booklet tests, 79–80
Sheep and goats
  differences analyzed, 64
  ways of expressing ESP, 57, 59, 220
Sitter
  in experiment with Mrs. Garrett, 178
Smith, Sister Justa, 115
Soul, 32, 33, 190, 191
Speaking in tongues, 206, 208
Special subjects
  Delmore, 66
  Early (see Pearce, Linzmayer), 35–36
  Harribance, 66
Spirit, spirits, 18, 26
  definition of, 183
  in connection with the Ouija, 18
  in connection with poltergeists, 186, 187
  in connection with witchcraft 204
  or soul, 191
  possession, 206, 208

Spirit photography, 55
Stacking effect, 81, 227
Stanford, Dr. Rex, 83, 99
Stevenson, Dr. Ian, 202
Survival
  and apparitional and hallucinatory experiences, 26, 171–173
  and the soul, 32, 33, 169
  and the telepathy hypothesis, 180
  as in religions, 169
  complicated answer to, 170
  evidence from cross-correspondences, 176
  immortality, 169, 170, 190

Table-tipping, 16
  method, 96
Targ, Dr. Russell, 104, 105
Telepathy
  as a clairvoyant effect, 46
  as a process, 82
  detour to clairvoyance necessary, 30
  difficulty in double checking found, 44
  early case study and experiments, 28, 29
  experiences suggesting it, 84
  experiments in dreams, 85
  in spontaneous experiences, 43
  malignant?, 199
  mistaken idea of, 201
  name, 27
  "pure," 43, 44, 46
  test for, major objective, 31, 32
  test procedure, 36, 42, 45, 47, 48, 53, 84, 86
Temperature and PK
  Schmeidler's experiment, 102
  thermister, description of, 102

Tests
  for spatial relations (Freeman experiment), 80
  for reasoning ability (Freeman experiment), 80
Thomas, Mr. John F., 174–175, 176, 177
Thouless, Dr. Robert, 59

U.F.O.'s, 12
Ullman, Dr. Montague, 85, 88
Unconscious
  Aspects of mind, 12
  difficulty of converting into consciousness, 97
  in direct contact with reality, 139
  in the ESP process, 58
  in the PK process, 59, 165
Unrealistic experiences
  illustrative case, 136
Unusual mental states See Altered Mental States

Van Busschbach, Mr. J.G.
  classroom tests, 74–75
Vasse, Madame Christiane
  dice tests, 107
  experiment on plants, 106–107
  school tests, 77–78
Verbal Material
  method of evaluating, 87, 178

Watkins, Graham and Anita
  experiment on resuscitation of etherized mice, 115
  use different healers, K.G. & L.H., 116–117
White, Miss Rhea, 74, 75, 76, 77
Witchcraft, 16, 204, 205, 209
Worth, Patience, 94